Fruits of Our Labor

by Kathy Kahn

FRUITS OF OUR LABOR
HILLBILLY WOMEN

FRUITS
OF OUR
LABOR

By Kathy Kahn

G. P. PUTNAM'S SONS
NEW YORK

Research for this book was made possible by financial assistance from: G. P. Putnam's Sons, *and the* National Endowment for the Humanities, *U.S.A.; and in-kind contributions from*: U.S.S.R.-U.S.A. Friendship Society *and* Novosti Books, *U.S.S.R.*

The epigraphs beginning "Bobbin and Loom," "The Mavericks," and "Tarzan Fan" are lines taken from songs written by Kathy Kahn.

Photographs, including jacket, by Kathy Kahn

Library of Congress Cataloging in Publication Data

Kahn, Kathy, date.
  Fruits of our labor.

   1. Labor and laboring classes—United States—Interviews. 2. Labor and laboring classes—Soviet Union—Interviews.
I. Title.
HD8072.5.K33   305.5′6   81-22708
ISBN 0-399-12698-8   AACR2

PRINTED IN THE UNITED STATES OF AMERICA

FOR ALL OUR CHILDREN

And with gratitude
to a friend of all the world's people,

RICHARD MORFORD

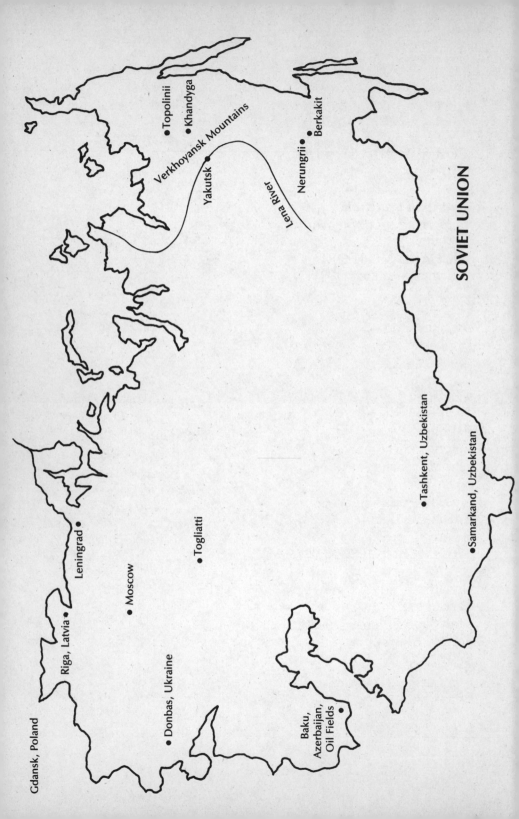

CONTENTS

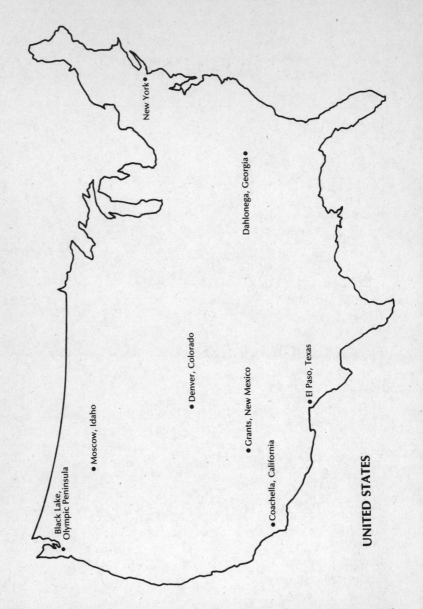

The U.S.S.R. is the largest nation in the world, covering 8,649,490 square miles. The U.S., less than one-half the size of the Soviet Union, covers 3,618,467 square miles. The U.S.S.R. intersects eleven time zones; the continental U.S. intersects six time zones. The population of the U.S.S.R. is approximately 267 million; the population of the U.S. is approximately 227 million.

Introduction

These are stories of life and labor, told by Soviet and American workers. They are partly bold fact, partly ancient fable. They are sometimes humorous, but just as often, chilling reminders of calamitous times. Some are laced with whispered innuendo and others are so graphic they almost bite. These personal ballads are all sincere accounts of citizens who represent many nationalities, cultures and traditions in two powerful nations. As they speak about the ever controversial subject of work, its liabilities and rewards, these laborers' voices do not always blend in one harmonious chorus; they often disagree about what causes humankind's problems and how to solve them. But their stories share one key element: these men and women all perform constructive labor that keeps their nations supplied with basic goods and services. With sweat and sacrifice, they have invested in the future of two nations they love. While they work for a living, they wonder if the same privilege will be passed on to their children. With foreboding, they think about the future of the world; with optimism, their hands continue building a dream.

Soviet society glorifies workers and America marvels at products that come from their hands. Their labor sustains humankind, but what material and spiritual rewards do their technologically advanced societies offer them? Representing a microcosm of labor's occupations, this book aims to break down the myths and stereotypes that surround today's American and Soviet workers, to open a fresh line of communication between them, unencumbered by either nation's propaganda mills. And these voices, speaking for themselves, may help pinpoint some ethical standards that must replace archaic political machinery if the world's workers are to move securely into the 21st century.

Today's American and Soviet workers know very little about each other. Cold War hostilities between their rulers have prevented a free flow of accurate, unbiased information from one nation to the other. Soviets are told very little about the brighter side of American workers' lives, and Americans tend to be skeptical about heavily weighted negative reports of life in the Soviet Union. Are the denunciations leveled by Soviet dissidents against their homeland accurate accounts of life in the U.S.S.R.? And is it true, as some Soviets think, that American workers are preparing to fight a war against them? Eager to learn more about life on the other side of the Bering Strait, Americans have read Soviet publications and Soviets have tuned in pro-Western shortwave broadcasts. Unfortunately, both of these government-controlled sources present one-sided glorified pictures of their citizens' lives and labor. Citizens know they are being fed propaganda about "the other side," and they wonder what to believe.

Is it possible that truth is simply an illusion hanging like an opaque curtain over the Bering Strait, perceived differently from each side of the DEW line? Is it possible, in the era of Cold War and nuclear hot spots, to view both sides of the Bering Strait rationally if not dispassionately?

In the autumn of 1980, I decided to write a book about

American and Soviet workers. If they could talk to each other, I wondered, what would American and Soviet workers say about their lives and work, about the societies they serve? With less than a grain of interest in political "isms," I wanted to skirt official rhetoric, to hear workers' voices and learn firsthand how they perceive their own future and that of their nations. If the world was going to be radiated out of existence, I told myself, I did not want to face Doomsday with lingering questions about a people who would be victims of U.S. nuclear weapons. And I wanted to know more about workers in the United States, who are potential victims of the Soviet Union's nuclear arsenal. Since my sympathies lean more toward laborers than toward bosses, I would have to make an extra effort to objectively report labor's condition. Since I have no emotional attachment to any political system or its rulers, I could objectively report on the liabilities and rewards these systems offer workers. At least, it seemed worth trying.

With a small publishing advance from G. P. Putnam's Sons, I traveled around the United States, interviewing men and women about their daily lives and about the work that sustained them. Concentrating on traditional occupations such as mining, herding and farming, I visited some of the more remote areas—New Mexico, north Georgia, Alaska and rural Texas. Some of the workers I spoke with were in trades that are rapidly becoming automated and which may be removed from human hands within the next few decades. Besides talking about their lives, I asked them to comment on their philosophies regarding today's society and current world affairs. I also asked them what they would like to know about the lives of their Soviet counterparts. Their replies were revealing.

"I don't know anything about Soviet workers," a farmworker told me. "You never hear about them. So, if you ask what I want to know about Soviet workers, well, it's all new to me."

"I know they've got salt mines over there in Siberia," a railroad employee told me, "and the workers make lousy wages. But there must be something they like over there. You never hear of workers' revolts in Russia."

An unemployed auto worker approached me on a train traveling west from New York. "I heard you're going to visit the Soviet Union and talk to workers over there," she said. "Do me a favor. Find out if they've got any job openings over there." I asked her if she would seriously consider going to the U.S.S.R. to live and work. She thought about it for a minute and said, "Well, probably not. This is my country, the United States. Anyway, I'm too old to adapt to a different country. But if I was younger, I'd sure check out that scene. I read somewhere that Soviet women get bonuses for having babies. Now, I think that's a great idea."

The questions American workers raised, both about their own society and the one few Americans have ever seen, guided the direction of this book. I had my own criteria as well. The men and women whose stories would appear in this book had to be free to express personal opinions, whether or not they agreed with those of their employers or government or union officials. Workers who had been previously interviewed by the mass media, or who held high-ranking union or political positions, were excluded from the selection. In all cases, I made the final selection of persons I would interview. Altogether, I spoke with hundreds of laborers in both countries and interviewed about fifty.

The idea of comparing working and living conditions in the United States and the Soviet Union seemed feasible and even terribly important. From a purely statistical point of view, I learned, these comparisons are virtually impossible. The Soviet government does not publish statistics on work related issues, data for example, on industrial accidents, injuries and deaths. These figures for American workers are readily available from government agencies, but like the U.S. Census, their accuracy is highly questionable. This book contains few statistics. Nor is it a scorecard of living and working conditions in the two countries, although some comparisons are made. Several of the Americans and the Soviets work in the same occupation. All work either on the land, in factories or in service work. But as similar as their jobs might be, their personal testimonies defy rigid comparisons.

As I sought American workers for interviews, during three cross-country journeys, so many were enthused about the project that a wealth of material resulted. Their interviews were arranged through labor unions, corporations, personal acquaintances, or just by walking into a town cold and asking around. Since no time limits were placed on the interviews—as would happen in my Soviet experience, when officials placed limits on my discussions with workers—the American interviews were comfortably informal. Many were done around kitchen tables, over cold beer and homemade tamales or cornbread. A few were done on passenger trains, in bus depots and coffee shops. Some were done in workplaces. The Americans were always hospitable and anxious to help the project. They frequently insisted I spend the night in their homes instead of in motel rooms, and these gestures to a stranger greatly relieved the financial burden of the project. With a treasure of information about the condition of labor in the United States, I returned home and prepared to leave for the Soviet Union.

Through a group called the National Council of American-Soviet Friendship, which I first located through New York's Yellow Pages, I had applied for permission to visit the Soviet Union and interview workers there. I specifically asked to visit regions that were not often seen by foreigners. Early in 1981, I received a press visa and permission to work for five weeks in six Soviet republics.

As the date for departure grew near, I did not have enough money to cover even round trip air fare. I called Vladimir Belyakov, an information officer at the U.S.S.R. Embassy, and told him I had failed to raise sufficient funds for the project. He sighed when he heard this news. "Katya Kahn," he said, "we have done everything possible to arrange your work in the Soviet Union. And now you say you can't even raise enough money to buy your airplane ticket. What can we Soviets think about you?"

I was tempted to go back and leaf through the Yellow Pages, but a few days later Belyakov called, and with another sigh, said, "Katya Kahn, you will purchase for yourself a one-way ticket to Moscow. We will take care of the rest." And so, on April Fool's Day, 1981, on a one-way ticket, I arrived in the Soviet Union, seeking out plain truth about Soviet workers, told in their own words.

The U.S.S.R.-U.S.A. Friendship Society and Novosti Books, both based in Moscow, had offered to assume the costs of my travels within the Soviet Union. Novosti, a state publishing house, said they would provide an interpreter to accompany me. They also agreed to ask local trade unions to pre-select workers for interviews, since my press visa was good for only five weeks and I would not have time to do this preliminary research. Nor would I have received permission to just wander around the Soviet Union seeking out persons to interview.

The editor-in-chief of Novosti's book arm was a gentle, almost fragile man named Alexander Pushkov. His office was responsible for arranging my itinerary. Pushkov made a point of telling me that there were no strings attached to their offer to cover my travel and hotel expenses. In other words, Pushkov said, they required no written documents or verbal promises that I would write in a pro-Soviet light. Their interest, Pushkov said, was twofold; they hoped that I would write fairly and objectively about Soviet workers, and, if they liked the book, they might want to publish a Russian-language version of it. That was all. I have never had any reason to doubt his integrity and sincerity; nevertheless, all was not red carnations and sunny smiles during my visit.

The interpreter assigned to accompany me did not speak English well. In plain fact, she was more of an escort, whose credentials were better suited to security work. It was also immediately apparent that had I demanded a different escort, one fluent in the English language, the project might have been abruptly terminated. This escort had obviously been carefully selected as the best qualified to serve as my traveling companion. If I had asked for a different interpreter, months of bureaucratic red tape would have been required to make the change. Fortunately, all the interviews were being tape recorded and could later be retranslated by someone fluent in both languages. And on the brighter side, my Russian improved rapidly, out of necessity for survival. My escort was able to translate the rough equivalent of conversations, and as the weeks passed, her English improved. But another source of strain had developed. She was overprotective.

The unfortunate fact is, Soviets are so accustomed to hostile Western journalism that they often are overly defensive about their society, even to the point of distorting its positive features. Soviet officials tend to "protect" workers from Western journalists, a practice that contributes to the great vacuum of information about Soviet workers' lives. My escort often tossed a protective blanket of distortion over workers who were eager to speak openly with me. She was as vulnerable as any American is to the lashes of hate propaganda and was anxious to present her country in the best possible light. She was doing her job. I did, however, experience moments of tremendous frustration when I met Soviets who had not been addled by attacks aimed at their system, who spoke impeccable English, and who might have better served as the interpreters of their people's heartfelt words.

When I returned to the United States, I found an

American woman, Fay Lila Greenbaum, who speaks fluent Russian. She agreed to translate the tapes verbatim as each worker spoke. Comparing these translations with my Soviet escort's translations on the tapes, some interesting patterns emerged. The Novosti escort had done a pretty good job of translating the essence of what was said, but throughout was unable to do so exactly. Isolated incidents occurred in which the escort would, for no apparent reason, change the meaning of what was spoken, either by adding a word the worker did not use or by altering complete sentences. In a few cases, she actually cut the person off. Fay's translations caught these discrepancies, and what appears on these pages are accurate translations of the Soviet interviews.

Soviet workers were not as candid as the Americans. This fact is boldly illustrated when their stories are compared. In fact, any adverse comments Soviets made on-the-record about workplace or society were purely accidental. There are a number of reasons for this. According to the Soviet Constitution, "it is a matter of honor for every Soviet citizen to uphold and defend the Motherland." This constitutional article is taken very seriously by workers. Whereas representatives of the intelligentsia spoke more openly about social problems, the workers I talked to on-the-record almost never raised criticisms about the system. I did, however, have many chats with Soviet citizens which were more relaxed and open.

Perhaps the Soviet workers feared some sort of reprimand if they censured the status quo. In two or three instances, this anxiety seemed present. I observed the same anxiety in American workers selected for interviews by U.S. companies. Several told me, "I'll tell you what goes on, but don't print it because it will get me into trouble at work." In both societies, workers know that criticizing the status quo can cost them their jobs. Four of the persons whose stories appear in this book have been given pseudonyms in order to protect them from possible retributions by their bosses or by government officials. Two are Soviet immigrants living in the United States. Two are Americans.

There is yet another reason Soviet workers do not often criticize the system. Conditions in the U.S.S.R. have improved enormously since 1945, when the land lay in ruins, devastated by World War II, twenty million of its people the victims of Nazi murderers. The abject poverty that followed the war is gone; the quality of life has improved.

Soviet culture has impressed a certain ethic upon its citizens—family problems are internal matters, and in the national family, this ethic, healthy or not, holds as well. Americans whom I met for the first time rarely hesitated to speak candidly about their personal lives and their workplace problems. But I am compelled to wonder what might happen if a Soviet author approached, as I did, an American farmworker on a Trailways bus riding through New Mexico, and asked her for an interview. The Soviet workers who I interviewed were meeting the first American they had ever laid eyes upon. Like my escort, they were anxious to make a good impression.

When I asked workers in both countries to relate their personal philosophies on labor and current world problems, they were all modest. When they finally spoke, they were eloquent.

Another difficulty arose during the Soviet trip. Though not as unpleasant as some problems I encountered, the tradition of greeting guests with vodka or champagne toasts frequently interfered with my work schedule. I am not speaking of a few polite sips; each occasion called for several toasts, each toast equaled a generous bottoms-up double shot. My first experience with this hospitable custom, in the little Siberian reindeer herders' town, Topolinii, resulted in disaster. After that, I quickly learned to hold my vodka and keep the tape recorder loaded and rolling.

Once I returned to the United States, I had the good fortune to receive a grant from the National Endowment for the Humanities. These funds allowed me to complete research for the book and to do the actual writing.

This picture of life and labor is by no means a total one. These are twenty-eight true accounts of workers' lives, stories that illustrate the wealth of information American and Soviet workers could share if only given opportunities. These voices all agree that humankind stands on the threshold between war and peace. They all have a genuine desire to hear each other's point of view. All these men and women could be called patriotic. Each has a love for country, Motherland or homeland, a love for material and spiritual ground that transcends allegiance to any particular set of political leaders. Ironically, these workers from two nations on the brink of the ultimate confrontation possess the same dedication to an idea called democracy, and to the concept of freedom and justice for all. But because of different historical conditions and varied perspectives on today's world, from either side of a radioactive veil, American and Soviet workers do not always agree on which "ism," if any, truly represents the best interests of their homeland. An important quality each of these workers possesses is the desire to be free to hold a personal opinion that does not infringe on the rights of others, and to live accordingly. Their ideas are the substance and heart of this book; their voices speak sometimes softly, sometimes like thunder, from the core of American and Soviet society.

In southeastern Siberia, a huge new hydroelectric plant is being built. I went there to talk with the construction workers. An older worker, about fifty, sat beside me during a roundtable discussion. While the younger workers pelted me with questions about life and work in the United

States, he sat silently, head bowed, a troubled frown creasing his brow. The younger workers' questions were very specific: they wanted to know about American workers' income levels, employee benefits, shift schedules and so on. Suddenly the older man raised his head and said, "Look, we want to be your friends. Tell me, why do American workers not want to be our friends?"

"Where did you get that notion?" I asked him.

He shook his head sadly and studied tips of calloused fingers. "We read it in our newspapers. We see it on television. The American people are supporting a war effort that will kill us Soviets."

I set him straight—as best I could, anyway—and before I left the camp, he kissed me on the cheek and said, "Please send my warm greetings to my fellow workers in the U.S. Tell them I hope they have success in their lives. Tell them I wish every day for peace."

A few months later, I was riding Amtrak through the Pacific Northwest and happened to meet a young woman serving in the army. We began talking about the Soviet Union. I asked her what she thought about Red Army soldiers. She sighed and leaned her face against the train window. She said, "They're probably just like me, I guess. Only what I can't figure out is why they want to make a war with us."

An American union organizer gave me a miner's safety belt to present to Soviet miners. The Soviet miners gave me a hard hat to give to the U.S. miners. American union members poured buttons, t-shirts and handwritten notes of union solidarity into my suitcase before I left for the U.S.S.R., and I returned laden with gifts and messages from Soviets to distribute among Americans. For weeks I was a pack mule bearing tidings of friendship between people who have been divided by an ocean of political hostility they did not create.

Here on these pages, twenty-eight workers bare the

bones of two systems and examine their health. They speak for themselves about life and labor on a complex piece of rock called Planet Earth. Like the soil they turn, they have substance. Like the jewels they mine, they reflect sturdy beauty. Like Planet Earth, these workers occupy a unique position; they are at once vulnerable and powerful. In their own words, they tell us why.

Salt of the Earth

Topolinii

"The Moon is putting on his furs."
                              —Siberian weather report

Every winter, Arctic frost lays a slick arm across the Bering
Strait and, with Nature's eternal disregard for governments' Cold War squabbles, firmly bonds the United
States to the Soviet Union. When the ice bridge joins
Alaska and Siberia, a pedestrian on snowshoes could cross
the Strait's narrowest point in minutes. In any season, a
bush plane could fly from Alaska's shore to Topolinii,
Siberia, in a few hours. But a cautious pedestrian or bush
pilot avoids crossing the Bering Strait. Guns poised there,
on both sides of the International Dateline, warn that more
than the time of day inclines hostile governments to keep
their peoples divided. So an American trying to reach
Topolinii's reindeer herders must take the long way
around.

From America's East Coast, a Topolinii-bound traveler
can board an Aeroflot Ilyushin jet that flies from Washington, D.C., to Moscow in eleven hours. In Moscow, a

TU-154 jet will carry the traveler further around the globe to Yakutsk, Siberia, a twelve hour flight. From Yakutsk, capital of the Yakutia Autonomous Republic, the traveler boards a Yak-40 for a short, smooth ride—in clement weather—to Khandyga, a Siberian outpost on the banks of the River Lena. In Khandyga's little wooden airport building, the newcomer might be confused, noticing the clock on the wall runs on Moscow time, but a little arithmetic reveals the total travel time between Washington, D.C., and Khandyga, Siberia, is twenty-three hours, and the trip nearly circumnavigates the globe. The Bering Strait route would be more practical—except for the guns.

At Khandyga in winter, when the temperature has plunged below minus 30 degrees Celsius and ice coats every inch of ground, a wise voyager will imbibe alcoholic beverages to shore up blood circulation for the last leg of the journey to Topolinii. At least that is what Konstantin, Khandyga's airport manager, told me one Siberian winter morning as he helped me into a tiny silver biplane.

Bound for Topolinii, Polar Aviation's World War II vintage cargo biplane was crowded. Swelling sacks of mail and fresh vegetables—Yakutsk hothouse gold—bulged against six straight chairs of varying colors, shapes and durability. The chairs supported seven people, just as varied, though better built. A Siberian Even family cuddled together on two wooden chairs, the baby's face so thickly muffled in wool scarf that only two glistening brown eyes were visible. She might have been a reindeer fawn. Her brother, dwarfed under a rabbit fur cap, stood leaning into his father, emphasizing their perfectly matching features. The Evens had high broad cheekbones, diamond teardrop eyes that smiled and smooth yellow-bronze complexions. Near the hatch, a spindly Yakut man wrapped his galoshes around chair legs and pressed a red accordion to his chest. He smiled like a musician feeling rhythm. A fat bag of cucumbers crushed up against his legs, threatening to overflow into his lap. Directly across the cabin, a toe length from the Siberians, sat a huge Georgian journalist and his elegantly clad, pale Muscovite comrade, sharing anecdotes in earnest, soft tones, as if guarding their Russian nouns from the Siberians. The Even family politely pretended to hear nothing beyond their baby's soft, muffled breathing, and the accordion man was in another zone, fingers lightly caressing keys on the folding red box.

Perhaps I ought to have cared what the Georgian and the Muscovite were so fervently discussing, since they were my chaperones on this flight to the top of the world, where Siberian reindeer herders lived. But I was reeling from several vodka chasers I'd downed at Khandyga airport's little back room, swift belts from the Georgian's bottle. "In Siberia," he had counseled me, "you must drink to keep warm." I sat forward in the cockpit, shoulder to shoulder with two Yakut pilots. They played with switches and levers labeled in Russian. I watched the prop rotate to a fine invisible whir. We taxied over Khandyga's ice strip, tipped nose up, and a ptarmigan on ice skates could not have lofted more gracefully.

East of the Lena, we flew over shimmering turquoise pools that snaked around ice floes in the Aldan tributary. Jagged glaciers fought a downstream battle against a late winter sun, but Earth still hibernated under a thick white blanket swiss-dotted in tiny tundra trees. Mountains raised a lumpy backbone, creasing the blanket where the Earth curved. Peaceful winter sleep.

It is forbidden, without special permission from the state, to take aerial photographs over the Soviet Union.

Sounds of chattering journalists drifted up from the cargo hold. The prop whirred, chopping at clean, crisp air. The pilot pointed straight ahead out the window. "Alaska?" I asked him.

"Da."

After a while, the copilot took the controls. Hugging the

27

mountains, the biplane dipped into a deep valley and landed smoothly on the frozen Delin'ya River. From the air, Topolinii was a small speck on the ice. By land, the reindeer herders' village did not look much bigger.

Reindeer slaughterhouses and corrals skirted the town. Red flags ribboned Topolinii's square, leftover decorations from the annual winter festival. Neat and simple wooden buildings sat back up behind the flags, each wearing a square identification plaque. The Primary School. The Library. The Birthing House. The Yakut State Reindeer Farm Office. Town Hall. Midmorning sun only teased the deep ice crust that covered every inch of ground. Breath crystallized. Slick ice footpaths and the square were deserted. An Even man named Nikolai, fragile featured, soft-spoken and dignified, wearing a fur hat and a navy blue topcoat, ushered us into the town hall.

The Khandyga vodka had nearly worn off, and I wasn't in the market for more alcohol, but toasts are customary when visitors arrive anywhere in the Soviet Union, and Topolinii's Town Chief, a Yakut man in a green Hawaiian print shirt, had a bottle handy. He explained that alcohol helps the body's blood adjust to Siberian temperatures. Nikolai, who was the reindeer farm's manager, concurred in a gently persuasive voice. The Chief broke open a fifth of White Dynamite and led us into his office, a rural version of every office I saw in the Soviet Union. An elbow-worn wood desk and a long conference table made a T. Walls were plastered with Five Year Plan charts and graphs, and framed snapshots of Model Workers. Lenin, wearing a peasant's hat, a suit and tie, waved and smiled from a poster. A partly unfurled red flag revealed a gold hammer and sickle emblem. A table in the corner supported a miniature mock-up of the future Topolinii, an industrial outpost designed with advice from the Eternal Frost Institute in Yakutsk. Yakutia is coated with permanently frozen ground, and construction is a risky affair on what Americans call permafrost. Improperly designed, a heavy structure melts permafrost layers, causing the structure to sink in bog or just tumble over, creating environmental chaos. Topolinii's mock-up displayed several large buildings, scientifically designed, the Town Chief told me, to prevent damage to the eternal frost.

He led me over to the conference table, where Nikolai was already pouring White Dynamite into double shot glasses. We drank three toasts. We drank to the health of the Town Chief, to the arrival of an American, and to peace and friendship throughout the world. Afterward, stepping outdoors was almost bearable, but my bones still refused to defrost. Nikolai smiled and pointed at my feet. "It's those boots you're wearing," he said.

"Can't be," I replied, "these boots are heavy leather and fleece lined."

Nikolai nodded. "That's just the problem. Here, try *unti*."

Unti are felt-bottom boots made of reindeer leg skin. They are soft, warm and comfortable as clouds. Almost instantly my feet defrosted and my whole body felt acclimated to Siberian winter. Having proved his point, Nikolai directed me to board an *uazik*, a Soviet land rover, specially designed to glide over ice roads. "Get in," he said quietly, "we're going for a little ride."

We sped out of town on a narrow ice road, a silver ribbon winding through scrubby tundra forests. The uazik carried three Yakut, one Even, a Georgian, a Muscovite, and one American. Somehow, conversation flowed. In Russian. Nikolai explained in his reassuring manner that although Topolinii seemed almost deserted this morning, quite a lot of activity was taking place behind closed doors. The Yakut accordion man who flew in on the biplane was now rehearsing with the town's amateur cultural club, preparing a program planned in behalf of a visitor from America. Children in school were also preparing for the event. Most grown-ups were either indoors working in various town enterprises or out on the tundra hunting or herding.

I asked Nikolai where we were headed down this ice ribbon road. He smiled and shook his head. "Just going for a ride." I shivered a little and looked at my Muscovite escort, who was crushed in between the Georgian and Nikolai in the back seat. She wore a slightly confused expression, so it seemed pointless asking her where we were bound. "And so," said Nikolai, "to continue our discussion. I want to inform you that tomorrow morning you will have the pleasure of meeting the Even woman, Prascovia Neustroyeva. She is a hunter, one of Yakutia's best. She shoots her game square between the eyes, so their sleek coats are always unspoiled." The uazik skipped over a bump on the ice, and Nikolai adjusted his fur hat. "Now I will tell you something about Siberian reindeer herding."

Siberian reindeer herding, he explained, provides a solid economic base that supports about one hundred and twenty thousand native Siberians. The estimated number of reindeer in Siberia is about eight million. Herds are broken into units of fifteen hundred, with one herder for every two hundred and fifty reindeer. Reindeer herding is the traditional occupation of Yakut and Even families in Yakutia. Moving over treeless or sparsely wooded tundra, reindeer graze on ground lichens and lowbush berries. Herders move with the reindeer, and breeders work in the corrals and slaughterhouses. Every part of a slaughtered reindeer is used for human consumption. Reindeer meat is high protein, low fat, and can be prepared in a variety of dishes. The hides make warm coats and good mattresses if you know how to care for brittle fur. Leg hide and fur make unti, the best boots in Siberia. Doeskin makes the softest shirts for Yakut and Even babies. Hides make warm tents. Most important, Nikolai said, are reindeer antlers, when they are new and soft, in summer. In the old days, he explained, shamans used the blood of soft reindeer antlers in heady concoctions that cured the sick and made the weak strong. He did not mention the aphrodisiac properties traditionally attributed to a powder made from ground reindeer antlers.

The land rover halted suddenly. Straight ahead, sun poured over the ice highway, blinding gold. Skinny pines and larch trees formed thin woods on both sides of the road. I had the strange sensation of being stranded on Siberian tundra and liking it. A hush fell over the passengers in the uazik. Not an uncomfortable silence, but expectant. The Muscovite and Georgian wore puzzled frowns. Nikolai and the Town Chief stared straight ahead. The driver studied his fingernails. Total silence. Minutes later, soft, tinkling music drifted out of the tundra, like icicle chimes, gentle at first, then gradually louder. A child's Christmas Eve dream. Sleigh bells. The snap of a whip. The "Eeyi-haw!" of a master herder. The tundra swelled with music. I looked out the window and a reindeer with bells on looked in.

A man approached, dressed in thick furs, carrying a rawhide whip. He was Yakut, more Eskimo than Mongolian, bronze complexion so smooth it defied age. He had two teams of reindeer hitched to long wooden sleds. A young Yakut girl in a fur-lined parka sat in the driver's seat of one. The Yakut man pulled me out of the land rover and led me to his sled, arranging me in the rear like someone arranging groceries in the back of a pickup truck. Satisfied with his work, he flung a fur blanket over me, took the driver's seat, placed a pair of dark sunglasses on his nose, cracked the rawhide whip and cried, "Eeyi-haw!" We flew toward the North Pole. Deep in the tundra, the sled halted beside a low, canvas tent, pitched on the ice, bolstered with larch logs. Two women and a little girl stood at the entrance, smiling a welcome. A little boy with a red nose hugged his mother's leg. Introducing me to his family,

31

Igor Pogodaev, the Yakut reindeer herder, spoke his eloquent, streamlined native language.

Igor Pogodaev

I am the leader of my family. By sled, we have come here to my home. My family wishes to welcome you. We just sit on a blanket, but below the blanket, *listvennitsa* [larch] branches make the floor very warm. You pile the branches maybe five centimeters deep, just to cover the snow.

We are seven in my family. Wife, sons, daughter-in-law and grandchildren. We are reindeer herders all our lives. I wish to tell you about my life as a reindeer herder, as leader of a Yakut family. But first, it is necessary to drink a toast. The leader of household always makes the first toast. It is a custom when Topolinii's Town Chief visits our tent to drink for his health. So, please take the vodka—we will drink to the Town Chief.

Next, it is proper to welcome guests. As leader of the family, I make another toast: to our American friend who travels across the world and sits now with me and my family in our home. I wish she stays a long time here with my people. Please, drink. It is also proper to toast our Soviet guests, and drink to their health. We must drink again, to Nikolai, our brother Siberian. And now, a toast for all who gather in my home; family, friends. For long friendship. Finally, we must have a special toast for peace between our countries. May our people live and work under clear skies. Especially, I toast America's reindeer herders. Now it is wise to eat something.

Please, have a small snack prepared by my wife and daughter-in-law. *Brusnika* [wild cranberries] taste very good frozen and with sugar. Reindeer meat, frozen chips, yes, raw, make strength. It is better to eat reindeer meat frozen in the Siberian winter.

I will speak later about my life. But first, I can tell you

something about reindeer herding, for that is the occupation of my family.

Reindeer is the main supply of food for Yakut and Even people. Reindeer meat is fat free, very good tasting, very healthy.

In early spring, reindeer sprout horns. In summer, the horns are still soft. Summer, we cut the horns and ship them to medical industries for making medicine. Yes, it is called *andalin* in Russian. Very good medicine. We use all parts of reindeer—fur, horns, meat, sinew, every part of a reindeer.

The biggest problem for reindeer is the warble fly. Warble flies bore through reindeer hide and drive the animals crazy. The herds stampede, and many reindeer are trampled to death. Now our Soviet scientists have come up with medicine to protect reindeer from the warble fly. Now we have no more problem of warble fly for Siberian reindeer.

Reindeer eat lichens and lowbush berries on the tundra. We move the herds in a migration pattern. This allows the lichens to regrow. Lichens take fourteen, fifteen years to grow. Moving reindeer herds scientifically is the main secret of Yakut and Even success with reindeer herding. Usually we go by sled or on foot with reindeer herds. But we have helicopters for herding now, and sometimes we use a helicopter.

When the reindeer are ready for slaughter, we herd them into the corral. Breeders feed grain to the reindeer two times a day, for one month before slaughter. This makes reindeer fat, makes better meat. Feeding corn, the reindeer get much bigger. Maybe a hundred kilos or more.

Now reindeer herds are bigger, more healthy. Long time ago, we learned to tame reindeer, but we had problems with the warble fly, and did not use scientific herding patterns. It was not easy changing our habits of herding. We Yakut and Even are independent people, and like to do things our own way. But we are glad now to have the help of Soviet scientists. We have gone to school, learned about injecting warble fly medicine, learned migration patterns. Our state farm is well organized. Before, we herding families just worked independently, but we didn't succeed so well with our herds. And now, our state farm is expanding, growing bigger. We have health clinics and our children go to schools, learn many occupations. Don't think change came easily to Yakutia, it didn't. But we Yakut and Even people, we made the decisions, we made the changes in our lives. And, of course, the state helped us.

We keep some reindeer for sled deer. And still today, we prefer reindeer milk, although we have cow's milk too.

Can reindeer fly? You have felt their swift movement pulling the sled. Reindeer are very fast, run for hours with no stopping. Young fawns keep up with their mothers. Can reindeer fly? Tomorrow, when I come to Topolinii to visit you, maybe I will answer this question. But you see, time has so quickly passed. We had a good visit. Now I must go out with the herd. The sun is down and it becomes very cold. You must return to Topolinii now. So my life story must wait until tomorrow. Please expect me at nine o'clock.

We will drink a toast now. Please, take some vodka. It is cold on the tundra.

The whole town turned out to hear the Yakut accordion man and local cultural club perform Arctic ballads, haunting homespun melodies and ancient songs of the hunt. Afterward, though it was near midnight, a crowd of jolly children dragged me into Topolinii's town square, a glistening mirror beneath the full moon. As we played children's games, I noticed the youngsters were almost all mixed nationalities, a rainbow of the human race. Many were both Slavic and Asian.

Americans are often confused by inaccurate media references to Soviet citizens as "the Russians," and to the Soviet Union as "Russia." Russia, in fact, is the largest of fifteen republics which are called the Union of Soviet Socialist Republics, or Soviet Union. Russia is the seat of Soviet power, Russia's Moscow being the capital of the U.S.S.R. Of over one hundred nationalities that live in the Soviet Union, Russians have the largest population, but Ukrainians in the European U.S.S.R., and Uzbeks in Soviet Central Asia are rapidly catching up. Like the United States, the Soviet Union is a nation of many nationalities. Topolinii's children, varied shades and hues, represent the broad integration of Soviet peoples, especially in the new Soviet towns on the Siberian frontier.

We were playing a Siberian version of Red Rover when Nikolai found us, and with one gentle word sent Topolinii's children flying home to their beds. In the guest chalet, Nikolai presided over a Siberian midnight snack—mounds of frozen reindeer slabs, brusnika and more White Dynamite.

"Eat heartily and drink up," he counseled, "and don't stay up too late arguing politics with the Georgian. In the morning I will tell you some facts about Topolinii and our reindeer industry."

The following morning, though I had not heeded his advice about early retirement, Nikolai kept his promise. He began by telling me that the Even language has over twenty words to describe snow.

Nikolai

Har means snow. The melting kind of snow. *Tonga* in Even is top-melting snow. *Kutana* means snow which is soiled on the surface. So there are many words for describing snow. Wet snow is *irina*. When it's snowing wet snow. *Pulga* means blizzard.

Here in Topolinii, fifteen hundred people live. About one

third of our population is children. Here there are Even, Yakut, Russian, Ukrainian, Kirghiz, Buryats . . . we have many nationalities represented in Topolinii. But the reindeer herders are for the most part Even and Yakut. Russians, Buryats and others might take a wife, a Yakut or Even wife, and begin working as reindeer breeders. But the herders have been Even and Yakut people.

Now we are changing our approach to reindeer breeding. Now we use industrial methods. Basically, that means we make use of technology. Thirty percent of our herds can be reached by roads. So we can transport supplies, people, by truck technology. And the herders can use prefabricated portable houses, not only the old skin tents. The prefabricated houses hold up well. So now we're herding reindeer on an industrial basis, right? So that means we give them special feed which raises their live weight. Once they're fattened up, right?—we weigh them, every one of them, seventy-three hundred reindeer at one time for slaughter. Now we breed reindeer weighing a hundred and six kilos. The average weight of a reindeer in Yakutia is eighty kilos. So we're improving every reindeer by twenty-six kilograms. We improve the quality of feed, and this changes the reindeer meat. They did research on our reindeer in Moscow and proved our results. So we're switching over in the direction of an industrial foundation, right? We use all parts of the reindeer, the skin, the antlers . . . we plan to build a number of factories for this purpose, to make warm things, souvenir crafts. We even use the reindeer skin which covers the legs. For sewing hats and unti. We supply the medical industry with reindeer antlers, and they use them to make the remedy andalin, which strengthens the body's organs. Reindeer antlers now are like gold. We have special cars and trucks designed for use in Siberia. And snowmobiles and helicopters, and airports where we receive supplies.

In this state reindeer farm, we have seventeen herds, with twenty-one thousand, two hundred and sixteen head of reindeer. We have about a hundred and twenty herders. We are still in the process of building the town, and so now we have a lot of construction workers, temporary residents, when they finish here they'll move on. . . . We have a maternity house, a small one, but we're currently building a new two-million-ruble hospital. You have seen the plan for the new town. We have two libraries here, a bookstore. We have a number of reading halls. All our supplies are mail order, brought in by plane. Right now we are organizing a centralized system of supplying libraries in the U.S.S.R. According to this new plan, we receive books and newspapers. Our central library is in Khandyga, the books are distributed from there. When the people in a village have read the books, a small library sent to them, we change the library. So there is a circulation of small libraries. If you need a book from Yakutsk, or from Moscow, from the Lenin Library, you send a letter. You'll receive the book in about a month.

We have a small hospital here. And a clinic with three doctors and a number of nurses. And an ambulance. All the medical people here are local people who we sent to study at an institute. Same with the teachers. As everywhere in the Soviet Union, all medical care and education is provided free to every citizen. Our teachers are also local people who we sent to study at an institute.

Prascovia Neustroyeva is here to talk with us now. I am going to help her because she does not speak Russian. Prascovia is pure Even. She was born not far from here. She grew up as a reindeer herder. Now she's a hunter. In a little while, Igor will come by. He is anxious to visit with you again. Remember, Prascovia is a little bit shy. She probably won't mention her Hero of Labor award. Anyway, here she is now.

She had entered the room so softly, with her hunter's light footfall, that Prascovia Neustroyeva might have been stalking polar foxes. She had wide, high cheekbones and dazzling teardrop shaped eyes that shone from a weather-worn face. She was squarely built and looked strong. She wore a dark wool suit with a straight skirt and flowered blouse, a rabbit fur hat and unti. She was very shy and seemed uncomfortable when offered food or refreshment. She declined politely, and with her eyes, Prascovia Neustroyeva said she was more comfortable out on the tundra where words are not so important.

Prascovia Neustroyeva

As a child, living on the tundra, I was quite sure the rest of the world was the same. The same nature, the same people, and everyone in constant movement, changing places and living with the animals. I thought all the rest of the world was like this. My mother and father were both reindeer herders, and their favorite expression was "We are always following the reindeer." Back then, there were no such big villages as Topolinii, where I live with my family now.

I was born in a small village just north of Topolinii, called Tompo, in 1928. Many times as a child, I heard about the Even giant—for I am an Even woman—the giant who protected my people against evil invaders who tried to interfere in the lives of my people, who tried to harm them. The Even giant was a hero in my people's villages.

It was necessary for our survival that even the children worked. I helped with the reindeer herding and I looked after the younger children. I had plenty of housekeeping to do in our tent, too. I had the job of making order in our skin tent and preparing meals for my parents. We moved not as one single family with the reindeer, but three or four families moved together. Our central supply was in Tompo. Usually, we herded the reindeer year-round, changing our location every two days. In two days, the reindeer had eaten all the grass and so we had to move on.

Our nature in particular is difficult. Each season of the year brings its own difficulties traveling among the trees. In 1942, we had an especially difficult trip. That winter, the temperatures reached minus 65 degrees* and the snow was very deep. But the northern reindeer is used to living in his natural conditions, so even one and a half meters of snow doesn't matter for a reindeer. It can still reach the lichens by digging with its hoof down through the snow where it reaches a special kind of lichen called *yagel,* or Iceland moss.

Since 1945, since I was seventeen, I have worked here for the state reindeer farm. When I go hunting, my working day begins at six o'clock in the morning. I can go either on foot or on the back of a reindeer. I pack traps, iron traps, traps made of rope, traditional traps, and meat for bait. And I have a trained dog for hunting squirrels and sables. I hunt several kinds of animals, and I take along different guns depending on the animal. The dog is trained to listen to my order. It knows from listening to me which animal to go after. I make the sound of the animal, and the dog understands the difference between, say, a sable and a squirrel. For example, if I'm hunting a sable, the dog is trained to hear the sound of a sable, and goes after it, chases the sable up a tree and bays at it so I can find it. Then I shoot it.

One day I caught twenty-five squirrels and two sables.

My tent is in the woods. I'll travel twelve to fifteen kilometers hunting game. When the weather is bad and there are no signs of animals on the ground, I don't go out. On those days, I stay inside my tent and do other work, like seeing to the skins, preparing them for tanning.

My family lives in Topolinii, my husband and children, and my husband also works on the state farm. I have seven children and of course I have taken all of them hunting

* $-65°$ celsius $= -85°$ Fahrenheit.

with me when they were small. But it was different for them than it was for me when I was young. Back then, life was more difficult for herders and hunters on the tundra. Now one of my daughters is studying sewing in Leningrad, and a son is in the army. Another is a reindeer herder. My younger children, Sergei and Alona, are still in school here, and another daughter is a teacher in Topolinii. Now Sergei and Alona live in a boarding school, and that's very convenient for me because when I go out on the tundra, I'm sure they're being well cared for.

Prascovia is not a pure Even name, but my mother had a close relative called Prascovia and she liked the name, so she gave it to me. The Even and Yakut names sound like Russian names, yes. They are the same names. Now we have no pure Even names.

I was told that in the United States there are lots of reindeer. But I know from the American Eskimo herders who came here that nowadays reindeer breeding is not so good there. This was several years ago, when I met the Eskimos. I don't know much about reindeer people of the U.S., about their methods of work, about their culture. But I would like to know about them. I do know they're having troubles in their occupation, and I hope they can become more successful. Being Evenki* people like myself, I would like them to be successful in reindeer herding.

I never got to hear Igor Pogodaev's life story. At nine o'clock that morning, he was tending a herd of reindeer out on the tundra, and I was tending a severe hangover back in Topolinii's guest chalet. I wanted to wait around the corral for Igor to return, but my Muscovite escort said, rather sternly, that a weather condition was forming over the mountains, and it was necessary to fly out immediately. Her firm hand at my elbow steered me out of Topolinii.

*Evenki are seminomadic northern Siberians, of which the Even are a subgroup. Prascovia is expressing her knowledge that, centuries ago, Evenki and other Siberian peoples crossed the Bering Strait and settled in Alaska. She feels a kinship with Alaska's Eskimos.

Riley Wreck

Riley Wreck reindeer camp is nearly at the top of the world, perched above the Arctic Circle on the shore of Kotzebue Sound, an inlet of the Chukchi Sea. The village of Kotzebue, central supply town for northwest Alaska's reindeer herders, is a thirty-minute bush plane ride along coastal waters. By air, Siberia is less than two hours from Riley Wreck reindeer camp. It sits on a narrow peninsula between the saltwater Sound and a freshwater stream. You can walk from the stream to the Sound in less than a minute. The beach is rocky except for a thin strip of sand at water's edge, and if you notice strange footprints in the sand, beware of brown bear. And wolves. The reindeer camp has three canvas tents, pulled taut over wooden skeletons, a communal kitchen, an outhouse, a fish and hide drying rack that supports a child's swing, and a sprawling reindeer corral where wooden gates open onto lowbush tundra meadows. There are no trees on this tundra. Even so, on a midsummer eve, Riley Wreck is Arctic Paradise. Midsummer night, the sun never really goes to bed, it just lies down for a few hours on the northeast horizon. Life at the top of the world will confuse and disorient a *cheechako*, stranger to the Arctic.

Johnson Stalker, an Inupiat Eskimo, has been outside Alaska once. In the fifties, Mr. and Mrs. Stalker flew "down below," to Birmingham, Alabama, where Johnson was honored as one of America's Outstanding Farmers, an award he received because of his skills as a reindeer herder.

Today, Johnson Stalker herds reindeer for the Northwest Alaska Regional Corporation, known as NANA, which took its name from the Northwest Alaska Native Association, the now-defunct group that founded the company. Although no longer subjugated to the Imperial Russian and Anglo-American fur traders who savaged Eskimos and their homelands, some native Alaskans have nevertheless accepted the economic system imposed on their ancestors. NANA is one of several regional corporations that developed out of the 1971 Alaska Native Claims Settlement Act, which returned 44 out of 375 million acres of land to the original inhabitants. On this relatively small piece of ground, native corporations are attempting to preserve their culture while simultaneously developing natural resources for the economic gains so long denied to Alaska's natives. Some Alaskans, including Anglo Americans who have lived in the State all their lives, oppose the Native Land Claims Settlement. Some of the opposition is patently racist; resentment of non-Anglo natives who are finally winning some of their rights. But most of the opposition seems to come from environmentalists who believe the native corporations will be no different than the Anglo companies who came before them and who damaged virgin land while developing it; and from Alaska's secessionists, who oppose any federal authority in Alaska. Some native Alaskans who are eligible to join the native corporations and possibly find employment through them, have rejected the notion of "working within the white man's system," and have opted instead to stay out of the controversy altogether, preferring to live subsistence lives off the land. But NANA executive Pam Herman told me that when the corporation was founded, virtually everyone eligible to become a stockholder signed up.

NANA's purpose and goals are best described by the symbolism its founders adopted: " . . . an Eskimo hunter moving aggressively toward a successful future in a vast, beautiful, and sometimes harsh world . . . NANA is all of us together as one hunter, successful if we are of one mind and purpose, hungry if we are split by doubts and mistrust of each other. As one hunter is small and insignificant when compared to our environment, so is NANA when compared to the corporate and governmental environment in which it must hunt to survive. The same qualities of courage, confidence, humility, respect, integrity and sharing with others that have allowed our people to survive as great hunters in a harsh climate are necessary for NANA to be successful. We as stockholders must develop these qualities in our corporation in order to insure its success."*

Milton Cross, NANA's bush pilot, and, incidentally, the mayor of Kotzebue, the town where NANA's offices are located, believes the organization has already made positive improvements in the lives of his people. "NANA's main goal," he said, "is to provide employment opportunities for our people. We want to preserve our culture, yes. At the same time, we are being careful to preserve the land, not damage it. We are thinking of the future."

NANA is indeed investing in the future. By 1980, its corporate operations included oil lease investments on Alaska's North Slope and in the Beaufort Sea. In joint ventures with other native regional corporations and Standard Oil of Ohio, NANA has a contract to operate oil rigs for SOHIO. NANA also operates a tourist hotel in

*NANA Regional Corporation, 1980 Annual Report

Kotzebue, and produces traditional crafts with jade from their Jade Mountain mining operations. In 1980, NANA purchased the assets of the bankrupt Kotzebue Fishing Cooperative and is now using the plant to process and package hides, horns and meat from their reindeer herds. NANA, in short, is no cottage industry, but a large corporation whose stockholders are people like Johnson Stalker, the reindeer herder.

Neither Milton Cross nor other Inupiats I spoke with in Kotzebue have misconceptions about quick and easy solutions to problems of rising inflation, and the neverending land controversies that complicate the lives of Inupiats today. Jimmy Carter's 1979 Land Act prohibited corporations from further exploiting vast areas of Alaska's land. These areas were taken out of State control and labeled National Forest Preserves. The native regional corporations' land was not affected by the federal land seizure, and native tribes were permitted, through a special provision, to continue hunting and fishing on the preserves. This access to hunting and fishing areas is crucial to natives who eke out subsistence lives from the land. But the provision excluded other Alaskans, who consider themselves natives, and yet do not fall into the eligible categories of Eskimo, Indian, Aleut or Athabaskan. These Alaskans are furious at being denied access to lands they too depend on, either for subsistence survival or for recreational activities. Adding fuel to the fiery issue, Ronald Reagan's secretary of the interior, James Watt, has announced his plans to turn the federal preserves over to major energy corporations for development, a move which among other things could adversely affect migration patterns of Alaska's reindeer herds. If Watt's dreams come true, all Alaskans will lose their rights to use these lands, and how Inupiats will survive is a question NANA's leaders will have to confront.

Native corporations have brought some relief to their

memberships, but inflation has placed a heavy burden on all Alaskans, one that is not easily lifted. The price of a hamburger at the Kotzebue Dairy Queen has risen to four dollars, and a new house there costs an estimated ninety thousand dollars. NANA has sought to relieve some of the economic stress by organizing a local housing authority which developed a low-income program to build prefabricated houses. Johnson Stalker, the reindeer herder, will soon have his first real home. Improving education and health programs for Inupiats has been another aim of NANA. Free health clinics, financed by the State, serve NANA's villages and the reindeer herders. As educational opportunities slowly improve for native Alaskans, the demand for better jobs grows. NANA leaders recognize the frustrations of their young people, who have received educations that prepare them for employment, only then to discover jobs are scarce. According to Milton Cross, the lack of job opportunities is the major cause of alcoholism among native Alaskans.

When NANA decided to go into the reindeer herding business, a handful of its members received permission to visit Topolinii, Siberia, and to consult with Yakut and Even herders there. The rare meeting of Inupiat, Even and Yakut reindeer herders took place in Topolinii in the early seventies. Since then NANA's herding operation has adopted some of the Siberians' methods.

Until recently, reindeer herding in Alaska has been a risky investment, mainly because the animals have a habit of dancing away with their Alaska kin, the wild Barren Grounds caribou. Harsh winters have also cut back the numbers of Alaska's reindeer, which were first imported from Siberia in 1891 by Dr. Sheldon Jackson, a missionary. After experiencing cycles of private ownership and government-regulated herds, Alaska's herders have only recently begun transforming their art into a full-fledged industry. Today, NANA's reindeer herds number about ten thousand head, and the meat is sold to local villagers, who depend on this protein source for survival. But reindeer antlers "in the velvet," sold in Oriental markets, remain the most lucrative aspect of reindeer breeding.

Milton Cross flies his bush plane out to Riley Wreck once a day, carrying in supplies and ferrying herders from one camp to another or into Kotzebue on their days off. He offered to take me along one day, to introduce me to Mr. and Mrs. Stalker and to Mrs. Stalker's reindeer stew. Flying over Kotzebue Sound, I asked Cross the same question I had asked Igor Pogodaev in Siberia. "Milton," I said, "can reindeer fly?"

"Sure," he said smiling. "In fact, I've had three reindeer in my cargo hold, going to Kotzebue. They flew just fine."

Johnson Stalker, the reindeer herder, has probably eaten a lot of reindeer stew in his lifetime. There is no food shortage at Riley Wreck reindeer camp, and his wife, Rosie, has a golden touch with the meals she prepares in the camp's kitchen. Her reindeer stew and elaborate sourdough pancake breakfasts would satisfy a healthy-sized polar bear. Johnson Stalker enjoys his wife's cooking. Still, he is a lean, wiry man, who gets more than his share of exercise out on the tundra. Under the Midnight Sun, we all sat around the camp's kitchen table, and Johnson Stalker talked about his life in the Arctic Circle.

Johnson Stalker

My dad was John Stalker from Noatak. He's been a reindeer herder ever since I was a kid, my dad. He used to even carry me on his back when I got tired, that's how small I was when I first started, and ever since then, I've been a reindeer herder. And when it got time for school, my uncle got some reindeer from the government, and I didn't even go to school, I be with the reindeer all the time.

Sometimes all alone by myself. A little kid. And I been in reindeer ever since. Ever since I was born in 1935.

When I was nineteen, my uncle want me to go in partnership, to get loan reindeer from the government. So my daddy sign the papers for me, till I get up to twenty, twenty-one. So after that I have partnership with my uncle, you know, half and half, he do the business and I take care of reindeer for him. Then they turn over the whole thing to me, the reindeer. I was pretty young yet, I guess, twenty-two. I start my own business with reindeer, still working on government herd.

The caribou migrate one time. Maybe forty thousand caribou go through my range, night and day they travel. You can't stop them. One day we had nothing but reindeer it look like. But they're all mixed with caribou. How can I get them reindeer out of caribou? I had three boys with me. I give them all ammunition so they can save my reindeer somehow. So we tried going around the caribou to get the reindeer out. I feel like crying because there is no more business right there if caribou take reindeer away. No way you can stop them. So we tried. We saved about three hundred. Caribou took the rest—the fawns, they all mixed up, excited, they thought their mother go with caribou, they go back and forth, all mixed up. That was in November 1966, when caribou took the reindeer away from me.

It's not only me, other herders besides me, from each village, absolutely run out of reindeer. Six herders from each village. Like York Wilson and Sheild Downey and all those guys. Caribou just migrate, you can't stop the caribou which way they want to go, they're not scared. And besides, they keep traveling, they can't just sleep in one place. The first ones lay down and the other ones keep moving. That's the way the caribou travel. They don't stay in one place. Unless you stop the first bunch. You stop the first bunch, they might turn the other way. But when first one goes through, no way you can stop the rest. That's the way I lose my reindeer.

When I lose my reindeer, then BIA's* trying to get me for a model herder. I didn't understand what the hell's a "model herder." That's in Nome. One year, they ask me if I want to go to Nome, you know. So I did. And I drive from Shishaulik, I drive reindeer to Nome. Snowshoes and dog team. It was shortest way I go too. Thanksgiving Day I start out, Kotzebue to Nome. I get to Nome just before Christmas.

It's experimental reindeer in Nome. I'm working with veterinarians and all that. If they want reindeer in the corral, I have to put 'em in there. Give 'em shots, studied 'em. They studied about the feed. Universities, they make a fence around the moss, how long that be good for reindeer. And like that. It's the kind of work I be doing with reindeer for BIA. Then NANA starts to get reindeer. And me and my wife, we're from Kotzebue. We get kinda homesick. Then NANA ask me if I want to work for them, with reindeer near Kotzebue. And BIA said, "You're gonna take our reindeer away." I says, "Yeah." Well, better pay, and so I drive reindeer back home.

I never have my own home, like settle down, see. We move around all my life. Now I'm gonna get a home at Buckland. It's NANA housing, low income housing. They're hauling it right now. It'll be my own home. That's where I gonna have home, at Buckland. It's easier for me to work then. 'Cause I don't take my family out in wintertime. Kids have school. I go by myself.

I never speak English as a kid. We speak Eskimo. When I tried school one time along the way, they didn't want us to speak in Eskimo. One time I got blasted on my lips

---

* The Bureau of Indian Affairs administered federal reindeer breeding programs before native associations were founded.

'cause I talk Eskimo to one of the kids. So I don't have to talk Eskimo. We talk like we were born, talking Eskimo. That's why I hardly talk English myself.

I was adopted when just a baby. My father, he was white man. They tell me he's my father. He was a miner up in Kiana. He had horses, they said he used horses and all that. They said I got a daddy who's a miner. This father, I saw him one time. He said, "You're gettin' to be quite a boy now, huh?" And he wanted to see me again, I think he wanted to give me his mines, me and my twin sister. But I didn't care for it anyway. I never belonged to him. My father who adopt me is a reindeer herder, a native.

The old men taught me how to be a reindeer herder. Nowadays when we herd reindeer we use snow machines. Long ago we use our legs and snowshoes and dogs. The old-timers taught me if you go reindeer herding you got to get the whole herd. If you miss any reindeer, tell us. They always have chief herder, you know, and chief herder's the boss. They wake you up early in the morning, and you have backsack with you and how many hours, two days maybe you have to stay with reindeer. And sled deer. Old-timers taught me about sled deer. Sometime I have blister over here from holding the rawhide. Reindeer pulling sled.

Before I was born there must be great reindeer herders. Like I heard about Iluktin Trix. He brought some reindeer from Lapland. They don't know about snow machine yet. He learn to be reindeer herder in Lapland then bring his reindeer over here. He is Eskimo. He make our collars and draw our pictures. In fact, they got today a Laplander's house still standing here this side of Buckland, that's where they used to stay. It's got an upstairs. Laplanders make a fence, long fence, you can still see that fence. It's maybe eight, ten miles long. Laplanders built that. And they had herders from this area, Eskimos.

They say reindeer much bigger back then. The old sled deer, they pretty big. It's a steer that you castrate and you

49

call it a sled deer. When you castrate a bull, we call it a steer. York one time had thirty sled deer, load the sled and went to Kotzebue. Long row of reindeer. He deliver meat to Kotzebue from his camp.

In August when the warble flies bother the reindeer, they go towards the wind, you see, and when the wind hits them, they go real fast and hit the beach. One day I pay no attention and reindeer go towards the wind. I'm eating breakfast. There was a fishing camp about two miles away. They have line on the beach for fishing, to pull the net up. So I run after reindeer, and I have reindeer dog. So reindeer stop on fishing line and lay down. I was a shy kid, you know, I don't stay in town, most of time I'm outdoors. So when I finally catch reindeer they're laying down on line belongs to fishing camp. Fishing camp people ask me if I'd go have coffee with them. I used to go past that camp and see a girl. I didn't know her name even. So I go and drink coffee. That's when I met Rosie. Find a girlfriend right there. Drive the reindeer back home. Now Rosie and me been married twenty-three years.

Rosie, she first don't know about reindeer. She try to drive reindeer sled one time, I give her tamest, most gentle reindeer. Still she was scared. But she learn. She really help me after we get married. Her and I all alone sometime stay in camp, take care of fifteen hundred reindeer. We didn't have no kids at first. We were happy when a fawn was born, just like a little kid. Now we have four kids. Johnson Junior, he was almost born in reindeer camp. Rosie started to have pain. I have sled gear for emergencies. So I leave one herder with reindeer and drive sled thirty-six miles to Kotzebue, take Rosie to Kotzebue. Before we have snow machine, we have to have emergency sled gear, in case something happen.

Snowmobiles start coming in sixties. At first, one that have most money get them. First snow machine I get was '65, with BIA. If you know about using machines on the snow, it's good to have snowmobile with reindeer herds.

It's easier to ride than walk anyway. But before snow machines, reindeer were more gentle. You have to know how to use snow machine with reindeer. When you do it helps. Maybe herder out seven or eight miles from camp with reindeer. And it take time to change herders. You have to walk all that way. It help to have snow machine then. Before snow machine, reindeer were tame. Whatever you want to do, you do right there. You start to butcher 'em, they don't panic, they don't try to run away.

Nowadays, these reindeer we have, they're all mixed. I get those from Nome, those from Espenberg, all kinds of mixed-up reindeer. When I first bring reindeer from Nome to Kotzebue, they try to go back home to Nome. They know where they come from. Hard time trying to keep them. That's the way reindeer are. Even if you would bring reindeer from Russia, I think they would try to go home. They know which way it is. Then we have to go out and get them. We know which ones to get because they got brands, markers on them.

Reindeer get used to snow machine. But I think now we don't watch our herds like before. You have to work with the snow machine real slow. But if you let reindeer go free whole summer and then try to corral them, that's the time they'll be wild. If a reindeer goes stray, that's the time a snow machine helps. If you use a snow machine slow, I think the reindeer would be easier to handle. Sometimes the guys go fast, they want to go home quick, go have supper or something, and they go too fast on snow machine. And if they move reindeer too fast into corral, they get excited, real excited, then they stray out. So we have to open up the corral until they really get tired and bring 'em back. Sometimes they're hard to catch even with snow machines. They can outrun you too if there's enough good trail. Helicopter is better even than snow machine. Easier yet. Now we have helicopter pilot from New Zealand. They use helicopter for red deer down there.

We cut horns in July. And we give 'em shots. This

October, we're going to give 'em their shots. And separate the butchering reindeer, the ones going to Kotzebue for slaughter. Over at Church Rock camp, that's where we'll do it. We'll separate the bulls from the steers. The ones we'll butcher, they have a red tag, so you know, you don't give the ones with the red tags shots. We castrate the steers so they won't fight and get skinny. So they'll get fat all winter. And you get some females to butcher, the old ones, pretty soon they'll be good for nothing, they don't have no fawns. And you can tell reindeer apart. They're just like human beings, acting different than each other, a lot of them.

When fawns start making horns, next year they make the same ones. And when they get older and older, they make the same shape horns, same as ever since they were born. Unless something injure their horns. Every year, even the old bulls after they drop their horns, they'll make the same type of horns. Because they use their hind legs on their horns, you know.

The horns stay soft until about September, October. Right now the females' horns are soft yet. We take the horns off before they start fighting, that's about September first. We take horns off by August. The bulls will fight. If there be one strong bull amongst the reindeer, out of a thousand reindeer there might be one strong bull that will fight. And he might be fighting over a female. And while he is fighting, some other bull might take that female. When they fight, they can't even eat, they put mud on their lips, they're fighting so much. Some of 'em, they cripple others. About a month they're fighting. You have to watch 'em, but there's not a whole lot you can do. If two strong bulls meet each other, which is which, who will be the boss? If they're just about equal, they'll be fighting for a long time. And the one that lose, if he lives, he won't bother the stronger bull no more. He's scared of him. That's the way these reindeer are mating. Fight. They tangle up sometime. If they get their horns tangled up and couldn't come out, they'll starve to death. Once in a while they do that.

Reindeer are smart. They're even smarter than me anyway. When I went to Nome one time with my uncle, we had eleven deers and we got to Nome and tied 'em up for a while at the airport there. Shopped around, and then it got kinda late. Real stormy. But we have to go home. So we start out and we have to know which way to go. So I think I know more than these crazy animals. So I try to lead them, riding in the sled, uncle riding in the back. I try to turn reindeer. They don't want to turn. So I said to my uncle, "I know they're going the wrong way." My uncle says, "Yeah, they take us wrong way. But let's let 'em go, see where they take us." And they get fast, 'cause we don't try to turn 'em. We had halters on 'em, double trees, single trees. But we don't try to turn 'em, just let 'em go wherever they want to go. And we drive through storm about half hour. Then we see light my wife put in window each time it storm. Right to our camp reindeer lead us. And I say, "They're smarter than me." And they are.

In June or July we take the bull horns. They're in honeycomb, more soft, more bloody. That's "A" grade, that's highest value horn. Because it's not bony yet. We take off the horns, box 'em, weigh 'em and send 'em out to wherever they're going. Johnny Wang, he buys 'em, takes to Korea to sell. They use 'em for some kind of medicine. Or some kind of hard-on, something like that. And they drink the blood from horns. We had some kind of Japanese [Koreans] here, they come all the way up here, twelve or so of them, just to drink the blood from horns. They come out to the corral where we was taking the horns off. We had to wait while they got their little paper cups and they had some kind of vodka or Jim Beam for a chaser—make Bloody Mary out of it, mix it with blood. They take the horn just cut from reindeer and maybe soak a paper towel in

53

blood and drink it, or just drink right out of horn. They close their eyes and start sucking that blood. Take turns. Then there's a big bull come out, and they all went after that. Then after they drink, they take off, fly out of Kotzebue and don't come back. Just come to have blood.

No, Eskimo never did that. Now, like when you kill the reindeer, you hang it up and cut the throat. We used to have blood from the throat. You know when you cut the throat to bleed it out, so it will be white and clean and won't be bloodshot, you always cut the throat. And my uncle used to lick the blood from it. And I have too. Just put your mouth there while it's spurting and drink. It's rich, pretty rich. But I never have it from the horn.

We used to eat the points of a horn. Just the points on the tip of the horns. Cut it with a knife, chew it. They're pretty good. Nowadays it's too expensive.

We use every part of reindeer that can be used. The leg skin we make *mukluks* out of. Use reindeer hide for mattress. We use reindeer mattress right now. If you've got a wife that can sew, then you can use the skins. If your wife won't sew, then it's no use saving them unless you give them away. You lay the hides out in the sun to dry. When I used to have reindeer herd of my own, I used to sell the hides to Goldbergs. They'd soften, tan 'em, make gloves, things like that. Mukluk is English. In Eskimo, we say *kammik*. Now the kids around here, they don't even understand Eskimo language. Inupiat, that's what I speak.

See, our reindeer here, they're half-breeds too. Now the caribou and the reindeer, it's just like Eskimo and white, you can notice the difference. And you can notice a half-breed reindeer from the regular reindeer, half-breed person from the regular whites. They're in between. You can notice that too. Just like human beings.

The best parkees they make from three year old fawns. That's warm, light. They use water and soap, make it soft, make parkee out of it. My daughter have albino parkee one time to wear to school. Fawn skin inside, all white pretty fur outside. Some albino reindeer have sour milk, some of them blind, some have pink horns, some don't live, you know, they like to sleep. You have to go wake them up.

As long as they live, reindeer make another horn every year. Old-timers tell me reindeer live up to fifteen years, even more. But nowadays, females live longer because we butcher the bulls when they're young. But we like to keep the females 'cause they have fawns. But when they start to get old, maybe twelve years, their horns start to get smaller, they can't get any more fat. Old age.

Reindeer, they drink salt water, they even eat salmonberries and ptarmigan eggs, they'll lick it. Not all the reindeer, there'll be some reindeer who'll lick ptarmigan eggs. Reindeer mostly eat lichen on tundra. Now we are trying to feed them grain. Reindeer like salt. When you're out on the tundra, inland, where there's no salt water, they dig around tent, they try to have piss, try to have salt. Not all the reindeer. If you had about a thousand reindeer, you'll have about half a dozen trying to do that. One time I tried to make a sled deer from a reindeer that liked salt. So I made a loop of rope in the snow and peed right in the center. Then I took one end of the rope in my tent and waited. Now he start coming, coming through the snow. I peeked through my door and watched, and when he finally step into the rope, I pulled my rope and caught its leg. Just like a trap. It's a yearling, it's not female. I have to castrate it, put halter on it and make a sled deer out of it. You have to know how to tie rope around wild deer. If you make it too long it will break its neck running. I made that sled deer. He turn out to be good sled deer. His name was Pisslover.

I always try to name sled deer. Honeycomb or Sweetheart or Happy Home. Pisslover was a good sled deer. I have to gentle it down. He'll fight at first. Then you can pet it. Some of them tickle. You can tickle them when it gets used to you. At first he'll try to hit you, fight back. But you don't have to be scared of him, otherwise he'll get meaner and meaner. Pretty soon you'll think he win from you. But if you hang on to it, pretty soon he'll get real calm, just like a horse.

We had a big steer in Nome, he weighed about four hundred and fifty pounds. They usually weigh between two hundred, three hundred pounds, the steers.

Now they start butchering over at NANA's fish co-op in Kotzebue. They butcher reindeer there. They're talking about using hooves too, and the sinew and all that. I don't know for what they use the hooves. Long ago, they used them for eyeglasses to shade eyes from snow's glare. They make little hole, just about see through there and wear 'em over eyes. Before they have sunglasses, they did that.

I was never a fisherman. I know how to net, but I never knew how to cut it and clean. But I know about the reindeer. When I'm off, I go to town, go into a bar, and everybody knows I'm a reindeer herder.

Sometimes you have a lot of fun with the reindeer. Just like people. If I like a reindeer and I don't see it for a long time, when I find it again I'm happy. Just like an old friend. And when I miss them from the herd, I go looking for them. If you miss one reindeer from herd, that means many are missing. If you miss two or three, there might be over a hundred missing from the herd.

Hardest time is storms. Sometimes you can't find the camp. Sometimes you can't even find the reindeer. Sometimes you get lost and can't find camp or reindeer! Maybe lost for hours. And sometimes we have trouble with wolves. Bear. Smart wolves. They wait for storms. When it get storm they go to our reindeer and kill many and eat. We put kerosene lamp near camp, and put red cover over it so reindeer have light, so they see the camp, don't get lost. Don't get killed by wolves. And brown bear. Yeah, in fact I almost got a bear once. See, he was killing all the little fawns. And I saw the bear running and I was so mad at him because I see the mothers, they're crying for their fawns, you know. So I go after the bear on snow machine with shotgun. I chase him and he really get mad at me, and then I turned the snow machine and when he start after me I turn back, and where he go I go after him. I think finally he get tired, I shoot him with gun and he's dead then. Buckshot. But you know, the old-timers said, "Don't go to the bear just 'cause you think you killed him." I heard this from the old-timers. So I go around him, he didn't move, I go around him again, he didn't move. I had this one guy with me, he was on a snow machine too. He didn't have a rifle. I have to get close to the bear to kill it, and all of a sudden that thing stood up and came towards me, its hair up, making big noises. He's coming after me. I shot at him but he never stopped. And then my snow-mobile, it stalled so I jumped off and we both took off on the other snow machine. From there I know I'm not gonna fool with him anymore, but I was always mad at him. This was in 1973.

We saw a bear the other day. Right here, near Riley Wreck. But wolves are the best skin. I got two wolves last year.

Now they teach us new ways to herd reindeer. We get up at five o'clock to herd reindeer. They don't teach us about sleep, but teach us about reindeer. Long ago, I used to sleep with reindeer. See, reindeer sleep two, two and a half hours. When they lay down, you lay down close to them, you know when they start stirring. Sometime they don't wake up, some of them. You gotta go and wake 'em up or they'll get left behind. You know, after they eat, they chew, they chew and they sleep. Long ago, when I travel a long ways with reindeer, when they lay down, I lay down, when they get up, I go. I never used to work with what we got here now, with these corrals. Long ago when I had herds, I just went with 'em. And we butchered 'em right out there, didn't bring 'em back to the corral.

A Logger's Instinct

On the northwest tip of the U.S.S.R., Latvia curves gently around the Baltic Sea. At Yurmala, on a typically gray drizzly morning, you can look out over the horizon and almost imagine Sweden's outline. The beach crunches underfoot, each step crushing dozens of miniature sea-shells, pink, white and gray, pale baby clams and scallops. A lucky beachcomber finds yellow amber rocks, gems of the Baltic. The coastline is five hundred miles long, and lined with dense forests that haunt the imagination.

One third of Latvia is swamps, peat bogs and marshes, low-lying floodlands that frustrate farmers. One third is pine forests reminiscent of old Latvian fairy tales of magic mushrooms and the "Finger-Sized Boy" tramping barefoot over damp land doing good deeds. The pines are tall, thin pencils in trembling green coats. No lowbush surrounds the trunks, just a thick brown needle carpet, soft enough to sleep on. The pines whisper chilly tales, true laments of battles waged among their majesty. Nazi troops stalking Latvian forests, following Himmler's command to "see to it that the Eastern Province is inhabited only by people with pure German blood." Nazi assassins stalking Latvian peasants, forest to peat bog, swamp to forest. The trees' branches were too high to grasp and climb, but trunks were big enough to hide behind. Many pacifist peasants hid. Partisans joined the Red Army that routed the invaders. The trees witnessed it all, and today still whisper among themselves about humankind's barbaric ways. Today the trees still protect, embrace and give breath to Latvians, who have always loved Earth's woodlands.

Nákotne means future in Latvian. Latvians would rather forget the battles waged in their forests and swamps; they prefer to think of the future, and the capital city, Riga, points the way. Riga rises out of a ring of forest named Yurmala after the seaside nearby. The Yurmala Forest is fondly called the "safety belt" by Rigans, because the deep woods help keep industrial Riga breathing and supply firewood for the city's hearths. Since peat is the only other source of fuel found on Latvian ground, most fuel has to be imported from other Soviet republics. Many Latvians, including Riga urbanites, still heat their homes with wood burning stoves and fireplaces. The Institute of Physics in Riga has its own atomic reactor to experiment with, and it may be a first step toward building an atomic power plant in Latvia.

Riga is still asleep in the crisp hours before dawn when Janis Bogdanov, a Yurmala Forest logger, leaves his urban flat and heads into the countryside to work. All the Soviet Union's forests are owned by the state, so Janis Bogdanov is a state employee. The job of a "green belt" logger is selective logging, to keep the forest trim and neat, to chop down any tree that spreads unruly, or trees marked by Forest Masters for firewood. Citizens are prohibited from cutting down Yurmala's trees, or any tree in the Soviet Union, for that matter, without a special permit. In Siberia, for example, one may chop down trees only in designated areas, and for every tree felled, two seedlings must be planted in its place. And Moscow's elegant white birch grove belt is state-designated protected land, guaranteeing no developments will deface it. Even Latvia's Yurmala Forest is protected by state laws. Meanwhile, the entire U.S.S.R. suffers a severe shortage of lumber for construction of private homes, and of firewood for heating homes. And in Riga, firewood is precious bounty. Rigans who heat their dwellings with wood can obtain a permit to chop firewood in designated areas, but the plots remain under state control because the government is wary of people hoarding building lumber and defacing forests. The firewood chopped by Yurmala's loggers is state property, distributed for public consumption. The opportunity for a black market firewood operation is thus wide open to high-ranking forestry officials who might be inclined to exploit their positions as overseers. But for workers like Janis Bogdanov, logging is very simply a job, and, incidentally, socially useful labor.

Janis Bogdanov did not choose his occupation for its "socially responsible" quality. He was born and reared, son of a logger, in Latvia's forests. Today he lives in a flat owned by the Yurmala Forestry Administration. Given the option, Janis Bogdanov might give up the amenities of an urban hot water flat and return to living in the forest. He is decidedly a woodsman who prefers moving among trees to negotiating Riga's traffic-jammed boulevards. At the Forestry administrative offices, a wall in the main corridor displays photographs of the last Five Year Plan's Model Loggers. Janis Bogdanov's graven image is not among them, nor is he a man to concern himself with decorations and awards. He is a logger's logger, Latvian kin to today's American woodsmen.

One mid-April dawn, I stood in Yurmala Forest watching Janis Bogdanov and other loggers working. The skies hung heavy with clouds that threatened snowfall. A small crowd of officials had collected in a clearing; the Forest

Chief, Ignats Grugulis, a couple of old-timer Forest Masters, a Latvian journalist and my escort. Ignats Grugulis was a huge man, a barrel-chested baritone with a full black beard. He wore the uniform of a state Forest Master, pine green and military creased. We were watching the loggers fell trees, the woods ringing with high-pitched whines of steel teeth against pine knots. A portable loggers' shack, gypsy home on wheels, sat nearby, its quaintness contrasting with a mammoth yellow tractor that had one long arm capable of lifting and loading twelve logs at once. The Chief Forest Master laughed. I asked him what was so funny.

Like low thunder, he chuckled. "Yesterday," said Ignats Grugulis, "I told the loggers they might stumble across an American in the forest this morning. They did not believe me. They thought I made a crazy remark. Now the joke is on them. They have never seen an American before."

Leaving the collection of officials behind, I walked into the woods, approaching Janis Bogdanov, the logger who had kept furthest from the crowd of officials, with his back turned. We had not been introduced, I did not know his name, but out of a half dozen loggers, he looked like the most experienced. I approached him cautiously, keeping an eye on his chain saw. He kept working as I drew near, but I knew he had me in peripheral vision. I leaned up against a tree and watched him trim green coats from logs he had felled. In a few minutes, the yellow tractor rumbled up and claimed Bogdanov's pile of trimmed logs. He began picking up the severed branches, making a neat pile, sweeping the forest's brown needle carpet clean. I said hello in Latvian.

"*Sveike.*"

"*Labrit.*" Keeping his eyes on his work, he said good morning. I might have been just another rustling tree in his forest. I didn't know many Latvian words, so I tried some Russian on him.

61

"*Ya iz amerike,*" I said. "*Amerikanskii* journalist."

"*Da.*" He kept working, displaying no interest in my presence.

The officials were back in the clearing, a hundred or so yards away. I was grateful for the opportunity to meet a Soviet worker on my own, without speaking through an interpreter, but to my frustration, this logger didn't seem to care a whit about me. I pulled out a pack of Riga brand cigarettes and asked Janis Bogdanov, "Where is it safe to smoke?"

He stopped working and motioned me to follow him along a narrow dirt path. Reaching into his jacket pocket, he pulled out a pack of Lenas and offered me one. We lit up and smoked in silence. Tiny flakes of snow wafted down through pine boughs and landed on his hard hat. He was a big blond man with pale skin. There were two rosy spots in his cheeks and a deep dimple in his chin. He wore several layers of bulky work clothes and high-topped leather boots. He shoved his hard hat back and glanced up at the clouds. I picked up a baby pine cone and broke off a section. Janis watched me, interested. I said, "Where I come from in America, the pine trees are bigger than these. And there's more underbrush. But your woods seem to tell a story I've never heard."

Janis nodded. "*Da.*"

"*Pozhaluista,*" I said. "Please, I'd like to ask you about your work in these woods."

He shrugged and said "*Pozhaluista*" in a way that means "Whatever."

Before I could ask a question, Janis Bogdanov turned to me, proffering another Lena, and said, "But first, I would like to ask you some questions about America." And he smiled.

As snow fell over the pine needle carpet, we sat in a forest official's car and Janis Bogdanov told me about his childhood in Latvia's forests.

Janis Bogdanov

That's why you walk through the forest so boldly. Maybe you like the forest like I do. I've been working in the forest for twenty-five years.

When I was born, well, in 1928, I was born in a small district town, Madonie. But the forest was also all around. Yes, all around. Yes, all around, the forest, great masses of forest. Yes, in general, yes I played a lot of the time in the forest. My father worked in the forest, even in our, as they say, capitalist Latvia.* I often went with my father to the forest. We went two or three kilometers, or even four, as soon as I'd return from school, we were immediately off to the forest. I helped him with the twigs, however I could. I was little.

We lived, the four of us, mother, father and brother and me. We had a small house, of course, there were two rooms and a kitchen. We had two cows and a horse, and five hectares of land there were. We grew grain and vegetables. These were the things our family had to eat, and my father added his earnings from working in the forest, especially in winter. There was nothing to do on the land.

The forest, the little nuts, these were my calling. And the mushrooms in the forest. As soon as autumn begins, mushrooms become my first order of business. *Boroniki* [white mushrooms with dark brown caps]. We made different dishes from them; we fried them, boiled them, dried them.

As a rule, not too many of my schoolmates were children of loggers. But you see, in earlier times, how it was to be a logger. They weren't such regular workers before. It was like this: Today maybe he'd work a day, and then for a week . . . maybe he'd move on further. It's probably like

*Latvia has gone in and out of the Soviet system several times since 1917.

that in America, too. Ts, ts, ts, well . . . when they worked in the forest what happened, you had to work . . . I remember my father woke up at four o'clock in the morning and went about in the dark, and he'd come back at eleven o'clock at night. It was dark there at night, so they would start fires and work by that firelight. Now, I work my eight hours, and then I'm free.

Yes, the Forestry gave us an apartment. And I have my health benefits. How could it be otherwise? To be sure, and each year we have to pass a medical examination as employees of a dangerous service. They give us this medical exam because our jobs are considered to be dangerous. What are the hazards of working in the forest? The power saw; it gives us vibration. For myself, for example, my fingers become white and don't work. The doctor already excused me once last year, and the year before, but I'm still working. I'm fifty-two. By law we can retire at fifty-five.

Yes, I was a very young child during the war. There weren't any battles here in Latvia where I was. When the Russians left and the Germans came there was almost a battle then, but I just saw the airplanes, but like, I didn't see the war itself. The most frightening thing that happened to me was when the Germans were leaving, they took me to dig trenches for them. For the trenches . . . They took me, they simply came to our place and said, "Let's go. Get your things together," and that was it. They took me away. I suffered for a whole week with them before I got away.

I was probably already sixteen years old. But I didn't work for them. They took me, but we never did any digging, because they were retreating the whole time. We walked and walked. At night we retreated and during the day they shut us in the barn.

While we were walking I met where my mother was. My mother had also been driven out, seventy kilometers from home. There was this city called Sausnia. There were horrible battles there. So she'd been driven there, and I found them in Matleno. That's when I escaped. I signaled to my mother that everything would be fine, and that she'd have a good journey. She still wanted to come to me to meet me, but I signaled not to, that everything would be okay. Later on, I came to her.

In 1956 I started working as a regular logger. Before that I worked with my father. Well, I helped my father. But I started working independently in 1956. I began my career as a logger at Sestinski Forest.

I started here fourteen years ago. I came here because I had small children and this is closer to Riga. Well, as everybody knows, the cultural center is the city. One daughter graduated from the institute. She works in the Riga City Council, and the second daughter is ill. She got sick . . . I have no sons; two daughters.

There is nothing in particular I like about this work—no one thing stands out. Before I came here to the Forestry, I worked in Riga for six months, but I couldn't take it. I got sick of it. I prefer outdoor work. Definitely. And besides, out here I'm free. No problems, everything is just fine.

I get twenty-four days vacation every year, and every three years I get two months. It's called a "two-monther." Every three years. This year I'll be here fifteen years, so that means this is the fifth time I'll be getting two months.

I'm not a traveler. I am not fond of tourism. On vacations—whatever—I go somewhere to visit friends, or I go to the lake to catch a little fish. No, my wife doesn't like fishing. She yells at the fish.

The green belt where I work surrounds Riga from one side to another. In these woods there are often little wild she-goats and small hares. There are elk around here. It reaches the town of Kaltinii, maybe one hundred kilometers away. It's a very wide belt, interrupted from time to time by small settlements. We have lots of forests in

Latvia. Latvia may be small, but it has lots of forests.

Sometimes I have apprentices working with me. Yes, it's happened. They work with me for a while, then they go for special courses, and then they work independently.

I don't do anything but cutting. I don't decide what trees get cut. A Forest Master goes through the forest and marks which trees are to be cut. I don't disagree with him. It seems to me that he's—well . . . sometimes when he's marking he misses some trees, and in this case I cut them. It's possible for me to use my judgment.

We work from eight o'clock until four thirty; we have a thirty-minute dinner break. That's all until eight o'clock the next morning.

Effects of war? There were lots of them. Lots of villages were burned down, and lots of Latvian people were killed, and lots of them were taken to concentration camps to work. If they thought they were on the side of the communists or if they found someone who didn't want to go into the German Army, and there were lots of them, they shot them.

As for my family, nobody was killed. My father hid. He also didn't go into the army when the Germans wanted to take him. He hid in the forest. He wasn't a partisan, he was just hiding.

There were girls and fellows taken with me. The Germans took us. Of course, there were lots of us youngsters, around two hundred people. No, we weren't so organized. Each person escaped on his own. However, wherever, whoever could. And we would always run away at night when we were walking on the move, retreating. The Germans were few, and straggled out, and it was dark, that's when you could make your break.

There were the girls, they even cried. What we'd say, we'd say, "You have to escape. When a moment arises, run. The main thing is to go alone. You mustn't go in groups or you'll be caught right away." And when I met my mother, there were less than one hundred of us left and it was more difficult for me to escape.

They didn't capture my mother. They drove them out. They threw them out, evicted them, and drove them on ahead about seventy kilometers. And the Germans took away all the cows. I left my own house. They burned everything afterwards. There were only smokestacks. I came back after the war and all that was left were chimneys.

I escaped not during the day, but at night. There was one German. The rest of the Germans had pushed ahead, they had to repair some road. I had boils on my neck. I stayed with the cook and helped him with the potatoes. And we had, well, they rounded us up in this school. There was a school there. And it was about two hundred meters from the school to the forest. And I told that German, as if on purpose, "Now I'll run away!" I went ahead about one hundred meters, and I don't know, either he was a good guy or something. I went ahead one hundred meters, but he didn't do anything, didn't react to me. And when there was only one hundred meters to go to the forest, I started running, and the German didn't shoot. And when I ran into the forest, there were these German supplies, and I thought, "Well, now I'll run into the Germans again." But there wasn't a single German there. And I went through the forest and ran away to my mother, and that's all. She showed me with her eyes the direction to go when I passed her. She occasionally stayed beside the road. And I had to pass through about two kilometers of forest to reach her. It was unfamiliar forest to me. I found my way. I had learned to orient myself in the forest since my earliest years. No moss; I just guessed from instinct.

Black Lake

"Watch out for the Widowmaker."
—Logger's Warning

The Pacific Northwest, with its fern-tangled rain forests, desolate storm-torn ocean beaches, its Cape Disappointment and Deception Pass, its Mt. St. Helens volcanic eruptions spewing hot, gritty ash over the land, is a dangerous place to live. Rainfalls are so heavy that automobiles must be specially equipped with gills. Summer, when you go outdoors, you don't tan. You rust. These and other Pacific Northwest legends are concoctions of natives, who hope to discourage newcomers and save Paradise from a population explosion.

Today a Pacific Northwest native watches warily as log trucks haul Douglas fir and pine logs out of the forests—a familiar childhood memory, yet some element of the nostalgic scene has changed. The logs got smaller as the native child grew taller. An illusion caused by growing up?

No. The trees are being taken younger now. The forests of childhood memories, tree trunks big as houses, are losing ground to population booms, industrial expansion, McDonald's stands and sprawling humdrum housing developments. Even federally controlled national parks are taking abuse. A native is sorely tempted to adopt the unfamiliar stance of activist and join the West's latest ecology movement, whose advocates want to save the trees from federal free-for-all clear cutting programs and simple neglect. Private timber corporations also own vast territories in Pacific Northwest forests, and the native who once welcomed the timber barons who brought jobs to the area now wonders if like a forest fire, their greed for profits has swept out of control. Who is responsible for the demise of Pacific Northwest forest lands? The most qualified person to answer this troubling question is a native logger.

Nobody loves the forests more than a logger. That is, a native logger who grew up in the woods. The Pacific Northwest, like Latvia, is rich in forest legends. Lumberjacks inspired youth with their fierce independence, their Paul Bunyan appetites for food and adventure. Loggers who loved forests more than towns, trails more than boulevards, whose tales of bear attacks and snake ambushes raised the hair on youthful heads. I once knew a logger who swallowed racing turtles, alive and whole, to demonstrate his voracious appetite and plucky spirit. The silent loggers were even more awesome—woodsmen philosophers who rarely went to town, and when they did, brought words of wisdom as refreshing and clear as running brook waters. Yesterday, a native child was fascinated with lumberjacks' tales. Today, a concerned native seeks a woodsman's wisdom.

One summer evening I was visiting my cousin Bill Munro at his home in the Olympic Peninsula forests. "Do you know any loggers in these woods?" I asked Munro and his wife, Ann.

"Of course we know loggers," Ann said. "Everybody knows each other around these woods. But there aren't many human loggers left these days. The big timber companies are pretty well mechanized." She frowned and puckered her lips. "What sort of logger are you interested in?"

I thought of Janis Bogdanov, the Latvian logger in Yurmala Forest. "An independent logger who's not connected to the big timber companies. Somebody who knows the work of cutting timber and hauling logs, who can explain what's happening to our forest land. Someone who really likes working outdoors."

Munro shook his head. "Everyone on this Peninsula likes to be outdoors. That's why we live in these woods. But most folks have had to take indoor jobs, for the State over in Olympia, or at the Oly Brewery in Tumwater. Not much outdoor work left, least of all logging work. Most folks have given up independent logging. It just doesn't pay anymore. Unless you're a Weyerhauser vice-president."

We sat in reverie, staring out the kitchen window at a grove of young alders. Munro squinted as if imagining convoys of mechanical woodcutters marching through his alder grove. I wondered how many young alders could be hoisted by one Latvian mechanical logger. Were there any independent loggers left in the Pacific Northwest?

"I know one," Munro said suddenly. "Name's Emerick. Milt Emerick. He's self-employed, works for himself, and has a mind of his own. He works on logging trucks now—mechanic—but he used to haul logs until the big companies took over logging in these woods. Emerick is the logger who can give you a straight story on the industry."

Munro was right. The next evening I met Milt Emerick at his home near a mysteriously dark body of water called Black Lake. Milt Emerick was a soft-spoken, philosophical man of about thirty years. He wore torn, faded blue jeans, a red plaid flannel shirt over long underwear, and heavy steel-toed boots. He had a thick black beard and a glint in

70

his eye. In front of Milt Emerick's mobile home, several horses nibbled at the ground. Milt's was a yellow quarterhorse named "Yellar" by its previous owner. Milt Emerick was kind enough to let the horse keep its name. Besides, he had more to occupy his thoughts than thinking up new names for old horses. Living in endangered forests, a logger can't help being a little preoccupied with the change coming over his land. The trees surrounding Milt Emerick's home on Black Lake were bigger than Yurmala Forest's pines, and there was more underbrush. But if Janis Bogdanov could have visited Milt Emerick in these woods, the two men might have swapped some petrifying lumberjacks' tales and some prophetic woodsmen's wisdom. Listening to Milt Emerick talk about the forests he loves, I realized that if trees could vote, they would elect someone like him Forest Master.

Milt Emerick

Used to be, when you looked around Black Lake, you saw a lot of open green, just trees standing right up to the edge of the water. My sister used to sit down on Black Lake for hours picking arrowheads out of the beach. Indian arrowheads that were there. This must have been a place to fish at one time. The tips of the arrowheads were broken off. Like they were shooting at something with arrows, probably hit the bottom and broke the tips off on rocks and whatnot. Black Lake is kind of a murky lake; it's got lots of algae. It's not really bad to swim in—I've never known anyone to get sick from it—it's just murky. You can't see into it. I took scuba diving lessons a few years ago, and I started diving out at Hood Canal. Then I decided to come out here and try Black Lake. I went down about two feet—you just don't see anything. It's black. Must have been a scuba diver named it, because it was pure black.

There's a few fish out there, perch, crawfish, and they've

been supplying it now with trout. Black Lake gets fished out fast now, though, because of the population around here. My grandfather used to take us fishing up here every Christmas and Fourth of July. He'd take us down to the lake and there used to be lots and lots of catfish—we used to catch catfish this long. But that was before it got real crowded.

You take a nail and drive it through the catfish's head, and you ring them around the head and peel the hide off. At least, that was my grandfather's method for peeling catfish. And my grandmother cooked it up. She floured it, threw it in the frying pan, and it was good fish.

Now there's not a piece of property left for sale here on the lake. When we first moved here you could still see the trees coming down to the shore. Now it's apartment houses, and there's a new school going up across the street. This area will be city before we know it. This was all real country-country, where you could let your dog run free and didn't have any trouble with the neighbors, because neighbors were so far away. Now it's neighbors right on your back porch, and their dogs and cats.

This was my grandfather's acreage. Before we lived here, we moved around a lot. My father hauled logs. He started out in Aberdeen, Washington, and hauled logs all the way from there down to California, into the big timberland, when redwood was really being logged. He hauled lots and lots of redwood down there, and then it just started slowing down. Too many haulers, too many contractors were competing for the same jobs. So he gradually moved back up the Coast, and here we are, we ended back up in Olympia.

When I was younger, you know, I grew up around logging. I knew they were taking the trees, yes I did. When we were on the Smith River, Dad kind of quit hauling then, and he went to work for an outfit that was a tugboat company. They rafted and towed logs down the river. They unloaded the trucks, dumped the logs into the river and rafted them, and then pulled them down the river. Our house was right in front of where the dump was, and you could see what was going on. They used an old apron type dump, where they ran two cables underneath the logs, tripped the stakes on one side of the truck and dumped the whole works into the river. I used to go over there when school was out and I could sit and watch them unload logs for hours, and I could watch the logs hit the water like a ton of bricks. I enjoyed that.

Most of the people who lived around here, when I was growing up, were businessmen, State people. This area is the capital of Washington State, so we got lots and lots of State workers. Lots of kids in this area were not too happy with loggers. Not unhappy with them, but they felt that loggers were not really the class of people you would want to hang around with. It wasn't difficult to get along, or anything like that, but they could think of better occupations. On the other hand, I couldn't think of any, and I surely couldn't enclose myself in an office like some of them do. Now especially. I do like the outdoors, and I would much rather work outdoors at any job.

I can remember the first time I loaded a log trailer. I was twelve years old. My dad was hauling for Simpson Timber Company. We went up, and we were doing the maintenance on the trucks. And he let me load the truck. I was in my height of glory. And I started driving early. In fact, I was driving when I was nine. I was able to keep it on the road anyway. I don't know how. I think it's probably just as well.

I started working for Dad when I was big enough to pack wrenches. On my time off, I had two dairy cattle that I showed at 4H. Dad thought it would be a good idea if I had something to do in summer. So I had these two Brown Swiss. I sold milk first, that was before I drew wages from Dad. Work . . . I felt like it was a family duty. My dad bought the cattle for me, of course, so I guess I shouldn't complain.

I milked the cows and sold the milk and eventually I earned enough money to buy a car. Then I bought the car, sold the cows, and went to work for Dad. Seemed like it was all just that fast. And I thought it would be better to work in the woods, I could probably make more money.

I've always been mechanically inclined, and so in school I determined that I would be a mechanic, or own big equipment even if I didn't work on it, just to be around it. I've always wanted to be in equipment or logging, something to do with heavy equipment.

These areas have been logged, clear cut is what they call it. They do lots of that, and it's ruined some areas. It's the most efficient way of logging. I think some areas should be clear cut. Selective logging is nice, but it's a very expensive way of logging. But in a lot of cases too, you've got to leave something to look at. There are areas that should be left alone. But sometimes you have to clear cut. Like down at Mt. St. Helens.

I was rafting in Wenatchee the day it blew. We stopped for lunch and someone had a radio on. We heard the mountain blew. We didn't believe it until we got down the river further. The sun never really came out that day, and all of a sudden the stuff started falling from the sky, and we finally realized it must have been true. We tried to go home and we got stuck. The dust started falling and all of a sudden it was an inch thick—had to drive with the windshield wipers on. Like winter, like it was snowing, only it wasn't snowing at all. Gray. Like it was Christmas, and running around in short sleeves. A weird feeling, not very comfortable at all. It was just dark out. Just gray.

I worked for a while in the ash down there. It was absolutely necessary to clear cut down there because the areas they were clear cutting were burned, scorched and all. If they don't get it out, don't move it, it's a fire hazard.

And if a fire gets going down there, it will spread. I was working for a road building outfit. We built roads so they could log their wood, logging roads. It was miserable. The ash was in your eyes, in your nose. We tried wearing masks but those little paper masks plug up so fast, it just wasn't worth it. Your equipment wears out real fast, chain saws cut down two trees if you're lucky before they wear out. The ash contains lots of glass and it wears everything out, anything that moves or turns wears out in the ash.

Weyerhauser owns lots and lots of timber and lots of logging around here. They are very smart business people. They make lots of money by manipulating. They have lots of pull where it counts. I can't really say I like the company, but they are a very smart company. I know lots of people who disagree with me—"Weyerhauser's beautiful people." They do create a lot of jobs around this area, but I think jobs would be here whether or not Weyerhauser was here. I believe Weyerhauser has some control over the Fish and Game Department, because they let them overkill every year, as far as I'm concerned. The hunters are killing more animals, there's too many licenses issued, too many tags issued for the area. There are just too many animals killed, to save their trees. Something about young trees, deer like to eat them. So it kind of gets in their pocketbook, I'm sure. I can remember seeing game all over this place. There's deer and bear up in the Black Hills, but not as many as there used to be. I'd be afraid to go out hunting now, because of the hunters. Opening day is dangerous, people get carried away and shoot each other, shoot at anything that moves.

Weyerhauser has lobbyists and they control our State a lot more than anybody would really like to think. Big money always seems to . . . I'm not saying anybody really gets paid off, but you can be intimidated. I'm not a naturalist by any means, but there's a lot of things I don't believe in. There's got to be a happy medium. Some clear cutting and some areas left untouched. I think Weyerhauser has probably taken too much wood. We don't get it, not the good wood. Fact of the matter is, if you go to a sorting yard where they sort logs, they have export piles which is all the nice big wood, and they have domestic piles, the stuff we keep here in the U.S. We get all the junk wood. This is Weyerhauser.

The Japanese will pay the premium price. I can see their point, I wouldn't want to haul bad wood over there. If they are going to take a load of wood over there, they want it to be number one, they want to fill their ship with number one wood. Where over here, we can just saw it and throw it in a pile. We don't have to haul it, we don't have to ship it. but they do. It kind of drives our market up too. We don't get the quality of wood the Japanese get. We're paying number one prices for something less.

Weyerhauser can control prices to a certain extent. Like right now when the market is really down bad—of course it's that way in any business—Weyerhauser takes real advantage of it. They really don't slow down all that much. All they do is offer less money for jobs. And to the logger who wants to work, or has to work, when you've got equipment you have to make payments on . . .

Loggers get work from State sales. The State or say, Burlington Northern [Railroad] or other landowners in this area will offer a good piece of timberland, they'll ask for bids on it and the loggers will go look at it. It just depends on whether or not the landowner wants the wood or wants to sell it out. Either they have somebody come in and take it out, find a market for it, or you can just log and haul it for them. They'll put a closed bid on it, everybody sends in a bid—what they'll do the job for. For the most part, the bidding's honest. When the market's are not so good, like right now, the companies will log their own. Like Weyerhauser's doing now. They're keeping their own men busy, and they do get contractors in there too, for a third less than what they'd normally have to pay.

One thing about Weyerhauser, I believe that they are reseeding as much as they can possibly afford to, because it's their income, and they're a growing company. In a lot of cases, Weyerhauser is a good company. I could take you down the road here, there's Weyerhauser's seedling trees. Acres and acres of young trees, just that high. They're really making an attempt to reseed the forests. I have to commend them on some things, they're probably spending more money than the State on reseeding.

There are different weather problems with hauling logs. This snow up here is the worst there is for hauling logs. Because it doesn't get cold enough. Down in Oregon, where it gets real cold—they say as long as you can see the frost on the tires you've got traction. Not too many years ago, we were hauling logs down there and it got down to 26 below. As long as the sun didn't come out, you could drive on it. In Oregon, it's nicer to haul logs in wintertime, especially if you've got a heater. But the type of snow you get up here is slick. That's why it's not a good idea to haul logs over this country in the snow.

I don't think our forestland is in danger. It's our farmland. This side of the mountains, most any place you can grow trees, even if it's steep country or way back in the woods, you can grow trees as long as you've got the rights to the land. That's about all that will grow. I'm more worried about our farmlands, that we are covering up every day with housing and industry. I think maybe they ought to build on the hillsides and leave the flatlands alone. Forests—I think that we could have good trees forever if we don't sell them all overseas. I really think there's a possibility of regrowing the whole thing.

Unfortunately, I see hard times. I really do. There's getting to be so many people, it's going to get hard to find jobs. That makes our quality of life go down a lot because there just isn't going to be that much more work. Other countries are . . . their industrial capabilities are growing, such as Japan, and that's hurt us. I don't know what we're going to do, but I think there has to be some changes made someplace in order to keep society together here. People want to work, there's lots and lots of people that want to work. And there's lots who we're giving free rides to, and I think that should stop. I think that everybody should earn their keep one way or another. I don't mind giving people things that they need to survive, but I think there has to be a line drawn somewhere.

Utilities, Exxon, Standard Oil and all those people, they've got built-in tax loopholes. There ought to be, when a company gets a certain size, there ought to be a standard tax. You will pay this percentage of what you take in. It will have to happen, just to make it so simple and plain and blunt that they can't get out of it. Because the biggest problem I can see in our society right now is that we confuse ourselves with words. In arguments, you write something up, and write it as plain as you can put it. And an attorney will turn it around for you and make it sound like just the opposite of what you wanted to say. I think if we get back to basics and worded everything so there was no other way of terming it, no other way of making it sound, we'd be a lot better off. Things would be a lot more simple.

Our government's too big. I believe that. They're taking a big chunk of our money, lots and lots of it. We'd probably all be better off if the government didn't have control of some of the things they control now. I just think that private enterprise is the way to go . . . much better managed than government. But the big corporations . . . say a guy has developed a good product, a quality product, and then a big corporation comes in and buys him out. The quality goes downhill because there's nobody in the corporation who's interested in the quality of the product. Too many politics, I guess.

I think without the family unit we wouldn't have a society at all. I think it's getting worse and worse, shows more and more in our society. I guess maybe that's one reason why I still like to work in the woods, why I still like to be out and away from society—not society, but some of the bad characteristics . . . it seems like there's a lot of young kids that get left alone, get nothing out of life.

I don't know where we're headed. I'm really afraid . . . I'd like to see everybody calm down, but unfortunately everybody doesn't think the way I do. There's too many countries that are absolutely enemies, that will be enemies forever. I don't know why, really, why they're that way. But eventually, I'm afraid there'll be a war that will do a lot of damage. I don't think any person on Earth wants it, but I think it's going to happen, through poor management or whatever, it's going to happen. One way or another, we're going to get overpopulated.

Down on the Sovkhoz

"To have a better view, go high up into the mountains.
When admiring a mighty tree, bow low to its roots."
—Uzbek proverb

Cosmonauts orbiting Earth report that at cotton harvest,
Uzbekistan seems buried under snow avalanches. Heart of
the Soviet Cotton Belt, Uzbekistan is sprawling sunbaked
plainsland shadowed by Central Asia's Pamir Alai Mountains, so imposing they are called "the Roof of the World."
Masters of irrigation technology, Uzbeks have been building canal systems for three thousand years and today's
Uzbekistan is crisscrossed with wide irrigation canals,
mountain spring-fed veins that drain into green farmland
oases. In Samarkand Valley, Uzbek laborers toil on cotton
farms, in fruit orchards and in vineyards owned by the
Soviet state and administered by the Ministry of Agriculture.

Islam has not completely lost its hold in Soviet
Uzbekistan, and a state farm, or *sovkhoz*, in Samarkand

Valley is one example of Uzbekistan's curious blend of ancient Moslem traditions and modern Soviet industrialization. In 1954, five Uzbek *kolkhozi*, or collective farms, turned their operations over to the Ministry of Agriculture, thus forming one giant sovkhoz named Payarik. As collective farmers, the kolkhozi had administered their own affairs, deciding which crops to grow, and how much of the harvest they would sell in public markets or to the state. The *kolkhoz* families did not own the land they tilled—private ownership of land is outlawed in the Soviet Union—but like all Soviet kolkhozi, these five collectives had held their land in perpetuity grants from the state. Once they turned their land over to the state, they gave up their perpetuity grants, and the Ministry of Agriculture claimed all the harvests and decided which crops would be planted. No longer tax-exempted collective farmers, the workers at Payarik state farm were tax-paying government employees.

Today there are about twenty-six thousand kolkhozi, or collective farms, in the Soviet Union, and about twenty thousand sovkhozi, or state farms. The government seems to be encouraging a transition from collective to state farms, arguing that state farms are more productive, by providing better farm equipment and housing facilities for laborers who agree to turn their collectives over to the sovkhoz system. Like the five Uzbek kolkhozi, many collective farms will fail to compete with the larger, more mechanized state farms, and will probably be forced to merge into megafarms like Payarik.

I don't know how successful these five kolkhoz operations were when they operated independently from the bureaucracies, but I visited Samarkand Valley one sunny winter afternoon and saw the new sovkhoz, Payarik's huge spread of farmland. Payarik is a model megafarm that officials are proud to show foreigners, where Uzbek farmworkers, many still wearing Moslem robes, plow the old Silk Route fields with big green tractors.

Fig orchards and trellised vineyards framed Payarik, and the freshly tilled cotton fields were framed with bright red poppies. A wide dusty road wound lazily through Payarik's central community, where rows of low, whitewashed adobe cottages seemed to bulge with active children spilling out into courtyards shaded by mulberry trees. At one intersection, a game of hide and seek was in progress. A fair Russian girl, towheaded and about four years old, stood shyly on a streetcorner, watching her bronze-skin Uzbek playmates dash in and out of their hiding places. A stray fat chicken stood in the road and clucked at a dusty black Volga carrying foreigners from Moscow to Payarik's headquarters.

Payarik is one of the state's largest cotton farms, its administrators told me, and harvests about ten thousand tons a year. Herb grasses, fruit, cattle and silkworms are also raised on the farm. Eighty percent of Payarik's cotton is machine harvested, I was told, and although chemical fertilizers and insecticides are in short supply in the U.S.S.R., the farm plans to use them widely when they become available. For the moment spared the health hazards attributed to chemical fertilizers and insecticides, Payarik's farmworkers must rely on organic substitutes, and they say these methods require more work and reap smaller harvests.

Ten thousand farm laborers and their families live on the Payarik sovkhoz. Most rent apartments; only about 10 percent have small private homes. The single most important difference between U.S. and Soviet farm laborers' lifestyles is that most of the Americans migrate from one farm to another and live in temporary housing during agricultural seasons. Payarik's workers, like the majority of Soviet farmworkers, live permanently on the farm.

Soviet farmworkers earn less income annually than industrial workers. The same is true for U.S. farmworkers. Soviet farm laborers earn about 1,800 rubles a year, while nonfarm workers average about 2,400 rubles. U.S. farmworkers are paid an average of $4,000 a year, but U.S. workers in nonfarm occupations average $11,285. The rubles and dollars a farmworker receives have the same monetary value as other workers' money, but do not have the same buying power. As anyone living on a limited income knows, it is difficult to benefit from bargain prices, to buy the "large economy size" items, with incomes that barely afford purchase of essential items in small quantities. In societies whose ruble and dollar values are calculated on nationwide average income levels, there is ample evidence that both Soviet and U.S. farmworkers are grossly underpaid for their labor.

The purchasing power of the dollar and the ruble cannot be accurately compared by simply converting monetary equations. Although a Soviet worker is paid fewer rubles than a U.S. worker is paid dollars, the buying power of the two currencies is different. The ruble does not float on the World Market like the dollar does. Its value is not determined by fluctuations on the exchanges. Although Soviet economists keep an eye on the international money markets, the ruble's value is set according to domestic financial requirements. If one wanted to exchange dollars for rubles in the U.S.S.R., a *very approximate* rate would be 1 ruble = $1.50.

100 kopecks = 1 ruble. A bus ride in Moscow costs 5 kopecks; a bus ride in New York presently costs 75 cents. A pair of women's stockings can be bought for 50 cents in the United States, but cost several rubles in the Soviet Union. The smallest domestically manufactured compact car costs a Soviet citizen 4,000 or 5,000 rubles, which equals about $6,000 or $7,000, just about the cost of a new compact car bought in the U.S. today.

Like the incomes of U.S. workers, the wages of Soviet workers are taxable, except those of collective farmers. Pensions are not taxed. As in the United States, family garden plots are taxed, except those of collective farmers, which is why a budget conscious farm laborer might prefer kolkhoz farming to the sovkhoz system. In any case, all Soviet land, whether or not it is tax exempt, is the property of the state.

The table below, which is based on figures from the U.S. Consumer Price Index and on Soviet statistical data, provides some comparisons of the cost of living for Soviet and American families. The figures are based on average income levels in both countries, including both nonfarm and farm families.

DISTRIBUTION OF FAMILY INCOME

(Farm and Nonfarm; figured on income average
of total population)

	UNITED STATES	SOVIET UNION
Housing	28%	2–10%
Utilities	11%	1%
Food	19%	25%
Medical Care	4%	Free
All Other Expenses	38%	64%

In both countries, low income families will end up paying more than the average cost for food, because they cannot afford to buy in bulk. In the United States, poorer families also tend to pay a higher percentage of their income for medical care and housing, and their "other expenses" are severely limited or nonexistent. Because medical care is free in the U.S.S.R., and housing costs are so low, Soviet families can afford to spend more of their income on food. While many Soviet workers tend to sock away funds for "a rainy day," many spend a big portion of their income purchasing black market items, clothes and foodstuffs which they are fond of but cannot find in state shops. In both countries, the tillers of the land reap fewer rewards than most for their labors. Soviet farmworkers are told that, in spite of chronically small harvests, a great portion of their crops must be shipped to Third World countries where malnutrition is rampant. The Soviet farmworkers I talked to did not grumble about this personal sacrifice, but expressed hope that their harvests would soon increase to meet both national and international demands. Hard labor, it seems, occasionally has its spiritual rewards.

But Soviet workers, both on and off the farm, are not above complaining about food shortages in their country. Although food costs are relatively cheap, often basic foodstuffs like bread, dairy products and meat, are in short supply. The fact is, Soviet agriculture suffers for a variety of reasons. Severe shortages of fresh produce and grains result from a tangle of red tape that plagues all bureaucracies, from rapid industrial expansion that channels more money to industry than to agriculture, and from food shipments to Poland and other Warsaw Pact countries and to Third World nations allied with the Soviet Union. Yet the nation which so benevolently parcels out food, produces only about one quarter as much as American agricultural enterprises.

There is another reason Soviet citizens must endure food shortages. Moscow, like Washington, concentrates a huge portion of government spending on development and production of war paraphernalia.

Many Soviet citizens are exasperated by the nation's food shortages, but, recalling postwar famines, have remained silent, patriotically patient with their government's slow agricultural progress. They also know their government recently signed a multibillion dollar chemical fertilizer deal with U.S. oil magnate Armand Hammer, a longtime friend of the Soviet Union. Chemical fertilizers and insecticide sprays, which increase harvests while poisoning farm laborers' skin and lungs, are the hope of Soviet agriculture's future. As the nation races to catch up with America in farm technology, it will confront a perplexing dilemma: how to protect the health and safety of farm laborers while spraying poisons on crops to increase the supply of food for a hungry world. And if the nation succeeds in mechanizing its field work, thus sparing humans contact with the poisons, who will employ the jobless farm laborers?

Some Soviets believe another factor contributes to their nation's food shortages. They are convinced the government is storing grain and other foodstuffs, as the Chinese are doing, preparing to feed those who would survive in the event of a nuclear war.

As mechanization and chemical fertilizers are introduced on the sovkhoz, food shortages are gradually being eliminated. Meanwhile, the Soviet Union ranks alongside the United States among nations whose people—as a whole—receive well above the average recommended minimum daily requirement of calories. Malnutrition is less of a problem in today's Soviet republics than it is in many areas of America's Deep South.

Sovkhoz laborers will benefit from elimination of food shortages, though many will lose their jobs to mechanical harvesters. They have been promised retraining in other occupations, though, and the farmworkers I talked to on Payarik sovkhoz seem happy about the idea of robots invading their fields and strange chemicals clinging to their crops. Meanwhile, Payarik's residents spend their free time tilling little private garden plots which, even in winter, seem to overflow with exotic fruits and herbs.

Each Payarik family has about one quarter of a hectare (1 hectare = 2.47 acres) of land for private use. Private garden plots are available to most rural and some urban workers, and are usually alloted by trade unions, which receive block land grants from the state. Since farm laborers are not organized in unions, the farm administration determines who receives land. A worker who switches jobs surrenders the plot of land too. The land remains in the control of the union or enterprise that holds the land grant. Private garden plots often have little wooden sheds standing on them, but the state discourages citizens from building dwellings on garden plots, preferring they remain housed in apartment complexes. For urban workers who covet a dream of a private dwelling, however humble, prospects of receiving a building permit for a garden plot cottage are dim. But farm laborers, those underpaid toilers of the land, have a better shot at living in a private cottage or semidetached adobe dwelling, like the lucky 10 percent on Payarik sovkhoz. Even a cramped flat on the sovkhoz may be preferable to a larger urban dwelling. If you like fresh air. At Payarik, there is plenty of it.

Payarik's technical specialists and skilled laborers have their own flats—cramped quarters providing a measure of privacy—while field workers and packers frequently must share flats. All of Payarik's housing facilities have running water and electricity, but indoor plumbing has not been installed on the sovkhoz and probably will not be until organic fertilizer is replaced by chemical agents. Mechanics and herders earn more than field workers—about 170 rubles a month. Personal income, as well as garden space, is taxable on a sovkhoz. Child care is provided free of charge for mothers who work in the fields. Some five hundred Payarik employees have retired and draw pensions while continuing to live on the farm.

It is on this cotton farm that the old man, Sultan-Murat Soliev, a retired cotton picker, lives. He tends a private garden, rules his family Moslem style, and goes every day, several times a day, to the Payarik mosque to pray. At home, a simple white adobe dwelling attached to his sons' similar quarters, Sultan-Murat and his wife maintain a modest lifestyle. Through a stone arch, glaring sun white-

87

washes a backyard garden plot and small fruit orchard. If you walk through the arch, following the sun's warm path, out beyond the fruit trees, you will be suddenly struck with pungent odors drifting from an open stable where Sultan-Murat keeps his milk cows and sheep. When the animals get unruly, as they do when a horsefly buzzes their ears, Sultan-Murat will stride into the stable and swat their hides with the corner of his *chapan*, a Moslem robe. Order is restored. He is master of this private plot and its inhabitants. He doesn't own the land, but he rules every human, beast and bird in this miniature Paradise. Even sovkhoz officials and sophisticated Muscovites seem slightly intimidated by the dignity of this Uzbek cotton picker.

Sultan-Murat commands immediate respect and reverence, though he does not demand it, and hardly seems concerned with such petty matters of the ego. He only admits to being a simple cotton picker and water bearer. Clad in Moslem robes, his head graced with a peaked cap swathed in white cloth, he greets a stranger with the full embrace of his humble possessions.

The official arrangement was for me to briefly meet Sultan-Murat. After getting an eyeful of this enchanting Moslem and his family, I was expected to be satisfied that all was peace and tranquillity on the Soviet sovkhoz scene. I was not informed until I arrived at Sultan-Murat's home that my picture of sovkhoz life would be limited to the old man's courtyard. Immediately I realized that attempting to compare what I saw on this one brief visit with what I knew of U.S. farmworkers' living and working conditions would be like comparing silkworms and onions—an impossible task. Making the best of the situation, I asked Sultan-Murat if he could spare a little time. He pulled a gold pocket watch from his robes, consulted it and nodded. His wife hastily prepared their home for a visitor.

The single piece of furniture in the two room house was a large, square Uzbek couch, covered with a satin quilt. She laid a fresh linen cloth on the quilt, and on the cloth placed plates of raisins, apricots and walnuts, dishes of thick cream, bowl-shaped loaves of *non*, Uzbek bread, and a pot of steaming hot tea. She plumped a fat pillow up in the corner of the couch where her husband would sit, and after surveying her work, made a hasty retreat to her son's house. Sultan-Murat motioned me to sit on the couch and nodded approvingly when I sat on his left in a half-lotus position. A practicing Moslem does not drink alcoholic beverages, and to my relief, no vodka was produced. Windows facing the courtyard cast bright sunbeams on our backs. I could almost feel the breath of Sultan-Murat's grandchildren, who leaned through open panes to stare at the proceedings.

Since Sultan-Murat speaks Uzbek, two interpreters were required for the interview. An Uzbek sovkhoz official translated from Uzbek into Russian; my Muscovite chaperone from Russian into English. Double translation is long and tedious. Even so, when I asked Sultan-Murat if he knew any old Uzbek folk tales, he did not skimp on detail, and never lost his train of thought while waiting his turn to speak. He seemed to fall into a light trance while the interpreters worked.

Uzbek folk tales are difficult to tell, and more difficult to translate accurately. The core of ancient Uzbek tales is the three-challenges plot. "The Old Man and the Dif," told by Sultan-Murat, is the story of how a simple peasant stumbled upon a Dif, a flying giant, and faced with the Dif's great physical power, three times outwitted him. The Dif, pronounced Deef, represents an evil spirit. The Old Man shows how human inventiveness can outwit an adversary. The *mullah*, Moslem holy man, represents Islamic justice.

Sovkhoz officials seemed astounded at Sultan-Murat's

89

ability to tell an old Uzbek tale that involved a "three times three" plot. Hardly anyone noticed as he spun the yarn that every few minutes he consulted his watch.

Sultan-Murat Soliev

For many years nobody has asked me about the old Uzbek legends. Now I am thinking of which of them to tell you.

Once upon a time, there lived an Old Man and an Old Woman. One day the Old Man asked the Old Woman, "Please, fetch me the ax and rope. I'm going into the woods to cut firewood." The Old Woman fetched the ax and rope, and the Old Man set out into the woods. When he came to a tree in the forest, to chop wood, suddenly a pheasant flew away from the tree. The Old Man saw there were a number of eggs the bird had left behind in her nest. So the Old Man took the eggs and put them in his pocket. Just then, he saw a Dif, a flying giant, approaching him. So he took the eggs and the ax and the rope and covered them up with grass, to hide them from the Dif.

The Dif asked the Old Man, "What are you? What are you?"

"I am a human being," the Old Man answered, "I am a man." Then the Old Man asked the Dif, "Who are you?"

And the giant answered, "I am a Dif. And I'm going to eat you up."

"Oh no," said the Old Man, "I'm going to eat *you*."

They decided to make a bet. The Old Man said, "If you are so strong, show me the bowels of the Earth." The Dif tried to show him the inside of his stomach, tried to open his own stomach to reveal the bowels of the Earth. But he failed, he couldn't do it.

Then the Dif asked the Old Man, "Now you show me."

This Old Man took the rope from its hiding place in the grass and threw it to the Dif. "There now, look." Then the

Old Man said to the Dif, "And now, show me the moon on the ground. The moon that's up there in the sky, get it for me from out of the ground."

The Dif could not. He spoke angrily, "And now *you* show *me* the moon on the Earth."

The Old Man took from the grass an egg which was catching glints of sunshine and showed this to the Dif. The Dif was very, very frightened of the Old Man's wisdom. Then the Old Man said, "I'll give you a third task. Please, produce from this large stone—butter."

The Dif took the big stone and pressed it between his gigantic hands, but he could produce nothing but sand. "And now it's your turn," said the Dif. "Show me."

The Old Man took the bird's eggs, crushed them and made a kind of yellow mixture. "This is butter," he told the Dif, "and so I am the winner. Now I'll eat you."

The Dif pleaded with him. "Please don't eat me. I want to be your friend."

"Well, okay," said the Old Man, "let's become friends. First of all, I'll sit on your shoulders." And he sat on the Dif's shoulders and the giant flew up into the sky with the Old Man on his back, and carried the Old Man to his home. When they entered the Dif's cave, the Old Man saw a big iron caldron on the open fire, and in the caldron was boiling meat. Big, big pieces. The Dif took one piece of meat from the pot. It was a large, large leg. He put it in front of the Old Man.

"Please, eat it," he said.

The Old Man ate and ate until he was filled to the eyes. Then he said, "That's all I can eat."

"But why?" asked the Dif. "You are such a strong man, why can't you eat more?"

The Old Man said, "Well, just before I met you, I ate a whole horse and her colt." Then he said, "And now I want to go home. Take me to my place." The Dif put him on his back and flew away to the Old Man's house.

The Old Man lived in a *yurt*,* in a skin house. It was a very small yurt and not so high. When the Dif went inside the yurt, he was so tall his head split a hole in the roof.

The Old Woman realized that they had a guest, and so must prepare something for him to eat. She said, "I'll cook you something. You tell me, what should I fix?"

The Old Man answered, "Cook meat."

The Old Woman stepped up to her husband and asked, "Well, what meat should I prepare for you?"

He said, "Boil the throat of the eldest Dif, boil the breast of the middle Dif, and if that is not enough, then bring me the ax and I'll cut a piece of *this* Dif's foot, and then we'll have enough."

As soon as the Dif heard these words, he instantly flew away through the hole in the roof. After the Dif left, he met a mullah, a Moslem holy man. And the mullah asked him, "Where are you running, running so fast? What has happened?"

"Ohhh, don't ask me," cried the Dif. "I've just escaped luckily from the place of an Old Man. I gave him a piece of gold. For this he wanted to kill me."

The mullah was on his way to give a lesson to his pupils at the Moslem madrasseh, the school. There were all in all forty pupils. And he took the Dif along with him. When the pupils heard how unjust the Dif was to the Old Man from the forest, they decided to put the Dif on trial. They asked him to sit there while they made their decision. But the Dif refused. Using their *chalmas*, they tied him up and took him to the Old Man's place. All of them—because he was a giant—dragged him to the Old Man's home. The Old Man came outside, and when he saw the number of persons visiting him, he was very surprised. Forty of them.

"What happened?" he asked them.

"We want to give you this Dif to make a trial," they answered.

*Yurts are circular skin tents used all over Central Asia.

"Well then," he said, "why only one Dif? You ought to all of you give me one Dif each. So you need to drag to my place forty Difs."

When the Dif heard the words of the Old Man, he broke free of the chalmas, and he flew away. And, as the Old Man said, "He is flying away to this very day."

If you'll stay with me, I'll tell you lots of tales.

The Dif was lying about the gold. He had been foiled twice by the Old Man's wisdom, once with three challenges in the forest, and once at the Old Man's home, with three threats the Old Man made. Following the pattern of ancient Uzbek legends, the Dif and the Old Man must have a third confrontation. The Dif set up the third and final confrontation by lying to the mullah about the gold. Representing the conscience of Islam, the mullah knew the Dif was lying and brought him before an Islamic jury. But lying about giving the Old Man some gold was not the Dif's only "sin." To the Islamic court, made up of the mullah and his students, the Dif represented an evil force that threatened society, a flying giant with no morals. And indeed, the Dif had threatened the Old Man's life, but the Islamic court did not know this fact. They brought the Dif to trial based on the mullah's judgment that the Dif ought to be prosecuted.

The Dif refused to accept the Islamic court's authority over his actions, and he disrupted the court proceedings. The mullah's students removed the scarves they wore around their waists, their chalmas, and bound the rebellious Dif. Since they had no direct evidence of the Dif's guilt, they dragged their prisoner to the Old Man's home, so the Old Man could testify against the Dif.

The Old Man, seeing forty Islamic students dragging the bound Dif to his home, decided that the court of law was just as foolish as the Dif. At the final confrontation between the Old Man and the Dif, the Old Man shocked the Dif's captors, just long enough to loosen their grip on the chalmas, by asking for "forty Difs." The same request also affected the Dif, who, out of fear, broke free from the chalmas and flew away. True justice, without revenge, was effectively accomplished by the Old Man's wisdom.

Sultan-Murat's fable had stunned his visitors with a message that defended neither Islamic nor Soviet, nor even American forms of criminal court justice. In the thoughtful silence that followed his yarn, I asked the old man to tell me something about his life.

My father was a *dehkan,* a peasant. He died when I was just a small child. My mother raised me, and she also took care of other children in our village. I helped her. We had a cow and a big bull. And I was the one who cared for that bull, gave him grass, gave him hay . . . as a small child I remember only hard work. There were no clothes to wear. As for me, for the whole year I picked cotton too, and it was hard work. The most difficult time was when the weather got bad in the middle of the harvest, when it rained or snowed.

On the collective farm, the harvests were too small. And the soil wasn't organized as well as it is now on our state farm.* On the collective farm, there was disorder every-where. And it was more difficult to work there because our collective farm wasn't so powerful as our state farm. The state farm gave us more machinery, more equipment. Now things are well organized.

Back when I was young, even the rich man did not have the things I have now. I have a car. There's cattle. There's enough bread. We have enough of everything, we live well. We can relax, we can study everything for free. And the main thing, now we have peace.

* Payarik uses a crop-rotation system, alternating between cotton and herb grasses; seven years cotton, three years herbs—for one hundred percent use of the soil, officials said.

We have freedom to do everything to improve our society—to study, to get medical treatment, to raise our education and send our children to schools, to work well and receive pensions. I receive my pension at home now. They say to me, "Please, don't come to the office, we'll bring your pension out to your home." They respect me. And if I feel myself a little sick, the ambulance comes right away.

Being a father, I raise my children in such a way that they will keep the Uzbek traditions. First of all, we must respect each other. My wife and I, now when we go somewhere, we go together. My wife tries to raise the children and grandchildren to respect their elders, both men and women. My wife was a state farmworker also, and now she receives a pension. She worked as a nurse in the daycare center here on our state farm.

I was a small child when I saw the veils on the faces of our women. And then they burnt their veils. I remember that our women from our farms, just after the revolution, they gathered for a great, great meeting in a place not far from here, and there was a man whose name was Mullah Hassan. He was a very educated person and he was famous among Uzbeks. Mullah Hassan explained to the women that it's not good to wear veils, and he explained why it's not good, why it's bad to go on with wearing the veils. Then all the women who had gathered for the meeting, from all the farms around, they took off their veils, and threw them into the fire. And they burned them.

Space exploration? Our country has gone to a very high level. I guess that's why we went so high in space exploration. Space exploration is useful for the people. I have a dream. I want one of my grandchildren to be a cosmonaut.

Sultan-Murat tapped the face of his pocket watch. The Moslem hour of prayer approached and he had to move quickly if he was going to reach the mosque on time. This afternoon, he caught a ride in the Volga with his house-guests. The Uzbek driver smiled into the rearview mirror at Sultan-Murat sandwiched between Western-clad jour-nalists and sovkhoz officials, like an ancient holy relic on a bed of decadence. I thought about a comment a mullah in Samarkand had made the day before. "Do socialism and Islam have common goals?" I had asked the mullah. "Yes, they do," he replied. "Both Islam and socialism believe in the dignity of every human being. Both Islam and social-ism, if they are genuine, seek to uplift all members of society." I asked the mullah if a true Moslem could become a member of the Communist Party. "Absolutely not," he answered, "because communism does not accept the existence of Allah."

"So a Soviet political leader does not have a democratic right to believe in Allah?" I asked the mullah. He did not reply.

Pungent, sweet scents clung to Islam's stone walls protecting the mosque's holy grounds. A single oak tree, older than the oldest Uzbek mullah, bent over a mirror smooth pond where plump goldfish glided, tracing thin swirls in the oak's reflection. Banks of pink roses in full bloom hung a lush carpet on a trellised wall. Moslem worshipers hurried to prayer, cloth slippers silent on stone pavement. Beige doves stopped cooing as if they knew the prayer schedule. Not a sound was heard except from a distance—swishing water. Sultan-Murat and his Moslem brothers were observing the cleansing ritual. The last time I saw Sultan-Murat, he was entering the bathhouse.

Bidding me farewell at his home, he had taken the chalma from his waist, the pale blue muslin square embroidered with orange and black thread, and, laying it on the couch, he smoothed it out flat. He placed a fresh loaf of non on it, filled the non with raisins and walnuts, closed the chalma and tied its four corners into a knot. He pressed it against me. "Please, take this for memory," he said, "because memories are the reason one returns. And when you come back, I'll tell you many, many more Uzbek tales."

Down on the sovkhoz, Sultan-Murat prayed to Allah.

A Bushel and a Peck

The family farm, that dim memory of golden harvests and laden tables, has crumbled in the wake of American agribusiness. Federal laws favoring large corporations over less competitive family farms have tilted the horn of plenty, and all the eggs have landed in one basket. Politically astute and often capable of buying legislation favoring his interests, today's corporate landowner holds millions of acres of America's arable land in reserve while families who still believe in the American Dream wonder why farmland is not more equitably distributed. Old MacDonald *had* a farm . . . once. Now God's Little Acre and the back forty have been mortgaged, reluctantly sold off to agribarons who, thanks to friends in office, got the land for a bushel and a peck.

U.S. megafarms are prospering as the price of grains and produce, meat and poultry, skyrocket. Agricultural technology promises even more profits for agribusinesses, which look forward to the day when they can let all their fieldhands go, when their land will be tilled entirely by machine, their crops harvested by robots.

American farm laborers receive few rewards for toiling on the megafarms, in an occupation that is rapidly being taken over by robots. Today, wheat, corn, soybeans—even tomatoes and some fruits—are harvested by machine. Increasingly, the more delicate fruits, like grapes, are being harvested by field robots, brainless mechanical slaves on wheels. Technology promises great advances for agribusiness, and promises to put tens of thousands of farm laborers out of jobs. Cesar Chavez, leader of the United Farmworkers of America, says the new mechanical harvesters are robbing human beings of the right to make a living, and has called the field robots "monsters." Agribarons argue that they are more efficient and cheaper than human harvesters. If the farm laborers were assured of retraining and placement in other occupations, perhaps they wouldn't mind being ejected from the *campos* and replaced by machines.

American farm labor is mostly migratory work. Field workers migrate from one megafarm to the next, following the season's crops south to north, then head back south to start the journey once again. For their toil, they reap nothing but calloused, acid burned hands, insecticide poisoned lungs, severely damaged backbones and the promise that tomorrow their livelihood will be taken over by machines.

Farm laborers were excluded from the National Labor Relations Act of 1935, which gave industrial workers the right to collective bargaining. Without legal power to bargain for safe and healthy working conditions, the job of farm laborer has remained America's least rewarding occupation. A migrant worker's annual income rarely exceeds $4,000. An onion picker in Texas earns 50 cents for picking 55 pounds of onions. The agribaron will sell 50 of those pounds for $16 on today's market. Migrant workers do not receive unemployment or disability insurance in most states, or retirement pensions or seniority protection, paid vacations or holidays, and frequently do not have a permanent home. They have no Minimum Wage protection, are often cheated by employers who fail to claim them on Social Security tax forms, and are excluded from the Occupational Safety and Health Act programs, which protect industrial workers. Women migrant laborers are paid less than men, and mothers must pay for child care in migrant camps. With rare exception, the campos are field slums, shoddy collections of buildings or trailers, often lacking running water and electricity in living quarters. Because the work is seasonal, a farm laborer averages about 130 working days annually. The average life expectancy of a U.S. farmworker is 49 years. These are a few of the reasons why U.S. farmworkers have organized.

Cesar Chavez' United Farmworkers and other affiliated farmworkers unions are demanding higher wages, health benefits, and better living and working conditions. Chavez' union only supports U.S. citizens and documented workers who hold Green Cards that permit them to work in the United States. The Texas Farmworkers' Union, and similar unions throughout the U.S. which are affiliated with but not part of Chavez' organization, also support the rights of documented farm laborers. But the independent unions go a step beyond Chavez, and actively support undocumented workers who come from Mexico seeking jobs. These men and women, while crossing the border, have frequently been assaulted by U.S. border patrols trying to halt the wave of immigrants. The unions have come across cases in which undocumented Mexican laborers have been held in physical bondage on Southwestern megafarms.

In Leningrad, I met a Texas farmworker, a member of a union group touring Soviet farms. I asked the Chicano man his opinion of Soviet farm laborers' living and working conditions. He said, "This is a totally different society.

Sure, the Soviets are better off than they were before their revolution. But you can't compare conditions here to conditions in our campos, in our fields. It's a different society here, maybe better in some ways, but . . ." He pondered over the question for a minute, then said, "You can't preach Lenin to American farmworkers, especially Mexicans and Chicanos. We haven't had the leadership we've needed for the past few years. But I'll tell you what— we have it now. And it's coming from the fields. We'll have our own kind of revolution, and it's not far off."

On the outskirts of El Paso, Texas, where onion fields were being tilled for planting, I met Francisca Carrillo, a Mexican immigrant who came to the United States seeking a better life for her children. She lived in a run down wooden house, with her husband and eight of their twelve children. They shared three rooms. Two electric bulbs hung from the ceiling, low wattage to save electricity, and a small television set was their only electrical appliance. Although she was not expecting company, Francisca Carrillo's rented home was neat and tidy, and the few religious ornaments on the walls lent brightness to the main room. She sat on the big iron bed, its thin mattress covered with a clean but tattered quilt, holding her infant grandchild on her lap. She wore a plain cotton dress, modestly covering her knees. Her hands were graceful as they played with the baby's fingers, hands that seemed never to have clenched into fists of anger. The palms looked smooth and polished, the fingers were long and slim and lied about her age. Her face bore lines, but they all seemed made from laughing.

"We are just farmworkers," said Francisca Carrillo. *"Los pobres. Mi vida no es muy interesante."*

We gathered around her table—Francisca Carrillo, my friend Paula Ruiz, who interpreted Francisca's Sierra Mountain dialect, and myself. Francisca's gentle voice, charged with some secret energy, transformed a dark tale into an illuminating parable. In the midst of poverty's sparse trimmings, she radiated spiritual beauty brighter than Pancho Villa's gold. She did not need the power company to shine, and her eyes said she knew it.

Francisca Carrillo

When I was a child, we lived in the Sierra Mountains. We lived in the caves. It wasn't until I was married that I lived in a real house. My favorite ball game was *canasta*, and I loved music, especially music from the violin.

When we had food, it was *somora—cabezas de plantas*. We would put the cabeza in the barbecue pit and cook it. With this we also had sweet cane and water. Or mint or herb tea. Even now, when I am not so hungry, I would like to eat this food. My mother would fool us—because our favorite treat was flour tortillas—she would make tortillas from vermicelli and tell us they were of flour. This would satisfy us.

To make a *tortilla de maíz*, you first take the corn from the husk, then boil it in lime and leave it overnight. In the morning, you would wash it and grind it on stone. Then you had your flour. You'd make the tortillas from this. Today the tortillas are not so good, bought from the store, but I can't get corn so I have to buy tortillas from the store. They have a bitter taste.

In the Sierras when I was a child, we would have fiestas on the Saints' days. On the Feast of San Isidro Laborador, the patron saint of wheat and corn, the village people would dance in the streets and wear masks. On the Fiesta del Cruz Santo, they would dance for three days and nights to the music of *la guitarra y violín*. In the Sierras, we just had the guitar and violin. Violin I loved best. The girls all wore pretty dresses and the men wore their best clothes too. We had a windup Victrola in the village, and sometimes we would have records to play music on the

Victrola. But we didn't have electricity, so there was no radio. Even today my favorite music is *ranchero*.

When I got married, I was fifteen years old, and I went to live with my husband's family on their *ranchito*. There I had my first baby, but before he was three years old, he died. His urinary tract was blocked and all his organs turned black. I was very young and did not recognize he had a disease. But all my other children lived. I have twelve *niños*.

My husband worked at the mines in the Sierras. He was eighteen when we got married. He worked as a mechanic in the mines where they mined gold, silver and other precious metals. It was very obvious that the company was taking this wealth from the land and that we pobres lived so miserably. They came from over here, the *jefes*, they came from the United States. And there were a few gringo *patrónes* who came to supervise the mines also. But we were never molested by them because we lived segregated from them. It was not until I came over here that I realized this same company, Asarco, has mines in the U.S., and the owners are from here.

The patrónes worked the miners very hard, but paid them very little wages.

We came over here in 1963 because we wanted a better life for our children. We crossed at Juarez. My husband and children had to get Green Cards first. Now my husband and children work in the campos. Mostly onions. Picking from six A.M. to two thirty P.M., with just one break at twelve thirty, for twenty minutes to eat lunch. I bring them their meals in the fields. The whole family picks onions and the patrón pays for whatever the whole family picks. In planting season, when the family is planting, they pay twenty dollars a day on the same work schedule. We get no housing, no health benefits. The patrón last year did not deduct Social Security, so we are unable to report that work for our Social Security. Picking onions is hard work for little pay. It is like when you are cooking and cutting up an onion—your eyes are bothered from the burning all day long.

I'm not a nervous person. Everything just rolls off my back like water. I suppose it makes life easier to take. I've never had *sueños,* dreams of how it might otherwise be. I just live from day to day. We have to live that way because we are los pobres. Los pobres always live from day to day. Sometimes when the children come home from school, there is nothing to eat, or maybe just a tortilla. There are many days when we go hungry.

Union? No, I haven't heard of that. I've heard of *sindicatos,* yes, I've heard of unions, but as for a farm-workers' union, no, I never heard about one.

We have always had to move around. My husband is also an electrician and work is very hard to find. My youngest niño is seven and he works in the campos. My oldest is in his thirties, and he too works in the campos. The older niños are married, and I have grandchildren, and even though they have their own houses they are always here with me. Because we are very close as a family.

My children, they are very good. We have never had problems with them. I don't have to worry about where they are or what they are doing. The children come home from school and do their lessons. One of my boys helps the priest after school. Now, my oldest *niña,* she is twenty and she is a senior in high school. It has taken her this long, you know, because we have had to move around to find work. She comes home and studies, she never goes out. I tell her she'll end up an old maid! After the children have finished their lessons, they will watch their favorite soaps on television. And you notice that picture of Jesus on the wall, my daughter painted it.

My husband, he is very *simpático.* He never gets into trouble, never fights with his friends. We are not nervous people.

I came over here because of my children. If not for them, I would go back to the Sierras.

In the Sierras, many people believe in magic and spirits. Not me. I don't believe in what you can't see. I never believed in ghosts. Once in the Sierras, I was frightened by the figure of a man, frightened because he appeared on the same night we saw the flame under our bed.

We were sitting across the room when the flame appeared. My husband said to me, "Do you see that flame underneath the bed?" I said yes, I could see it. It was a small flickering yellow and red flame, very bright. We thought it might be money—money burns. In the Sierras, we learned stories of Pancho Villa. He and his gang used to ride up into the mountains with their loot from bank robberies. They would dig holes in the ground and hide the money. Some of that loot is supposed to be buried in the Sierras still.

My husband said, "What is that flame under the bed?" I saw it too and so did my niño. I got up and went for water to put out the flame. I picked up my lamp and started outside to the well. A man was passing in the doorway. In the lamplight, his face, like a ghost, frightened me!

Water would not put out the flame. My husband began digging in the floor underneath the bed. We dug and dug, but we found nothing. We thought because of the legend maybe some of Pancho Villa's treasure was buried there. But no.

As a *muchacha*, I was a real tomboy. I didn't have time to think of the things of young muchachas. I was married before I had time to think about them! I went only as far as third grade in school. You know, we were very poor and had to move around a lot to find work. For my own daughters, I tell them, "Go to school and learn a profession so you can take care of yourselves, so you never have to depend on a man. Don't be like me," I tell them. "Learn to do something besides keeping house."

For me, a typical day is: I get up very early. And I am very grouchy. I pray. Work all day. If there is food, I fix it and take it to my family in the fields. Wash and iron, then go to bed early—*ocho o nueve*. Sometimes I just sit in the evenings with my niños.

Navidad—we have always had a good Christmas. The children are always healthy and we go to bed early. Sometimes the children get a little toy. Sometimes we have a few pieces of candy, and we usually have tortillas and beans to eat. Gifts? Our gift is that we are healthy, that we are all in good health.

All my children were born at home, except for one. My husband wasn't at home when the time came, and my sister-in-law didn't know what to do, so I went to the free hospital. Other than this, I have never been in a hospital, never had any surgery. Oh, once in a while my tonsils bother me when I catch a cold. But I have always been very healthy.

I've never had problems over here with the *gringos*. My children sometimes have problems at the school. But me, I don't have problems with anyone.

This house we live in now, we are paying a hundred fifty a month—for *que casa,* no? The owner has gradually raised the rent on us. Also, we pay gas, electric and water. Now the owner has said we must leave. We have thirteen days to find another casa, but we haven't enough money to make a deposit and pay the first month's rent. I do not know where we will go. My children, I don't want them to have to change schools again.

In the Sierras, the caves were very warm in winter. The snow comes all the way up to your knees outside, and no one goes outdoors then. But the caves are very warm. If they didn't have doors across the front, they had fabric like a tent covering the opening. So the snow didn't blow inside. We used kerosene lamps for light, like the miners used when they went into the mines. In summer, the caves are very cool and comfortable too. We had a stove. You make a hole in the roof of the cave and put a pipe up through it and let the smoke from your wood stove go out there—a chimney. It was very normal to live in a cave. Everybody else did.

I do not envy other people's material wealth. When I watch television, I can see what they have, yes. But those things belong to them. I don't envy them. As long as my children are healthy, as long as my family is united, that's all I care about. I don't wish for other people's things. If I could have one thing, one wish . . . it would be a home of my own. A place where my children could stay in the same school. A casa where we could live unmolested. I don't care if it was just a hut that we dug out of the ground. As long as we didn't have to leave it, I would be happy.

Sometimes my children will go over to Juarez for a Mexican meal. I tell them, "You don't have to go over there. You can get a real Mexican meal right here at home."

They tell me, "It's not the same."

And they go to Juarez.

On a Trailways bus, traveling across New Mexico's desert, I met Lucia (a pseudonym). Lucia and her son, Miguel, were going to Colorado to visit Lucia's husband, who was incarcerated in a federal correctional center there. Miguel was a friendly little boy, and asked me what I did for work. I told him, and asked him how old he was.

"Nine," he said, "and I have a job too."

"Doing what?", I asked Miguel.

"I work in the grape."

Lucia, her son, Miguel, and I sat in the Albuquerque bus station and talked about their lives as grape pickers in

California vineyards. Lucia's story is vivid and chilling, a simply stated account of the conditions of U.S. farm laborers.

Lucia

I grew up in Guadalajara. My mother and dad were farmworkers. They were separated and I lived with my mother. But she was always moving around with the crops, so I was raised by other people, by my grandmother until she died. Then my mother came and brought me to California. She was living in Mexicali and also in California. She didn't have papers yet to work in the U.S. But I had this godmother in California and she helped my mother with her papers. She brought me here about the time she got her papers. It was hard for me to get across the border because I didn't know any English. So when I showed them my birth certificate, they didn't think it was mine. See, I was born in California, but then was taken to Mexico when I was just a baby. My parents were always moving around.

So the Customs, they didn't think the papers were mine and they had to investigate me. I was just seven or eight years old, and they would ask me questions in English and I wouldn't know how to answer back. That was in Mexicali at the border.

In Coachella [California], my mother was working in the fields. Packing carrots and asparagus and other vegetables. Every year they go up north and work in the grape. They do that every year and they like it, 'cause they get away from the . . . from Coachella, I guess.

The first time I went up north to work, I was only like thirteen and it was something new to me, something different. It wasn't very nice, it wasn't really nice at all. It was real ugly, but we had to work and make some money, so we had to go, you know. It's always been grapes really.

The campo had wooden buildings. In one room there would be four or five families. We lived together. It was mothers who didn't have husbands, and their children.

One year, my mother had to leave me with a friend. I stayed with this woman about three years, and she became like another mother to me. She had a son, and later on we would get married. I didn't know English then, and they would make fun of me, so I learned it real fast. Not too good, but I get by. We didn't used to get along, my husband and me, when we were just kids living in the same house. He used to see me like brother and sister. Everyone where we lived in Coachella used to see us as cousins. His friends would ask me out to a dance or something and I would say no to them. Then as soon as he would ask me—'cause he was always hearing his friends ask me out—as soon as he would ask me, I would say yes. So we started liking each other and we stayed together.

The first year I went up north, we went up together. My mother and I went with his family, because they had a car. If you don't have a car you just have to get yourself a ride, or you can take the bus to wherever you have a job at. And once you get up there, it's your problem to get yourself a ride to where the camp is.

There's a lady in Coachella who's a foreman. She's a foreman and she goes up north every year. When the season's over down south, then we know she's gonna go up north and we ask her for a job up there. If she says yes, you go with her. Like last year for example, last year I went up north with her. I was pregnant with my baby, and I wasn't together with my husband. This foreman couldn't give me a job, she already had too many people. So my mother-in-law was already at this other camp, a Filipino camp. They weren't supposed to allow women there, but they still did. The foreman, he allowed women to stay there. This camp was different than the others.

The foreman lady's name was Sylvia, and she worked for

a patrón. The patrón provided trailers for all the people Sylvia hired to work in his grapes. First she drove us to Arvin, California, and we worked there for about three weeks. From there we moved up to Ducor, down below Delano. We moved on from there to an ugly camp where we shared an old, old house. This house had a lot of rooms, and the room we had was for two families. Each room was for two or three families, it depended on the size of the room. And then later the patrón provided trailers for the families. One trailer has showers and bathrooms, washing machines and all that. Another one is a kitchen with a cook and a dining room. All the other trailers have separate rooms, four to a trailer. If it's a big family, they get one room together. If it's only single people, then two or three or four girls get to have one room to share together. And then the guys are separate. There's no privacy at all really. Families are always fighting, arguing, and then the food, you know . . . They pay up to $45 a week for women's work. And you take your kids with you, like I take my two kids and now that I have my baby, I'll take her with me too. I'll have to pay a babysitter to take care of her there at the trailers. Plus I'll have to pay room and board for them. Not for the baby, 'cause she's really free, she can sleep with me. But for my son and my older daughter, I'll have to pay $45 for each, and then pay for myself, which makes more than $100, and I won't even earn that much in a week. I can't do it.

Last year I took them with me. And when I was at that Filipino camp, they were charging thirty-some dollars. I was up there about three or four weeks, and my children were helping in the work too. It was their first year in the grape, she was eleven and my son was about eight. I hated to put them to work, but they had to go with me in the fields anyway—I couldn't afford the babysitter. There wasn't anybody to leave them with, so they'd go with me in the fields and help me. The patrón's people, they knew my daughter was only eleven, but they gave her age to be sixteen so she could work. That helped me. Maybe it's better she got paid for it.

My son was in the grape for the first time when he was about four. It's . . . it's sad. It's really sad because you don't want for your kids to go through what you've gone through. It's painful.

There's two things you can do in the grape. You can pack the grape and you can pick the grape. I can do both. I pick the grape, then clean it up, you know, take the spoiled grape, the ones that are flattened, the rotten grapes out. And the green ones and the waterberries. Just cut it off at the vine, then clean it up and put it in the box, fill the box, seal it up and carry it out to the packers so they can pack it. And if you're packing it, then you just have to wait for the pickers to bring us the grape, then you clean it up. Then we pack it to make it look nice and neat, you know.

The grapes have acid and they eat your skin. And that stuff they spray on the vines—insecticide—that messes up your skin and burns your eyes, it ruins your clothes and gives you a really bad odor. When you're working all the time, it gives a person a real bad insecticide odor. Even if you bathe, as long as you're working there your clothes smell like insecticide all the time. You have to have certain clothes you use just for that work.

You know, one thing, people are afraid of the patrón. I don't know if it's right for him to be as strict as he is. He's so strict that as soon as the pickers in the vine hear he's coming they get all nervous, they start praying. They're really afraid of him, afraid they'll get fired. Everybody watches, you know, to see if he's coming. He jumps from one road to the other through the vineyards, through the grapevine. "He's coming! He's coming!" And everybody looks, everybody gets all paranoid. He's like in his forties or fifties, and he owns the vineyards. There's three brothers, I think, but there's only one of them the people are really scared of. His name is Salvador. The patrónes have a lot of land. They make wine. Up near Delano and Bakersfield.

The first time I went to the fields, I was like my daughter in a way. I wanted to be sitting down. It was real hot. In Coachella the weather gets up to 115, 117 degrees in summer. So we had to be picking grapes in that weather. When I had my daughter working I had her up north where it's not so hot as down in Coachella. But I'd worry. I'd look around and she'd be sitting down, she'd feel dizzy. It reminded me of when I was younger. Back then we were getting paid three or four dollars a day. Now I'm twenty-eight, so that was around 1965.

La Raza, to me that means we are united. We are all the same. Just the other day I was talking to a guy from Guadalajara, Mexico. And I introduced him to some of my friends who are Mexican-Americans. So I told him they were Mexicans. He says, "No, they're *pochos*." Pochos are considered Mexican-Americans. And then he started telling me, "Mexicans are the ones like me. I come from Mexico, so I'm a Mexican." But to me it doesn't make any difference. The ones who come from Mexico to live here, they would say they are Mexicana, or wetback, you know.

Pocho is a word for people born in the United States who don't speak good Spanish and they don't speak English well either. Like I speak Spanish, and I speak English, but not correctly. I speak Spanish wrong too. I speak it wrong yet I think I know it real good. That's what a pocho is. I have a dictionary, Spanish-English, English-Spanish. Sometimes when somebody asks me a word I don't understand, I go home and look it up. That way I really know what they are saying.

If I told you about the Farmworkers' strike . . . it was like a war. I was working in the fields. The strike was going strong. There were three sides, you know. There was the companies, there was the Teamsters, who were really the companies' union, and there was the United

Farmworkers' Union, Chavez' union. But we needed to work, we needed to make money. We didn't want to quit working and go out on strike. I knew it was for a good cause and I didn't want to let them down, the UFW, 'cause what they were doing was for the best. But we needed to work, you know. And most of my friends were out there on strike. So they would start calling us names and making fun of us and stuff like that. So we just had to get out, to quit working and go out there with the rest of them.

There was a lot of fights on the picket lines. There'd be the UFW on one side of the road and the Teamsters on the other side. They'd be calling each other names, and we were trying to call the workers to come out of the fields. The Teamsters, you know . . . I never got hurt, but you had to run to get away from them. The Teamsters were the company, see what I mean? So it was awful. It was good for us and bad for them. But then it was bad for us, 'cause we had to go through a lot, you know, fighting and war. Yeah, it was a war. Everybody just had to run. There would be trucks with Teamsters and they would get big rocks and they'd be going real fast on the trucks and throwing rocks at us. So then we would get sticks and we'd go after them. One time the Teamsters burned the buses some of the strikers were in. It was awful. No weapons or anything. But it was like war in a way. It started in 1970 and went on till about 1974, and it's still going on, you know.

One time I went to the store to buy lettuce. My girlfriend told me, "Don't buy any lettuce." And I said okay, I won't. But I love lettuce, you know, and I bought some. She was living with me, and when I got home we started putting away the groceries. When she saw the lettuce, she threw it away.

We need to work. But we need to be united, you know. To have a union.

Donbas Miner

This is the story of the Ukrainian coal miner Sergei Degtiariov, but the tale begins in the Lobo Canyon, New Mexico, in America's uranium mining country. Sam Tafoya is a mine workers' organizer for the Operators and Engineers' Union, and his territory is the Lobo Canyon. Shortly before I left for the Soviet Union, Sam gave me a tour of some uranium mines. As I was leaving the Canyon, running to catch a departing Trailways bus, he tossed me a miner's safety belt. "Here," he said, "take this to the Soviet Union. Give it to some miners over there." I promised that I would.

North of the Black Sea, the Donets Basin is coal mining country, mineral-rich steppes in eastern Ukraine. Donbas, as Soviets call the region, is the U.S.S.R.'s chief source of coal, although Siberia's vast coal deposits promise to outproduce Donbas during this century. Coal production has been reduced in Donbas recently, because the government is acutely aware of declining reserves. Still, coal is King in Donbas, or at least it is the major industry. Driving into Donetsk, a town of about one million people, a mammoth black statue of a coal miner looms over life there, reminding residents that in Donbas anyway, coal miners are labor's elite, and even if they aren't living like kings, they are renowned as heroes.

Next door to Donetsk, the twin mining town of Makeevka, with about half a million people, has no statue, but boasts an abundance of apple and cherry trees that, in early May, billow like low clouds over the avenues. In Makeevka, some mining families live in high-rise red brick apartment buildings, in modern but cramped living quarters. Others occupy low wooden cottages, primitive dwellings that look drafty and difficult to heat, and seem transplanted from a southern Appalachian hollow. Makeevka is dotted with black "terricone" slag heaps, so neatly sculpted they might be Ukrainian versions of pyramids. Scientists from the Donetsk Mining Institute are experimenting with grass seeding on the terricones, hoping to transform the volatile slag heaps into public parks. A dry, sulphuric tang hung in the air over Makeevka the morning I arrived there, dredging up memories of Harlan, Kentucky, and inciting a thirst for Kentucky moonshine. I had spent enough years in America's mining regions to know that most mining towns have a preponderance of bars and prothesis shops on the main streets. I looked around as we drove through Makeevka, but did not see any prothesis shops. And because it was morning, the bars were closed. Other than the lack of prothesis shops, and the neat and tidy terricone slag heaps, Makeevka, on first glance anyway, might have been Beckley, West Virginia, in springtime. I liked it.

The coal miner Sergei Degtiariov lived in a tall brick apartment building in Makeevka with his wife, Valentina, and their teenage daughter, Galina. Their apartment was spruced up the day I arrived to visit them, and although it was still early morning, bottles of Ukrainian champagne and Moldavian wine sat on the coffee table. Someone had laid out an elegant brunch of black caviar, smoked sturgeon, breads and cheeses. They were expecting company.

Sergei Degtiariov was a slightly built man, a dark Ukrainian, with deep cheek hollows and graying hair. He had wide, vulnerable eyes, like the eyes of a young boy who had seen no evil. But he had, as a young boy, seen more horror than most American children. This particular morning, though, Sergei Degtiariov was dressed in a sharp blue suit, with a white shirt and red tie, and had no intention of dredging up old nightmares. He was having company in his home, and wanted to put his best foot, and happiest smile, forward.

Valentina was a striking blond Russian, a kind hostess who understood an American's aversion to multiple champagne toasts before breakfast. Galina looked like Lolita but had innocent eyes. She was secretary to the Makeevka coal mine's chief executive, and told me she spent most of her spare time in discos. In her bedroom, two decorations hung on the walls: a crucifix and a disco "light box," which when hooked up to her stereo, flashed lights to music's rhythms. Her father built the light box using four hundred and sixty-eight bulbs from miner's lamps.

On this occasion, Sergei Degtiariov's home was crowded. A delegation of Makeevka mine officials and local Communist Party functionaries had greeted my arrival in Donbas and had dogged my heels ever since. Leading the delegation was Galina's boss, Vladimir, who had silver hair, slicked back, and a habit of winking at women. Two motherly women officials, dressed for a tea party, made no bones about their interest in meeting an American woman. A stunning young redhead named Tamara, a journalist and Party worker, said she had heard an American woman was going to visit Makeevka's coal mine. She had never been inside a coal mine, although she had tried to get permission many times, and seized this opportunity to realize a dream. Adding to the crowd at Sergei Degtiariov's home was Maxim Rilsky, a Kiev journalist who had boarded a train to Makeevka when he heard rumors about an American visiting the mines. Maxim did not speak fluent English, but spoke it well enough to say, "I'm going into the pit with you." My Novosti escort also planned to take the plunge, which was scheduled for the next morning, and as we approached Sergei's front door, the whole crowd was bursting with enthusiasm.

Sergei Degtiariov opened the door and blinked at the bubbly crowd. He seemed unaccustomed to such official gatherings in his home, and perhaps was expecting a smaller number of guests. He fiddled nervously with a champagne cork as he gave the host's customary first toast. He also did not seem used to drinking champagne first thing in the morning. Nevertheless, we toasted one thing and another, and then Galina broke out a box of chocolates big as a bathmat and dumped it in my lap. Vladimir winked at Tamara, and I realized the party had swung into full gear. As the crowd grew more jovial, and my brain began to fuzz from champagne, I wondered how I was going to interview Sergei in the midst of this gay merrymaking. I asked Galina if we might borrow her bedroom for the interview. *"Pozhaluista, pozhaluista,"* she said, opening the door for us. I motioned Sergei and the interpreter to follow. They did, and so did the rest of the delegation.

The situation called for immense patience and tact. One does not simply eject an entire delegation of Soviet coal mine officials and Party functionaries from a room where they want to be. I looked at Sergei. He shrugged. "Maybe we should go back to the living room," he offered.

"They'd follow us," I said.

Then Sergei had an inspiration. He switched on Galina's stereo and the light box. The room swam in flashing lights and vibrated to a heavy rock rhythm. The delegation retreated to the living room. We shut the door, turned off the equipment and began the interview.

Sergei Degtiariov spoke softly, with a heavy Ukrainian accent, about his childhood in the Ukrainian village of L'viv.

Sergei Degtiariov

During the war, we were called refugees. We lived in occupied territory near Kiev, my mother, two younger sisters and I. I was six or seven when the war broke out. My sisters were very young, one just an infant less than a year old. My father was away fighting at the front. There was nowhere for us to live, everything was destroyed when the Germans invaded. So we lived with strangers in L'viv.

In order to survive, I went, a little boy, to work for some people. They gave me five cows to milk. In return for tending the cows, the people gave us milk and fed our family. At first, the neighbors were afraid to give me their cows, but I wasn't the only kid in this situation, there were a lot of families without homes, without food. So we got together. The older kids were in charge, of course. Often when we were tending the cows, the cows and their calves, a German car would appear on the road. The soldiers would take the youngest calves away from us. We'd cry, because these were other people's cattle. But they would take the calves anyway. When we went back home and told the neighbors that the Germans had taken away the calves, they didn't scold us.

We children played "War" in the trenches left by the passing front. That was our playground. Our toys were unexploded shells, cartridges the soldiers had left behind. Many children died, they were blown up by these live shells. Before the Soviet military units could get there to clean up those unexploded shells, many people died. That was our playground.

Like all little boys, we loved to smoke. Maybe not all little boys loved to smoke, but we sure did. There was a field with a road through it, and the German cars used this road frequently. So we boys dragged water to the road and made puddles. The cars with German officers would approach, they would hit the puddles and skid. Their cars would get stuck. Officers always had what to smoke. They didn't climb out of their cars, they would call us over, and they would tell us to push them out of the puddles. And for doing it, they gave us cigarettes. Now I don't smoke.

Throughout the war years we wondered, "When will this war end?" Just that one thought. Everyone thought about getting something to eat. We children had a hero from our fairy tales. His name was Ilya Muromets, and he was a *bogatir*.* We waited for Ilya Muromets to come and crush the fascists. We little boys didn't have enough strength to harm them, so we waited for a bogatir to come and get rid of them.

We were evacuated from L'viv, on our way to Kiev by train. They had loaded us in. Our train started up three times, and each time as we would push off, the fascist planes would dive and blast the train cars. Each time they aimed for the middle of the train. And they hit it. My mother, my sisters and me, we were in the front of the train. As soon as one car was hit, the train crew would attach another one. The planes always hit the midsection. So that's how it happened, three times, and all the time we were in the front section of the train, the part that wasn't hit. We survived it, but lots of children died. And their mothers. There were no men on the train, only women and children. It's thanks to our mother that we lived through it. Although there was one instance when she said something that wasn't so good. There were three of us kids and

* Bogatirs are giants in Kiev Rus myths. Ilya Muromets was a legendary Ukrainian hero.

119

nothing to feed us. She was worn out herself and she didn't have any of her own milk left to feed the baby. That was the situation while we were on the train. So she says, "Please God, let this little one, at least, be taken to her own death." But the little one lived through it, and now she weighs more than all of us—ninety kilograms. Just to spite that war, she became the very healthiest.

These days I'm thin. I've got stomach problems. Maybe all that comes from those times. There wasn't anything to eat, we ate frozen potatoes from the ground, whatever we could collect. Then our units arrived, and I remember there was even a helping hand from America. American canned meat was given as aid to children who were without their fathers. And I remember the brown English shoes that were too big. And, with pleasure we ate the potatoes abandoned in the fields. We baked them in open fires. Then in 1946, there was a famine. We ate nettles.

After the war, we were left without an apartment. We moved to the Kuban, to my father's homeland. We went there, like all families returned to their fathers' homeland if they could. We went there to wait for our father's return from the front. My mother found a job on a collective farm. They gave her work, and since we had suffered, the collective farmers gave us a small house.

Everything had been destroyed. We had to plow the fields with cows, plant wheat by hand. And right after the war ended, there weren't any men to help in the fields.

We raised wheat and fruit, watermelons.

There was no paper. I remember when I was in the first grade, they gave us old newspapers that the grown-ups had already read, and we wrote between the lines with ink from a tree that's called *buzina* in Ukrainian, a tree you can make ink from.* We wrote our lessons between the lines of newsprint, and those were the first letters I was

---

*Buzina is an elderberry. Ink was made from elderberry juice.

120

able to make, with that buzina. They gave us books, one to a class, notebooks. We would come to school early or get together at someone's house in order to learn the lessons. We had to work collectively because there were not enough books to go around. Then more books and notebooks began to appear. Things began to get better and better.

Fathers began returning home from the war. Without arms, without legs. Every family was waiting for their father. As we were waiting for ours. One day my mother ran into some of my father's friends. They told her that he had died. He burned up in a tank. And our mother told us.

Although I didn't remember my father's figure—I was a small boy when he left for the front—I could picture him from photos my mother had shown me. But photos are photos, and since from early childhood I couldn't remember him, I carried his image in my memory. I wanted to follow in his . . . to be similar to my father, to be some kind of defender of our Motherland.

You could feel that the war was becoming more distant. There was industry starting back up, life was starting up again, the countryside was coming back to life. After a while, we schoolchildren began writing with lead. Not the whole pencils, just the lead part. And they broke easily. But it was a change. You could sense that many of our people had died. There wasn't enough manpower in the collective farm, and so the chairman asked us children to work. Right up until school, all summer we worked. None of us played, we helped because there weren't enough men.

One summer I helped at harvesting the grain. We took the grain from the combine on horses because there were no machines. But the greatest pleasure, the best job of all, was tending the horses. Because you could ride. This was such a pleasure for me. I was thirteen, fourteen, fifteen years old then, back in '48, '49. All those years I worked, until I finished high school. We never had summer vacations like kids do now. They would ask us to come to school on the first day of vacation, and then they'd ask us to work a little, at least for the harvest. And so we went to work, all through the summer, and through the harvest in autumn.

Since there were no men, my mother would send her single Woodchopper into the woods to chop wood for the fire. I was small at thirteen years, and the ax was heavier than I was! I chopped whole wagonloads. With tears. I would cry, "Mom! Have pity!" But I had to, there was no one else. All the men had died.

The town was small and it was not possible to build a big school for us. We had a small schoolhouse that went as far as the seventh grade. That was the only school in town. Then, when we finished seventh grade, we had to walk seventeen kilometers to the district school. But it was really a lot of fun, a very interesting walk, and we would often stop along the way and play. In the Kuban, there is hardly a winter season, but still, it got too cold in winter to walk that far to school. So we stayed in an apartment near the district school during those months. And so, I went as far as tenth grade in school.* And it was in the tenth grade that I first got interested in girls.

Simply, there was one girl that I liked. They lived well, were well off, and we were poor. And she felt that. But I had a friend, Pavel. He lived a little better, was a little better off than we were. And Pavel said to me, "Well, as a friend," he said, "give her to me." I wanted her to be my girlfriend, but as it turned out, I had to give her up. And she was also a blond, like my wife is now. For all that heartache, I fell in love with someone like her. You see, I'm dark, but I love the fair girls. My spouse, I loved her braids

---

*Tenth grade in Soviet schools is equivalent to twelfth grade in a U.S. high school.

when she wore them. When Valentina was young, she had this long blond braid. I was twenty-two when we met.

The difficult period had almost ended in our country. This was in the late fifties. But those postwar leftovers, it was still hard. The state had helped, they had paid for me and my sisters on account of our father having died in the war. And that was a big help to our mother. So then, according to our Constitution, when we boys are grown we should serve in the Soviet Army. I loved soldiers. My father was a military man. So when I finished tenth grade, they offered me . . . you see, they took all the children whose fathers had died into the military academy. We have the Suvorov and the Khimov academies, which give military training to the children whose fathers died in the war. They offered me a place in the Khimov Academy. But my mother didn't approve, she would not allow it. She said, "The father died. I don't want the children to die." She didn't understand that soldiers were needed for the army, even in peacetime. So I didn't go to the Khimov Academy, but then later on I received my draft notice and went on to serve in the Soviet Army. I was a radioman. Maybe because of my love for music, for radio has that experience at the root of it. I was stationed in Kiev. I was born there, so I served there. I worked the Morse Code.

In the army, it seems to me, there wasn't anything very interesting that happened. I was studying military matters. We worked on the radio apparatus. I learned to send and receive messages. And we had leave and time off on Saturdays and Sundays. Then we'd go into Kiev, into the city, and visit the museums or go to the cinema. We didn't meet a single girl. Not because it wasn't allowed for soldiers to meet girls, it was. Back then there was no television, and on the radio, well, you heard but you couldn't see . . . and the movies . . . well, I guess we just didn't grow up so fast back then.

The most popular song of the time was "Moscow

Nights." Do they know that song in America? It's a song from the fifties. There were many songs, but they've all "gone out," as they say. Like a person outlives his time, so does a song. Even if I named them, nobody would know them. Well, there was a song called "Saturday." And maybe some still remember the song from one of our films, "My Heart." Yes. "Your heart is light with a jolly song. It never lets you pine." The group Mox now is copying this song.

You know, during the war, although I was small, I saw many dead. It's somehow nice to see that we have now put up monuments so that we are reminded, even those who didn't see the victims. We have this good tradition, so that young people don't forget. On their wedding day, newlyweds put flowers at the eternal flame of such memorials.

If you'll permit me, I'll show you how Valentina looked in her youth. This is an old photograph from those years when we first met. She was of a pure Russian nature, it was the style then to wear a long braid. She was twenty years old here. And I really went for women with braids. In our country now, it's considered old-fashioned. I met her in a movie theater. But I have a kind of timid character, I'm kind of shy. I couldn't immediately . . . as the Russians say, only at the third attempt. She's really kind of strict. We had this clean-cut kind of friendship without any misinterpretations. And we were just friends for two years, purely comradely relationship. And then we got married. I was of an age. We understood each other. I couldn't live without her, and she liked me. The wedding, of course, wasn't as magnificent as they are now. That was right after I got out of the army, when I met Valentina. I was working in the mine.

Well, a group of the guys collectively decided to go to work in the mines. From the Komsomol [Young Communist League] appeal, we knew that many mines were being constructed in the country. And we decided to become part

of the youth movement after the war. We all wanted to . . .
our country was destroyed, in ruins. We felt that there was
a real need for coal, so that homes could be warm. It was a
time for our country . . . well, like now, the young people
who are building BAM* . . . so that we, with these, our
own hands would raise what had been destroyed. For us it
was even more so then, because our country had been
destroyed. And now, with BAM, they're building something new, they're supplementing what we already have.
But back then, there was no foundation, there was
nothing.

I've always worked in the mines here in Makeevka.
Many of our group wanted to build, to expand factories, to
build houses, but I decided to go into the mines. I served
with guys in the army who were miners. And that's why I
wanted to try it. They told me that it was hard work but
heroic. We received training here in the mine, they taught
us our specialty. It was like mining school. I studied
mining half a year, but at the same time, we were
apprenticed to miners. And since then, I've learned many
mining specializations. I can work as a mining/metal
worker, as a tunnel worker—I can handle any work
connected with mining.

At first I worked in another mine we have here, not so
deep as this one. This deeper mine they were just starting
to build then. But this deeper mine, when it was being
built, was famous all over the world. It was the deepest in
the Soviet Union. It set a world record for length of the
shafts at this slope.

The first day we went underground, we had the same
kind of feeling like we are all going down into a cellar, a

*BAM: Baikal-Amur Railway. Construction of the railroad began in the
mid-seventies, when thousands of Komsomol members volunteered to
go to Siberia to build it in answer to the government's call for speeding
up industrial expansion and developing the natural resources of the
region.

basement. It was dark. That mine wasn't so deep. But at the same time, there was a fear that the Earth's crust was so thick, it had to give way. I could imagine how it would crush a person. But nothing fell. We all got out.

The clothing was the same, only we didn't have the meters for measuring methane gas. Now it's measured electronically. Then, we had these little lamps. The lamps had little filaments and we could measure their brightness, they showed the level of methane gas in the air. But now we have an institute in Makeevka which specially concerns itself with labor safety. It was there that the apparatus for measuring methane was developed. It was started here, in the Makeevka Institute, and then spread all over the Soviet Union.

Our first day of work was like becoming acquainted, as with you becoming acquainted with our mine today. A person should know not just from books, from pictures, how it is to be a miner, but he should visually see where he will have to work. It seemed to me, of course, well, I had never worked yet then. I had mostly lived in the country. Mining seemed dirty to me. All the miners were covered with black powder. But at the same time, when you finish working and come out of the mines and wash off . . . maybe you've felt it, you feel that all the tiredness has left, and you have a pleasant sensation that you've done something good. We have a miners' song here in Donbas: "Only the miner who was underground all day can appreciate the sun and the high sky." We've got lots of songs about miners. It's very heavy labor, but that's why we're so respected. It's considered to be very honorable labor.

It's kind of like being in the army when you come to work your first day. You take a long time putting on your boots, figuring out how to put on your field shirt—you can't get the buttons straight. And then, after a while, it only takes seconds. It's just like that. If you count getting out of your street clothes, I could get dressed in about a minute, but you don't need to set a record getting dressed. I take my time getting dressed. The footcloths, we wear them because they are the most comfortable. Of course, footcloths go directly against the skin, without socks.

Now we have very complicated mining techniques. Composite. It's called the Winkle complex. I'm working now as an operator. I have to take care of the electric equipment and an oil station which maintains the pressure for the complex. Hydro cables supply the drills with oil. All the complex of equipment works is on hydro cables. To raise or lower them, it all depends on hydraulics. So the station where I work gives the atmospheric pressure. The pressure results from the oil. Like the brakes of an automobile.

The most difficult days are the ones after vacation, when you've relaxed. Then your legs and arms hurt. Like an athlete who doesn't work out. But it goes away.

I don't solve technical problems. That's for the mechanics and engineers. Everything is prepared in advance. Somewhere around ten people work on our line.

In 1972, we had a fire in the mine. One comrade saw smoke coming from the mine. He quickly informed everyone nearby. All the people were brought up quickly from the mine, so there were no injuries. The firemen were called, but the fire spread through the mines, and it was a few days before it was contained. I was in the mine when the fire started. We looked after each other. The team has a Mine Master who leaves the mine last. He counted us to make sure that everyone had gone up, that everyone was saved, so there was no possibility of danger to anyone left behind. There were no victims.

Miners are like cosmonauts, there aren't many people who can do their jobs. It seems to me it's just that. Not every man or woman should go to such depths. Not because he's afraid, but there isn't the opportunity. I wouldn't want my daughter to work in the mine, no. It's men's work. Women, like the sun, should shine above.

There's something about labor, I started to labor very early. I liked work—seven years I was a cowherd. Maybe that's why I went into the mines.

Vladimir, the coal mine director, sat behind his office desk, hands clasped before him, gazing down the long conference table where the delegation sat. Some were reading notes, others pouring fizzy mineral water into crystal glasses. Sasha, the chief mine engineer, was in charge of this meeting. He sat on my right, exuding a seasoned miner's sense of self-confidence. He would lead the mine expedition, and by now, a total of four women would be accompanying him into the mines. Sasha was secretly planning to take us into a rather shallow mine. Now, he addressed me at the conference table.

"Tomorrow morning," Sasha said, "we are going to take you into a coal mine. It is extremely important that you understand the situation underground. This is for your safety. So there are a few details we must discuss. First of all, women do not often go into our coal mines. We believe that mining is very damaging to a woman's health. Yes, it is true women used to work in some Soviet coal mines. But today it is not permitted for women to do this dangerous work."

I asked Sasha if Ukrainian miners were superstitious about women going into their coal mines.

"*Konechno,*" he said, "certainly, it is the same all over the world. But we make certain exceptions. For example, sometimes a mine safety or health inspector is a woman, and we must allow her into the mines for inspections." He coughed lightly. "Now, you will please tell us, have you ever been in a coal mine before? If so, please tell us when, where, and the circumstances."

128

"In 1974," I answered obediently, "in 1974, in the People's Republic of China, Tangshan Coal Mine. We went one mile down and five miles in."

You could bite the silence. Sasha rubbed his chin for a minute, then jumped up and hurried over to the telephone. He spoke into the phone, making a few changes in his plans, and returned to the table. "So," he said, "they took you down only one mile? Well, Katya Kahn, tomorrow morning we will take you into a *real* deep mine."

The Donbas miner's uniform was too big and they had to sew me into it. Sasha had told me that during the time we were in the mine, I would lose four kilos of body weight, or ten pounds. I weighed in before and after the expedition, and he was right on the nose. Before going into the mine, the miners fed us a huge meal that included slabs of raw pork fat, fish, meat and carbohydrates. No vodka.

I strapped the New Mexico miner's belt around my waist. Sasha checked our gear, and we stepped into the elevator, a dank, square, steel box, and shot down the shaft at about eighty miles an hour, cold air blowing like a hurricane around us. We made a smooth landing, over a mile down, Sasha opened the door and we stepped into the bowels of the Ukraine.

The tunnels were high and wide, with arched ceilings. Wind from ventilators blew swift and cold, but heavy layers of clothing and moleskin footcloths under our boots kept the body temperature up. I could feel sweat pouring underneath the clothes, the shedding of the big miner's meal. Sasha cautioned us, "Stay very close together, don't stray out. Keep right beside me or behind me. Keep your lights on, and if the women . . . here, give me your oxygen tanks, it's easier for me to carry them. Watch your step. Most of all, watch straight ahead of you." We walked for hours, it seemed, through the Earth's underbelly, damp, dark caverns, seeping water, leaks from hydraulic feed lines plunking water softly on the cavern floors, rotted timbers strewn about where new timbers had been raised. Sasha said, "This is our deepest mine, and the most complicated one." He said nothing more until, after endless trudging, we finally heard the sound of a hydraulic drill. "We're at the pit," Sasha said.

The continuous miner bored through hard rock wall. The pit was hot, men working there had stripped off several layers of their uniforms. In the light of our headlamps, I saw the flashing teeth and headlamp of one miner. When my eyes adjusted, I saw he was a huge man whose eyes twinkled out of a soot blackened face. Sasha introduced us. "So!" boomed the big miner, "an American has come to visit my workplace!"

He helped me work a chunk of coal off a seam. "There," he said, "now you have contributed to our production quota for the Five Year Plan." I pocketed half the coal. "And now," the big miner said, "please answer some questions for me." He barraged me with questions about deep mining in the U.S.

I explained that union miners receive retirement pensions and health benefits. I told him about the Mine Health and Safety Act, and admitted that it was not always enforced. In response to his inquiry, I described living conditions in eastern Kentucky and in West Virginia mining towns. Finally I explained that a serious problem American coal miners face today is layoffs, since many deep mines are worked out and surface mining is accelerating.

"Well, of course, our mines get worked out too," said the big miner. "Surely U.S. miners are placed in other mines or retrained? And what about fatalities in the underground mines of the U.S.?"

I told him that in 1980, over one hundred thirty miners were killed in mine accidents, cave-ins or explosions. I didn't know the statistics on uranium mining, but told him there had recently been a death caused by a cave-in in a uranium mine.*

Finally he stopped asking questions and I asked him a few. He said that Soviet miners work on a quota system, one similar to the American underground miners' "bonus system," and that Soviet miners are paid bonuses according to production levels. Miners work in teams, and teams have their quotas to fulfill. Because mining is a dangerous occupation, miners are allowed to retire at age fifty, with a full pension if they worked twenty years. Retirement pensions for coal miners are higher than for Soviet workers in less hazardous occupations. Widows and dependents of miners killed in mine accidents, and black lung victims receive full pensions. Miners' work gear is provided free of charge and trade unions pay for vacations, usually a month's time off. On holidays, Donbas miners frequent resorts on the Black Sea. The Donbas miner said trade unions have the right, as U.S. miners' unions do, of calling inspections of the mines, but not the right, as U.S. miners have (though they are often penalized by the company for exercising it) of refusing to work on an unsafe job site. This question must be negotiated through union officials. Soviet miners are required to have annual medical examinations, including X-rays to determine if the worker is contracting pneumoconiosis, the black lung disease caused by inhaling coal dust. Underground machine operators and water supply workers are required to have monthly medical checkups. In Donbas and Eastern Siberia, mine safety institutes train miners in life-support systems and emergency procedures. When a mine is

---

*In 1981, over 150 miners died from job related injuries. Between December 1, 1981 and February 13, 1982, 65 miners were killed in U.S. coal mine disasters. That averages approximately 6 miners per week who died from job related injuries, not counting the approximately 4,000 a year who die from black lung disease.

worked out, Soviet miners are guaranteed jobs in other mines or retraining in other occupations.

The miner said he did not know of any recent fatalities in Soviet coal mines, nor of any explosions, fires or other mine accidents since the '72 Makeevka fire. Even if he had looked for injury and fatality figures, he would not have found them. The government does not make public statistics on work-related injuries, disabilities and deaths, a practice which may contribute to, rather than reduce, the number of accidents. Workers with access to this information may be more cautious on the job. They also might refuse to work if the statistics suggested a job site was unsafe. And though statistics are often inaccurate, withholding them from the population can only breed distrust of the censors.

The Donbas miners and mine officials readily admitted that working conditions in Makeevka's deepest mine are not optimal, and since the '72 fire, they have doubled their respect for its complex and volatile nature. Men working there face more risks to their health and safety than in most Soviet coal mines. Among a population rich in heroes of labor, they are the elite.

There are no prosthesis shops in the Donbas. But in spite of the heavy emphasis the government places on miners' safety, some workers have lost legs and arms in mine accidents. There are no prosthesis shops because artificial limbs are provided to the victims, free of charge, in government clinics.

I unbuckled the New Mexico miner's safety belt and gave it to the big Donbas miner, telling him about Sam Tafoya, Maggie Martinez and George Rodriguez, three New Mexico deep miners. He listened intently, studying the belt, which was less cumbersome than his own. As we were leaving the pit, he said, "I have read a little about America's deep miners. It seems to me we Soviet miners are more respected and treated better. I know, for example, that in the United States, miners are not people's heroes. Ts, ts, ts . . ." He shook his head and said, "Tell my brother miners in New Mexico I send them greetings. Tell them a fellow miner hopes they get everything they need to live healthy lives and work in safe conditions. All miners must insist on these rights, we all must demand them. Tell my fellow miners in New Mexico I hope one day they will come to Donbas so we can meet and talk about our very dangerous and very courageous work."

"If they wanted to come," I said, "would your officials allow them to visit and to see your workplace?"

"I don't know," he said, "that's a question for the authorities. But they let you come down here, anyway. And you're not even a miner! So it seems to me they can come, *da*. And after they see my workplace, I would like to have a look at theirs."

I shook his soot blackened hand and turned to go. The big miner called out once more, his voice booming through the tunnel. "And tell your American miners that I think they need their own Lenin!"

"Hey, Zapata!"

"¡Que buen terreno!"
—Miner's dream

Mexican workers were once inspired by a hero named Zapata. Today, new forces are leading the American labor movement, and among the leaders who have emerged is uranium miner Margarito Martinez. Twenty years a coal miner, twenty years a uranium miner, Maggie Martinez led one of the U.S. labor history's most important strikes, an eight month long battle between the Oil, Chemical and Atomic Workers' union local in Grants, New Mexico, and Kerr-McGee Corporation, waged in the painted deserts of Lobo Canyon in 1973.

Kerr-McGee is one of several U.S. energy corporations that mine uranium in the Southwest. Used as fuel for nuclear power plants, uranium's "waste" byproduct, plutonium, is the key ingredient in nuclear weapons. Kerr-McGee and other companies have secured mineral rights and leased vast areas of land in the Southwest, land that is visibly, and perhaps permanently, scarred from uranium mining operations. In 1979, federal authorities began removing Navajo, Zuni and other native nations from their ceremonial grounds, clearing the way for the mining operations. Although the mines have provided jobs for some natives, uranium mining and milling processes are the center of heated controversy in the region. Environmentalists charge that radioactive emission and waste materials are polluting the land and skies there, and that the soaring cancer rate among uranium miners is proof that the big energy corporations are more concerned with profits than with health. Some native tribes in the area have joined the disputes and a few tribal councils have leased their land to the corporations. Other nations have promised to resist the inroads of corporations and federal officials.

Kerr-McGee, the largest uranium mining and milling operation in America, has hired mostly "ethnic" workers. Eighty percent of its miners and mill workers are Chicano, 7 percent are American Indian, and 2 percent are black. In recent years, eleven Kerr-McGee employees have died of lung cancer, one of several disabling or fatal effects of inhaling decaying radioactive particles in the mines. Jobs are scarce in the Lobo Canyon, but only a decade ago, Grants was a boomtown thriving on increased demands for "yellowcake," first discovered near Grants in the fifties by a Navajo Indian named Paddy Martinez, who never got rich. Today, the energy corporations hold huge stockpiles of uranium and are having difficulty finding buyers. Since the malfunction at Three Mile Island nuclear power plant in Pennsylvania in 1979, many communities have resisted nuclear power plant operations in their vicinity. With the demand for uranium at an all-time low, the energy companies are closing their mine shafts and mills, and at least for the present, are laying off thousands of miners. But Kerr-McGee is still operating, and Maggie Martinez still has a job. In spite of potential health hazards, he

135

would rather take risks underground than be unemployed.

Maggie and his wife, Pat, welcomed a stranger into their home one evening as though they were greeting kinfolk. The rambling six-room house reflected the prosperity of a union miner who draws good wages. Couches and carpets and a color television, paid for on time, and a kitchen filled with the appliances many Americans consider indispensable, typified an American workers' dream realized. Family photographs on the dining room buffet, religious scenes and union strike souvenirs hanging on the walls, revealed a family's spiritual values. The house glowed, and a stranger could feel the depth of warm family bonds.

"How did you find me?" Maggie Martinez asked. He was short and looked solid as granite. His voice was soft, his dark Mexican eyes shaded under thick lashes.

"George and Bonita Rodriguez gave me your name," I told him. "I was a stranger they picked up on the edge of town. I heard about a cave-in at a Kerr-McGee mine today, that a miner was killed. I asked George Rodriguez who could explain conditions in the uranium mines. He said if anyone could it would be Maggie Martinez. He gave me your phone number."

"Take off your shoes," Maggie Martinez said softly. "You might be here for a long time."

Margarito Martinez

Phelps Dodge Corporation owned a coal mine in Dawson, New Mexico. They're a copper company, but they used coal to smelt copper. They recruited all the workers from Mexico. Okay? They used to go to Mexico and bring them back in a train. In the hoppers. Anybody that wanted to join this train to Dawson was welcome. My dad and mother didn't have any children, so in 1915, they got on this train and came to the United States. My dad went to work in the Dawson mine.

There were twelve children, born one after another. I was born eight days after the explosion. My dad never did miss work, you know, but on the day the mine blew up, he told my mother he wasn't going to work. I was just about to be born. Course the ladies from Mexico never did question what their husbands did, so my mother said, "Okay, you're not going to work." At two o'clock that afternoon, the mine blew up. My dad was home. But I lost an uncle in that explosion. Three hundred and twenty-seven people at one shot. Everybody who was in the mine died.* My dad was part of the rescue team.

Everybody at that time, we were really—how can I tell you?—dirt poor, poor as church mice. Right in the middle of the Depression. I used to notice the younger kids would cry because they were hungry. I remember going to bed hungry. Now Dad, one time he went to work and this is what he took for lunch; some cabbage leaves that were growin' in the garden and a salt shaker. And you know what? There was many times I saw that. Let me tell you a better one, a humorous one. One time my dad, he was working swing for some reason, he was getting ready to leave for the mine. He opened his lunch bucket and there was four biscuits inside. He threw them down on the floor and jumped up and down on them. He gave the lunch bucket to my mother and said, "Now give me some *lunch!*" She told him, "That's it. That's all we have in the house. That's it." So he picked up the biscuits he'd stomped on, put them back in the bucket and went to work.

So that was how the miners lived.

We lived in a company town, and I'll tell you one thing, Phelps Dodge had good houses. They were fabulous compared to what others had. Listen to this; they used to charge a dollar eighty-eight for a ton of coal delivered to your house, a dollar a month for the light, a dollar a month

* The Dawson mine blew up in 1923.

for the water, and we had soft water, the best water. One time they wanted to raise the rent from eight dollars to thirteen, but we had an uprising and they brought it back down to eight. We lived very poor, but we lived comfortably in some ways. The company made sure you stayed, so that when the Depression was over you'd go back to work for them. They were only working the mines two days a week, Friday and Monday. In them days there was no way out of the company town, no way you could make the money to get out of there. Besides, who wanted to get out? Because it was unique. I know men who came to Dawson at age seventeen and are buried there. They lived to retire. That was unique. So we stayed in Dawson.

They had a company store and it had a buggy. You could charge anything you wanted at the company store. I thought back then prices were high. They weren't. Listen; a sack of flour, a hundred pounds, cost a dollar seventy. Tall cans of Pet milk—I worked in the store, so I know— thirty-six cans for a dollar. Outrageous, huh?

We were so poor that my mother had to put us to bed to wash our clothes . . . we had one set of clothes and we stayed in bed while she washed 'em. Laid 'em outside to dry, then brought 'em back inside and we put 'em on again. You know what? Our grandchildren don't believe that.

My daddy worked ten hours a day in the mines. For ten hours they'd pay a dollar fifty-five a day. Yes, the rent was low, but there was no money, especially during the Depression when the mine only worked two days a week. On a good week, they'd work Monday, Wednesday and Friday. But listen, they had it good compared to these other companies—they weren't working at all. There was no money and we lived from one day to another. My daddy kept goin' deeper in debt to the company store. The conditions underground, as I understand, were bad, real bad.

Back then you could take just so much, you know? And then you're gonna fight. All the people who are true at heart, they can take just so much. All of a sudden they're gonna say, "I don't give a damn who you are, I've had it." So they brought the union in. John L. Lewis, the United Mine Workers', and they went on strike. They were tired, they wanted more money, right? Their families were goin' hungry. So they called a strike, and what happens? The company went around trying to terrorize people into goin' back to work. They'd tell people, "Either you go back to work or we'll throw you out of your house." And there was nowhere to go, no money to go.

You stop and think about this. These people came from Mexico. Many of them never went back, not even to visit. Now you stop and think, you pull up roots to go to another country, never to return. How many friends did you leave? How many loved ones? How many sweethearts did you leave behind? How many uncles, aunts, people who loved you, who you'll never see again? So you got to admire them people. They were all alone, and Dawson was like a little island.

But they stuck.

Finally the day came, the company men came to evict my dad, they came to the house and knocked on the door. I was six years old, standing next to my daddy, looking at these guys. All the neighbors came out and gathered around. A company guy asked my dad, "Felix, are you gonna go back to work?"

My dad said, "Hell no, I'm not going to work." And he had that terrific accent, you know.

The guy said, "Well, Felix, if you don't go to work you'll never have nothin' and your kids'll go hungry."

My dad looked at him and said, "Well, I'll tell you what. I been working fifteen years for you, you sonofabitch, and my kids go hungry and we never have nothin'. So what do I have to lose? So fuck you."

139

Right then I knew, it was simple. We had to do something.

Even nowadays, I'll admit there might be some guys in the union who don't know what the word "solidarity" means. That's one word any company cannot understand, cannot comprehend, cannot cope with. Okay, there's a good example in Poland. The government, they come out there with cannons and everything telling people to go to work. And the people are saying, "Go ahead and kill us. Then who's gonna do the work?" See, you get to a point where you realize who you really are. You know who you really are? Without *you*, the patrón ain't shit. It takes a long time to sink in. Sometimes it takes a Depression, people goin' hungry. Okay, take Zapata in Mexico . . .

There's a big, tall guy, that's the patrón. Then there's Zapata, he's a tiny, tiny thing. The patrón says to Zapata, "Hey, Zapata, do this, do that, do the work!"

Zapata says, "Yes, I'll do the work."

But after a while, Zapata gets tired of this. And all the time Zapata is growing bigger and bigger. Finally Zapata sees; "Hell, without me, the patrón ain't shit." Zapata's getting bigger and bigger.

Then the patrón says, "Hey, Zapata . . . !"

Zapata says, "You know what? Without me, you're nothing. So now you'll do what I tell you because *we* are the bosses, the people that produces are the bosses."

It's the same with the miners, but it takes a long time for it to sink in.

So we never did get thrown out of our house, and the union won. The union won because—how could you use force in Dawson when 90 percent of the miners were Mexican? The first thing we had on our side, the minority was the majority. At first, we didn't know how to use our strength, but one day we said, "Well, bullshit, let's use our numbers, let's use our heads and do this together."

Back then, Mexicans didn't need Green Cards to work in

the U.S. The company brought them in from Mexico, so they were legal. See, Phelps Dodge had mining interests in Mexico, and they knew them guys knew how to mine.

Let me tell you about being a coal miner. You've heard this song about sixteen tons. Sixteen tons is nothing, man. You know what? In Dawson I loaded as much as fifty tons a day by hand. Alright, fifty tons is enough to load a boxcar. Sixteen tons would be like loading three carts. Hell, I loaded ten carts, and once in Colorado I loaded thirteen five-ton carts. How do you think my arms got so big? I did everything by hand, kid. Look at my arms. But understand, everything had to be in balance, the shovel I used was perfectly balanced. And I used to take honey, used to put it in my water and drink it. In the coal mine you take everything with you.

I was on the bonus, I made a lot of money. My goal was to make a hundred dollars a half—fifty dollars a week. Fifty bucks a week, and all that work, eh? All that work.

In those days you had explosions because technology was not up to what we were doing. Then technology caught up and we have federal regulations. Mining has always been a hazardous occupation, but so is driving along the highway. So you make it . . . I worked twenty-two years in the coal mines and I never got hurt, other than smashing a toe or something. In them days, the father used to take his son down and break him in. My dad broke me in, and he could holler at me if he wanted to, he knew darn well I wouldn't talk back to him. Isn't that beautiful?

I was making five dollars and ten cents a day. If somebody would've told me that some day I'd make twenty-seven dollars an hour, I would have laughed him out of the country. And that's what I make now, but twenty-seven dollars an hour doesn't do nothing for me because inflation's eating me up.

When I first went underground I was excited. It was a

job, money. I could buy Pat things I wanted to buy her. Don't forget we were just recently married. And I had that terrible thirst. Ask her, ask her about my thirst. But you know what? What did beer cost in those days? Two dollars a case, fifteen cents a bottle. So I had that thirst, that terrible thirst, but I never laid off work and I managed to take care of my family and some of Pat's brothers and some of my brothers. And I never went to quench my thirst without taking my money home first.

Yeah, there were problems with coal dust. My dad probably died of the black lung, but he never did collect. I have applied for black lung benefits, but they're hard to get because the companies are fighting them. A lot of our union members had black lung. I can say that I did use all the precautions. I used all the safety equipment. In a coal mine, the most important piece of safety equipment is water. All the machinery is equipped for using the water to keep down the dust. A lot of guys get too lazy, they don't want to put the goddamn water on. Not this Mexican. He put the water on all the time. No dust, see? Let me tell you something about being a miner; when you come home from work you're so tired . . . it's not the physical work you've done, it's the total concentration. All the machinery I use, I feel with my feet and my head, in my ear. All the hearing. So when there's a cave-in at a distance, you can feel it in your ear, it displaces the ear. You understand what I mean?

Cave-ins is one sensation . . . cave-ins in uranium mines is mild compared to coal mine cave-ins. See, the only thing holding up the ground is the coal. Once you dig it out, it's gotta fall. You want it to fall, you want to cave it in. If you don't, it adds pressure to the rest of the mine. You gotta relieve the pressure of the strata, and of course you do it when nobody's around.

I worked ten years for Phelps Dodge in Dawson, ten years for the CF&I [Colorado Fuel and Iron Co.] in

Colorado, twenty years in coal, and twenty years in uranium for Kerr-McGee. And I have been a miner all that time. From Day One. The first job I got in Grants didn't last long. I got fired for tryin' to bring the union in. That was in 1961, and in the same year I got a job at Kerr-McGee. I worked about four months and then we went out on a big strike. But that's okay.

See, uranium mining . . . you always hear from a distance that radiation causes lung cancer. You hear it but you don't see it. It always happens to someone else, you know. Well, when we first started mining uranium it was just a theory. And the companies didn't really stress ventilation. But if you've been a miner quite a while, you know if the ventilation's not good, you know it in a hurry, you start getting really wet with sweat. Ventilation comes first, without ventilation you're not gonna live. When we first worked here, we didn't know how many radiation levels we were working under because nobody monitored it, nobody give a damn. Finally, after we brought the union in, the union kept pressing and we got the radiation down to a .75 work level, three quarters of one working level, that's hardly no radiation. First we got it down to three and then gradually down to .75. See, when you come into a new industry the name of the game is money, you want to make money and the company wants to make money. Then after a while you say, "Hey, wait a minute, what about our health?" But the company didn't care whether you worked in hazardous levels or not. And at first the men didn't care either. Because, see, radiation is something you can't see, you can't taste, you can't feel. But once you get a dose of radiation it never goes away, it's with you for life. So that's the way things were.

You're on a bonus system, you'll take a chance. Money is money, the more you do the more money you'll make. Like me, I don't get paid by the tonnage, I get paid by the footage. I drive the tunnel, I average six feet a day. The base pay is about eight, nine dollars an hour, there's no limit to how much money you can make. You know what the bonus system is like? It's like a hang glider—once you jump off you're committed, you better stay with it. When you're halfway through a job area, then if something goes wrong and you take a few less taps, a few little short cuts, you might not live to tell it. That's what it's all about. A lot of guys have been killed by human error, mistakes, things people take for granted.

If the company has safety violations, when we find them, they get a citation, they gotta pay. But let me tell you, MSHA [Mine Safety and Health Administration] hasn't worked too good in the mining industry here because, for one thing, on the Advisory Board of MSHA, they don't have one person that ever was a miner. So they sit back and make rules for a game they never played. You got me? Now you know. And the people who want to become inspectors are sometimes people who weren't too good as miners. A good miner controls his own income. He also controls the income of the company. The guys who become MSHA inspectors are guys who couldn't mine, couldn't get along with nobody. And they have so many regulations that they're choking everybody. You gotta be realistic.

When I come here, Kerr-McGee had been operating about a year and a half here. And Kerr-McGee didn't have a union. Who organized Kerr-McGee? We organized them.

The company wasn't dummies. They invited all the unions to come in, they figured if we have one union here and another union over there then it can't be all one union together. But we brought the Oil, Chemical and Atomic Workers Union in here and that covered everybody working at Kerr-McGee. But we never could get the union shop out of them. This was the '61 strike, and we used to drink a lot on the picket lines. One night I come home with a bunch of guys off the picket line and Pat said to us, "You guys are really something. You can manage to get credit at the gas stations, you can get credit for beer and whiskey, but I haven't seen one of you ask any grocery store for a sack of potatoes on credit." She was right. You could've heard a pin drop. That strike only lasted a few months before we won it.

Let me tell you something about solidarity. In 1973, we went on strike. Kerr-McGee was trying to take all our benefits, everything we had fought for, take 'em back. I was president of our local. Seven hundred and thirty-six union members went out the gate. Out of seven hundred and thirty-six, thirteen crossed the picket line. Eight months we stayed on strike. That's solidarity. And we didn't have a union shop, just the open shop. But I found out one thing, open shop's not so bad if you got people that want to stay in the union. Eight months. Oh yeah, we did the picket lines. Hell, we got indicted. They hauled me off like a common criminal. They brought in Escort Service, too, hired guards. And they hired scabs. It got bloody. But listen, we whupped a lot of scabs, there ain't no question about it, we fought back.

The company was bleeding, losing their asses. They went and got tailings from the mines and run it through the mill, to make it seem like the mill was working. And in the middle of the night one night, some guys broke through the goddamned picket lines and went in and tore the mines up. Drove a goddamned pickup truck into a shaft. They went to all the mines that night and tore the whole damn thing up.

Speaking of miners, everyone knows how to use dynamite. During the strike, me and Pat were having a barbecue here at home one night and all of a sudden we heard a "BOOM!" I told Pat, "There went another scab." It was two, and a brand-new pickup, blown in half. Nobody died during the strike. Almost, but not quite. The company finally admitted they lost the strike, because we have seven hundred and twenty-three guys that stuck like glue. That's solidarity.

A lot of people ask me, "Why do you still mine?" I'm fifty-eight, you know. I like to mine. One thing that excites me is my profession. It *excites* me. It's a challenge.

To be a miner takes concentration. The miner's game is a game of inches, a game of death, eh? A game of Russian Roulette. It's an emotional damn industry. When I'm drilling to make a blast, I don't let nobody interrupt my concentration. Not even my helper. The only way my helper is going to get my attention is he's gotta shut off the air and the water. But there's one thing I want you to know. I'm going to be fifty-eight next week and my hearing is fantastic, my hearing frightens me. My hearing ability should've decreased but it didn't. It's increased.

The environmentalists wanted to shut these mines down. My son and I went to testify before the hearings. The environmentalists said, "We want to save this environment, it's the only one we have." Okay. But people gotta work too. We have to work somewhere. I told them, "My daddy was a miner, I'm a miner, and my son here's a miner also. Right there's about a hundred years' experience, so if you've got any questions, c'mon ask." They didn't have any questions.

When you mine uranium, the uranium is radioactive, and the only way you're gonna get a safe working environment is with ventilation. Everybody who works in the mines has a life support system, and you're dumb if you don't use it. It's easy to blame the company all the time, but it's not always the company's fault. There's miners that turn off the fan, the ventilating system because it makes noise. Some turn it off because they get too cold. Okay. We've got a working agreement that says no miner will ever do anything to endanger his health and safety. If the company violates the rules, the miner can refuse to work in unsafe conditions. But the miner has some responsibility too. The name of the game is money, and the company and miners play the game together.

This cave-in that happened yesterday, over in Section 19. The miner was making a slice, a trench. You make it deeper and deeper just like a ditch. See, this is rock, but the rock has fractures in it and you can't see 'em. So how are you going to support the ground? You don't have timbers like in coal mines . . . you use the bolt system, and even so, you can't see these fractures. There's a lot of ways to mine. I heard they weren't using the right procedure over in Section 19, and this miner had complained about it. He complained because there was a lot of open ground and there's no way you're gonna support that. He knew the rules, he should've refused to work. He had two or three options: the main option is to abide by the working agreement and refuse to work in an unsafe condition. Or he could've suggested some other way of supporting the ground, suggested they try it. See, we got foremen, bosses who never drilled a hole in their lives. Now you got me? And the miner wants to make a name for himself: "Look at me, look at the tonnage I got." His thinking is, "I'm halfway there, so I'm not gonna back off, I'm already committed . . . I'm gonna take this one little chance."

When the rock came down, he couldn't hear the rockfall. He was wearing earplugs. The rock came down and hit his drill and drove it into his mouth straight through the back of his head. He died instantly.

A death in the mine is always bad. Most are brutal. A guy who worked opposite me on the same section was killed in our workplace. His skull was smashed and his brains were all over the place. They came in and scrubbed the place down, but I couldn't go back to that spot for a long time because it stunk from the smell. So you see, those are things that happen.

A mine underground is a huge stretched-out complex operation. Me and my helper, we go to our workplace and maybe we don't see anybody else all day because we're a mile, two miles from the station. The mine travels out in different directions. See, when you're alone in the mine, when there's no boss around, you will have the tendency to take a few little shortcuts. But you better look out for yourself because the boss is too busy telling all the crews what to do, he doesn't have time to look out for you. You and your helper, you have a responsibility to each other and to your little section of work.

Let me tell you something about coal. Coal, it bursts. If you square down with a pick, it'll bust by itself, it'll push up by itself. In a coal mine, everything you turn out is coal. They call it a vein, huh? In uranium, it's in pockets. They've already drilled from above, they know where the ore bodies are. So you tunnel under it and then you mine up, tunnel up eighty or a hundred feet till you reach the ore. You've got your life support system with you, see, and once you get up closer to the surface, you drive air holes in, suck the ventilation in. You make it like a checkerboard and you load it right there. You go for the ore bodies, that's uranium, at one level, then you go to the next level and that's rock so you tunnel the other way. You know there's ore because they've drilled every fifty feet on the ground, they know exactly what's under there. And you know you're gonna find water, so you pump the water out and tunnel out right there. When you go down to the next level to mine, you never mine directly over the new tunnel, you leave support. We used to lay timbers for support but now we use the bolt system.

Look here. These are the safety regulations, I keep 'em with me all the time. Article 12.5: "No employee shall be required to perform services that may endanger his reasonable safety beyond the reasonable and normal requirements of his job."

Now look at the miner. He sees inflation's eating him up. So he's making the dollar, he's becoming a fanatic. He says, "Aw, one more time won't hurt me." And he'll keep pushing and pushing, then pretty soon something happens. It's not greed. You're trying to survive, trying to make it. I think I made thirty-five thousand dollars last year. Unheard of, huh? And I'd laid off like a madman 'cause I don't feel too good. And you know what? We didn't save any money.

There's a saying in Spanish that means, "No matter what you do, sooner or later you have to go to the bank." The Anglo, okay? No matter what you do, you're gonna wind up at the bank or the finance company. You go to the mine, the boss is Anglo. Kerr-McGee will discriminate just so much, just enough where they can get away with it. But discrimination, Pat and I know it will always be with us. You take it all in stride, but you know it's there. It's like radiation, you don't see it. But you feel discrimination. I go into a bar and there's an Anglo and he looks at me and says, "I like Mexicans," and I know he don't cause he's talking about it. Discrimination—they don't shout it from the highest rooftops. But it's the little things you notice. I know when the boss don't like me, but it don't bother me because I know I'm a professional in my job. When a guy really gets to me, I tell him, "I'll live through this holocaust yet." He knows what I mean.

They use "Mexican," "Chicana," "Chicano," "Hispanic." There's no difference. They use 'em till it gets crazy, but there's no difference.

Pat's family is descended from Chinese who went to Puebla, Mexico. She's part Chinese. My family is descended from Ponce de Leon. I guess that's why we never wanted to get old.

You know what I feel about the uranium issue? About the nuclear issue? The fuel that we are producing is ahead of its time. You get a fuel and what do you do? You make power. And yet there are so many things we use for war that could be used for peaceful purposes. The things we use for "peaceful means" are the most destructive. Nuclear can be the most destructive or it can be our best friend. We're on something, uranium, that's ahead of our technology. Then all of a sudden they ask, "Well, now what are we going to do with the waste materials?" Nuclear's here to stay, so instead of bickering, the labor movement and the environmentalists and the companies should all get together and figure out how to keep it safe.

I want to save the planet. Do you? I love life too much.

We cannot love one another and love the planet unless we accept each other as we are. There are some bosses, some agencies that don't understand—you gotta bop 'em in the mouth to get their attention. Well, I can accept those people, I just want them off my back.

I worry about nuclear war. I know if we ever have a nuclear war, that's it, we're finished. And the one that wins is gonna be worse off than the one that loses. How did we get this way? This nuclear fission is ahead of our time, it's ahead of us.

If I had it to do over again, I'd be a miner.

When you're a miner, if you've got good ground, we call it in Spanish *buen terreno,* you're a good miner. If you've got bad ground, you're a bad miner. "When you're hot, you're hot . . ." And when you have good ground you better squeeze for every goddamned penny you can get, 'cause opportunities to get good ground are few and far between. When you've got bad ground you just ride it out.

A miner is a mathematician. You got to be. I can figure out my contract in my head. And a miner is a superstitious *cabrón.* When I put bolts in the back [roof], my helper says I never put thirteen, I put twelve and if I have to add another one, I'll put fourteen. We're not machines, huh? And you know, miners can be a tough bunch, tough on each other too. There's a few guys who like to give other guys a bad time, who don't treat them really like brothers. But lately here I've noticed things are changing, people are

150

treating each other better. Maybe they've learned something, maybe we've all learned that it's not what you say but what you do that's important.

I had this guy tell me one time, "Hey Maggie, I heard that the Catholics are not afraid to die."

"You got that wrong," I said. When I go underground, I always make the Sign of the Cross. I said, "I'm a Catholic and I'm afraid to die. But," I said, "I'm prepared to die."

Technology's Harvest

Bobbin and Loom

So great is the rate of production
That many a time I have heard
The word go from worker to worker:
"Won't you pass me a Great Speckled Bird?"

Oh, we're turning on to turn off the nightmares
Crashing on a spinning wheel of lies
We've been brought up to fly like the bird does
Doubling on the twisting threads of life.

—Cotton Mill Candy

Whether a society glorifies workers or marvels at products
that come from their hands, workers' problems are often
ignored. Each year, the Soviet Union spends millions of
rubles honoring workers and their achievements, yet the
nation still lacks technology that can meet the demands of
rapidly expanding industry. The burden of Five Year Plan
production quotas thus falls on workers' shoulders. Without the aid of robots, rapid industrial growth places
tremendous pressure on Soviet workers. Americans,

155

meanwhile, are trying to cope with stress caused by layoffs, by the tens of thousands, and inflation's unmerciful bite. To insure company profits, American corporations are hiring fewer workers and raising their production quotas, negating any stress-relieving benefits that automation might offer.

Inside Soviet factories, workers are encouraged to compete against one another to become the "highest achiever." If they surpass their own production quotas and outdo fellow employees, they claim rewards managers bestow on "model workers"—vouchers to visit health spas, paid vacations, brand new compact cars, their photographs on the factory bulletin board, and lots of media attention. Material incentives, Soviet managers have learned, increase workers' production, especially when the rewards are items workers cannot afford to buy or which are in short supply. Competing for material rewards increases on-the-job stress, especially in noncompetitive persons who may be ostracized by their peers and belittled by management if they refuse to play the game.

Material incentives are not enough to keep production levels high, though. So entire factories compete against one another in the race to meet Five Year Plan production quotas, a race that challenges the patriotism of laborers. The winning enterprises receive some material rewards from the government, often cash bonuses which are divided among employees, but the real incentive is patriotism, a commitment to the government that raised the nation from the rubble of war to its present industrial might, and to an economic planning system that rhetorically glorifies labor yet often demands superhuman results from laborers. Factories compete to prove their loyalty to the Motherland, and a "true patriot" welcomes production speed-ups. A worker's reward is that deep patriotic pride that still seems to swell the hearts of many Soviets. And, an exemplary worker might receive the most coveted prize of all, the medal of a "Hero of Socialist Labor." In Baku, Azerbaijan, I saw an old pensioner whose jacket was so heavily decorated that he couldn't stand up straight. On the one hand it was touching to know this old worker had been honored for his achievements, for his patriotism and heroic deeds as a laborer. How many American workers who have faithfully served bosses for twenty-five, thirty years or more are honored as heroes? On the other hand, speaking practically, honoring workers with medals and other material incentives has served the interests of management; it drives workers to meet management's demands. Inside Soviet factories, heavy competitions and speed-ups that resemble old Charlie Chaplin films are grating on workers' nerves. As in all highly industrialized societies, accelerated production is a major cause of on-the-job accidents, many which are fatal. Soviet workers are under a great deal of stress. And after work, they take it home with them.

American corporations also encourage allegiance in their employees, not to a nation, but to boards of directors who pay workers' wages. Loyalty is exacted through various methods, including material incentives and the competition techniques Soviet managers are so fond of, and, perhaps the most popular management tactic, the old "carrot and stick" routine. Enticed by management's often false promises, an employee might really believe that being a "good worker" guarantees a promotion or raise in pay. Meanwhile, the manager can dismiss any employee whose loyalty might be deemed questionable. Some companies even resort to "patriotic" rhetoric to keep production rates up. Employees are reminded that the company's product is vitally important to America's well-being, and that personal sacrifice in the form of long hours for short wages is, after all the sweat and tears, necessary in order to assure America's continued stability. This may be true in some isolated cases, but any nation whose laborers are under

157

continual stress is not healthy, nor is its government stable. And while many Americans endure production speed-ups, thousands are losing jobs to automation and to recession's heavy hand. They too take the stress home with them.

Divorce and alcoholism have reached epidemic proportions in both the Soviet Union and United States. The U.S. has the highest divorce rate of any nation in the world, and the U.S.S.R. holds the record for alcoholism. American workers, who have easy access to drugs, are using them both on and off the job. I know a woman who works in a chicken hatchery in north Georgia, where the chickens are fed speed so they will lay eggs faster, and the women who collect and package the eggs take amphetamines, like the legendary "Speckled Bird," to keep up with the hens. Absenteeism is a big problem in Soviet factories, and some workers are drinking on the job. In Leningrad, I saw factory workers gathered around outdoor kiosks on wheels, swilling huge steins of beer on their noon break. As the rate of firings increases in the U.S., violent crime sky-rockets. As production quotas soar in the U.S.S.R., with its shortage of workers, the need for improved health care to treat physical and emotional stress becomes acute. Heart attacks and bouts of severe emotional depression are claiming younger victims in both countries. Personal problems caused by job tensions have become so common in both societies that factory management has hired psychologists and some have even installed personal problem hotlines.

Some positive steps have been taken to treat symptoms of job tension. A few American companies and Soviet enterprises have introduced new shift schedules in their workplaces. Called the Sliding Work Schedule (SWS) in the Soviet Union, and Flexi-time in the U.S., the new arrangement allows employees to set their own hours on the job. Planning together, in semi-autonomous production crews, employees arrange their shift schedules to meet each worker's personal needs while still getting the job done. Employees accumulate overtime hours which they deposit in "time banks" and withdraw when they want time off. Soviet workers contribute a portion of their time bank hours to a social fund which parcels out hours to workers who have not accumulated time but need it. Flexi-time and SWS allows workers the freedom to schedule other important activities into their lives, like visiting a health clinic or the dentist, spending time with children and older relatives in need of attention, or ironing out problems with a spouse—precious time that could save a marriage, or a life. This time management concept not only enhances workers' personal well-being while granting them more control over their lives. Managers who use Flexi-time and SWS have discovered that production usually increases, and the quality of the product improves, when employees set shift schedules.

While some managers respond to their employees' needs, often only after trade unions have demanded they do so, most still regard production quotas and profits as more important than their employees' welfare. The textile industry best illustrates this attitude, and sheds light on how the ever-controversial robot is negatively affecting some Americans' lives while Soviet workers, lacking automation, wish they had it.

American textile workers face a future of unemployment as the industry becomes increasingly concentrated in the hands of a few large companies that can afford to automate. Robots are already serving textile bosses in a big way, and industry forecasters estimate that within a decade or so, they will cut the work force by 60 percent. Just as well that the crippling cotton dust disease, byssinosis, or brown lung, will no longer kill textile workers, although no test I know of proves that robots aren't also vulnerable to the invisible dust that has destroyed thousands of textile workers in the 20th century.

Burlington Industries, the largest American textile manufacturer, leads the robotics movement, and according to textile union organizers remains the toughest nut to crack. Burlington has been slow to change its chronically hazardous working conditions, and since new Occupational Safety and Health Administration standards have been set to regulate cotton-dust levels, the company has rapidly moved toward elimination of human beings from their factories, preferring to invest in robots rather than in the future of employees. Burlington hopes to fully automate before textile union organizers succeed in unionizing the company's employees. In the meantime, textile workers continue to toil in some of the nation's most dangerous workplaces.

Carrie Bingham is a former spinner who worked at Burlington's Pine Tree Carpet Mill in Dahlonega, Georgia. I chose to talk with her about the situation at that mill precisely because she is no longer there. In spite of America's guarantee of freedom of expression, another Burlington spinner, Shirley Sommerour Westbrook, was fired from her job after I wrote a story based on her personal account of conditions inside Pine Tree Carpet Mill. She joined Carrie and me one day recently for a discussion about Pine Tree.

In Uzbekistan, cotton capital of the Soviet Union, the Tashkent Textile Mill, Tash-Tex, is turning out inferior products in order to keep dust from killing textile workers. Tash-Tex prewashes bales of cotton before bringing them into the mill for processing. This practice, recommended by medical experts who have studied ways to eradicate brown lung disease, eliminates much of the fine, invisible particles which attack textile workers' lungs and hinder breathing. Elimination of this invisible dust, which can be measured using collectors with microscopes, does not necessarily eliminate the larger particles of cotton dust which are often visible clinging snowlike to everyone and everything inside textile mills. The larger dust particles are hazardous irritants as well, but it is the particles which are invisible to the human eye that cause brown lung. Some textile companies have cleaned up their acts, and maintain work sites free of these visible clumps of cotton. But this impeccable appearance can be deceiving, since the killer cotton dust is the invisible stuff, which may still be present even if the mill is free of the larger, less deadly irritants.

Prewashed cotton, like that used in Tash-Tex, produces a weaker fabric, and many textile companies are loath to adopt this practice which might cause profits to fall. But even with the employment of this safety procedure, working conditions in Tash-Tex were deplorable when I visited. A lack of innovative technology seemed to place a heavy burden on the relatively small number of men and women operating machines. And robots are not exactly marching into Uzbekistan at the moment.

Karomat Jakubaeva is a young Uzbek woman who works as a weaver in Tash-Tex. She took me on a tour of her workplace one day. The noise there was so severe that it was difficult to be inside the plant for more than a few minutes without losing one's equilibrium. Ventilating fans and shafts were visible everywhere, but cotton dust—the visible stuff—clung to a stranger passing through. Karomat told me, "You get used to it." She is a young, energetic woman, so energetic that it was difficult to photograph her because she did not stand still. Speeded-up production rates often cause nervous stress, and medical experts have observed hypertension as a serious problem among women and men who work in textile mills, a problem that disappears when they leave the occupation.

In Moscow, I visited the Lyubertsy Carpet Factory. There, things were better than they were in mills I have visited in the United States, and a far cry from the Tash-Tex Mill. Still, Lyubertsy is planning a production speed-up. The manager there, Irina Leoshkevich, expounded management's philosophy with typical front-office rhetoric

161

the day I visited her. While I was sitting in her office, Marina Zhivora, a Russian woman, one of Lyubertsy's weavers, burst in and in rapid Russian began to admonish her boss about a problem related to the lack of medical personnel. I watched, fascinated, as this employee demanded that her chief, who was obviously uncomfortable with the scene, do something. Once everything was settled to Marina's satisfaction, the weaver and her boss shared an embrace, and later, off the job, a bottle of kvass, an alcoholic beverage made from black bread.

The American textile workers, Carrie Bingham and Shirley Westbrook, describe meticulously what it was like at Pine Tree. Although none of the Soviet women tell their stories in such graphic—and negative—detail, what Carrie and Shirley describe of Pine Tree's working conditions is similar to what I observed in Tash-Tex, with the one exception that management-employee relations appeared better. These four textile workers, and one manager—included for contrast—all have something important to say about textile work and about their lives, cultures and traditions. Listening to them, it became clear that this kind of labor did not enhance their lives the way more exciting and rewarding occupations would have; it was just making a living in two societies that are rich in human potential and sorely lacking in fulfilling careers. If every textile worker could be assured of a different, useful position in society, without sacrificing one day's wages, perhaps it would be both ethical and wise to invest public funds in robotics research, throw open the doors, and let the robots in.

Carrie Bingham lives in a mobile home perched on the edge of a country road in north Georgia's Blue Ridge Mountains. She lives alone, but her kinfolk come and go so frequently that the trailer's front door seems like a useless obstacle. Behind Carrie's trailer, beyond a field of sweet grass, a pine forest sifts beams of winter sunlight and casts long shadows over the trailer. On the lower side, the road that was once a dirt path traveled by Georgia's finest moonshiners now is paved and winds into Dahlonega, an old farming community that today is the home of Pine Tree Carpet Mill. One February afternoon, I sat at the Formica-topped table in Carrie Bingham's kitchen and listened to her and Shirley Westbrook describe conditions in Pine Tree Mill. They spoke fearlessly, because they had nothing to lose. Carrie does not plan to return to the mill and Shirley, who dared to speak out once before, felt no loyalty to the management that fired her.

Carrie Bingham and Shirley Westbrook

CARRIE: Father was a farmer and a sawmiller. We had a sawmill up in the country, and a farm up north of Dahlonega. And that is where I was raised. During the Depression. It was an L shaped house with five rooms. The loft upstairs wasn't sealed, it was lumber that wasn't nailed down. There was a stairway up to the loft and we kids used to hide up there. We lived mostly in the kitchen. It had an old cookstove and a fireplace too. The dining room had a long table with benches on each side, and every time it snowed . . . well, there was a loose shingle on the roof, so when it snowed the snow would come in on the table. We'd get up in the mornin' and there'd be a big pile of snow on the table. We'd all make a dive for it . . . snowballs!

In the very back of the house was our sitting room. In summertime, we'd carry guests back there. My older sister did her courtin' in this sitting room. Her boyfriend would come every Sunday and stay all day. We'd peep through the windows at them. Sometimes we'd go up in the loft and peek through the cracks in the floor. One time, one of my nieces stepped on a plank and went through on 'em.

Our father built us a Flyin' Ginny. You've probably never

heard of a Flyin' Ginny. It's a seesaw. Father chopped a tree down and bolted a big wide plank to the stump. We'd ride that all day. We had grapevine swings, we'd swing over the creeks. Vines that hung on the trees. We'd find a good vine hangin' over the creek bank, get up on it, and fly off the bank over the creeks. In summertime, we'd just jump in.

We grew cotton. Father would sell the cotton and buy food. He'd buy big barrels of flour, and we ground our own meal. We raised our own hogs and made our own grease. The things we'd have to buy for winter, Father'd use the cotton money for that. Now, Mom would make big barrels of sauerkraut and pickle beans. Any suppertime, we always had sauerkraut or pickle beans or both. And cornbread. We'd save flour for special occasions, which would be Sundays. We mostly fixed cornbread in the oven, but I remember Mother cookin' it in the fireplace. She had a black skillet with a lid on it, she'd put it in the ashes and let it cook.

We canned vegetables we had grown. We didn't have too much beef, but we had pork to eat. And we didn't have too much to eat, you know. Nothin' fancy. It was the Depression. Mother would plant peas and then we'd dry 'em and shuck 'em, then lay 'em out on a sheet on the ground and beat 'em with sticks till they come out of the shells. Mother'd save those to cook in wintertime. She'd put snuff in 'em to keep the weevils out. She dipped snuff, my mother did.

We picked cotton right up till Christmastime. Then Dad would buy what little Christmas we got. A little peppermint candy, oranges, maybe some chocolate drops. The only doll the family ever had, the only real doll, was the one I got for Christmas. It was made of hard material, not like rag dolls, and its eyes were painted on. It had a beautiful dress. I was about twelve when I got that doll.

This was during the Depression, see. Mother would get

cloth maybe once a year to make her a new dress. The only time she wore the new dress was goin' to church. She'd take her old dresses and cut 'em down for my older sister to wear to school. Mother'd grow shrubbery, boxwoods, and a salesman would come along and buy 'em. With that money she ordered cloth from Sears and Roebuck to make us dresses.

Now, this cousin of mine, he lived with us, and he made whiskey for a living. There was a big river that run through the farm and he made his whiskey far back in the woods on that river. We'd go out to the still and watch him . . . it was on a creek that run into the Ellijay River. The creek ran down a mountain. He had two long boxes, I guess about fifty foot long, filled with water, and big barrels set at the end of those. The sugar and the corn went in that. At the bottom of the barrel, the whiskey'd come drippin' out. You sat there and caught it in jars. He had a fire goin' under the barrels, cookin' this stuff up. It took a week to run off a batch. He'd hide the whiskey up in the loft, bring it in from the still and hide it. Then his customers, they'd come around on weekends and get 'em some whiskey. He'd pour it out in jars, and in the bottom there'd be these little black specks, you know, stuff in it. He'd give us the whiskey from the bottom. We'd strain it through a rag and make us a little jar, then he'd sell it for us right along with his. Maybe we'd make a couple dollars, and then we'd order a piece of material from the catalog. Make us a dress.

Late on a Saturday afternoon, he'd load up the rumble seat of his A Model and take off. We never did know where he run the whiskey to, but late on a Saturday afternoon, he'd load up and go.

If you bring a hoe inside the house, your hog will die. If you sweep the floor after sundown, you'll have a death before morning. Mother would never let us sweep after sundown.

Mother believed in herbal cures. Father had rheumatism real bad in his back. Mother would get garlic and cut it up in a jar and put lemon juice in it and water and he'd drink it. Mother'd make yellowroot tea and take that for a remedy. She'd give all the babies catnip tea. She used to bat her own cotton, Mother did. She made quilts and hooked rugs. My daddy did a lot of whittlin' just for a pastime. In later years, we used to make little baskets out of Coke stoppers. I had an uncle that made a radio once. We'd go over to his house on a Saturday night and listen to the Grand Old Opry.

We went to church on Sunday mornin'—most of the time. Then we'd go down on the creek and play. We were havin' boyfriends about that time and we'd go ridin'. None of the boys had cars, but this older man who lived right on the town square, he rented cars on the weekends. The boys would rent cars and take us for rides. There wasn't really very much to do. I remember going to Gene Autry and Roy Rogers shows on Saturday evenin'. But my father wouldn't let us go out at night. So we slipped out a lot without him knowin'. He always said all the meanness went on at night. He wouldn't even let us go to church at night, you know, when they run revival at the country church, we couldn't go at night. So we'd go spend the night at our half sisters', and they'd take us to church. I'm sure father knew what was goin' on, but he never said anything.

I went to tenth grade in school. I quit, and went to Clarkesville, Georgia, to a trade school. Took welding. They were training people for war jobs. Then I was sent to Savannah, Georgia, where the shipyard was. They had war jobs, and I worked there as a welder. This was in '42. I met my husband there and got married. I was seventeen when I got married. Seventeen. He was a welder too. Well, we had a family, I raised my kids while I was working at Pine Tree. Now I've been divorced ten years. Back in those times, in Savannah, I was workin' on a war job, but the war, it just didn't seem real. Except when you'd go to the movies and see a Newsreel. Then you'd know for sure it was real.

I come back to Dahlonega when my mother got sick with cancer. Brought the kids back, we all moved back here, and went to work at Pine Tree. And I've been in and out of that mill four or five times since then. I'd get mad and quit, then I'd go back. Needed the money. I worked there a total of about eleven years.

When Pine Tree came in here, back in the fifties, the town changed. Before then, this was a farming community, all the jobs were farm jobs, sawmill jobs, and there weren't many of them. In some ways the textile mill was good for people, in some ways not so good. A lot of people got jobs. A lot of people who before didn't have cars, now they could afford 'em. A lot of people partied more, bought better clothes to wear, bought new homes. They went into debt. The town changed. People's lives changed. People were job scared, afraid they'd lose their homes, their property.

I went to work at Pine Tree in the sixties, worked there off and on till just a few years ago. I had sisters working there, and at first I couldn't get on, but finally they had an opening and hired me. From outside, the mill looked very dirty. It was made of brick. Outside the building, it looked like snow scattered on the ground. That was the cotton.

I was very nervous my first day of work. They'd already given me a test, the speed test, puttin' little pegs in holes, little speed tests with your hands. Then the lady who taught me my job was very patient with me. The machines were scary, goin' so fast.

The yarn is comin' down through a little pipe. It's got rollers on it, you got to be careful not to get your fingers in those rollers. Sometimes the yarn gets wound around the rollers, you have to cut it off with a knife. Then when you get your little piece of thread running straight, you grab it with two fingers and twist it together, and then it goes down on your bobbin, you doff that bobbin off, and the machine will stop when your bobbins are full. You take off the bobbins, put new ones on, throw the filled bobbins in a buggy and somebody else picks them up. The new machines, they stop automatically.

Production wasn't run by how many bobbins you filled. It was run by so many yards. You had a little gauge on your machine, a time clock, that runs just like a speedometer in a car. You were supposed to do so many yards in one shift.

We worked eight hour shifts, five or six days a week. Rotating shifts. Graveyard shift, you do that two weeks. The next two weeks, you switch from three to eleven. You just about get adjusted to the change in your schedule, when you have to switch. It's hard on mothers, I know, that have housework and have to look after children. Now, they've changed that. People just wasn't happy with it and they kept trying to get it changed. There was even talk about bringin' a union in, but that talk got people in trouble. But they finally changed the rotating shifts, the people voted to get rid of them. And the company, well, they agreed to it. That was right after Shirley got fired.

The cotton got all in your hair, all on your body. It's very irritating to your skin. Some people were allergic to it, others weren't so much. Our carding area was right at the end of our spinning area, so we got a lot of cotton from there. We had four frames. Two girls to a frame. One girl would work on the outside of the frames, keepin' them tied up straight. The other girl would work inside. And we'd rotate that. It was easier workin' on the inside because you were right there close, you didn't have a lot of walkin' around to do.

We often worked three shifts in a row. So you know, you had to get a little help to get through that. I took diet pills. Sometimes we'd go in and work twenty-three hours before we'd go home. Then they made a rule that you couldn't work more than ten hours. Then they changed it to twelve hours. Now you can work a sixteen hour shift. Before, where you didn't get paid overtime, now after forty hours you get overtime pay.

You could say the word "union" out there and you could see the hair raise on the back of their heads.

SHIRLEY: Once we were carrying around a petition just to get a credit union around here, and they panicked. Because it said "union" on it. I had to go before them four or five times when we were just tryin' to establish a federal credit union, had to go in the office to explain why it said "union" on that paper.

CARRIE: If you passed around any kind of paper, they'd go crazy. The union tried to come in. They'd stand outside the gates handin' out papers. Then the supervisors would tell the workers, "If you even stop and pick up one of those papers you've lost your job." Threatening stuff. Some of them would say they were going to the manager, the manager would say they would close the plant before they would have a union in there.

People didn't want to lose their jobs. They were scared. One guy who worked in the mill, he had worked in a union shop down in Atlanta. He knew the advantages of a union. So I know he signed a card back then. After that, he quit or got fired, he wasn't around anymore. They had meetings at the plant, where management would talk to us, saying they was not going to have a union in there.

There were a few women in my department who had nervous problems. They'd have cryin' spells, stuff like that. They'd go into the restroom, everybody else'd kindly look after them and keep the foreman away so they wouldn't get caught. Protect them so they wouldn't get fired. Back then, most of the women who took pills, they used diet pills. Drugs wasn't too bad a problem back then. It's got a lot worse now. They got people peddling all kinds of pills

169

now. I used to take 'em myself. Sure did. They give you lots of energy, you just keep goin' and keep goin', you don't have to sleep if you don't want to sleep. The rotatin' was hard on people's nerves, your nerves was always frayed.

SHIRLEY: Pills were easy to get. All you had to do was pass the word around that you wanted one. The company had to know the drugs were there. You could tell by the rate of your work. Some nights you might be runnin' the same yarn that the girl beside you was runnin', and she might get off her limit of a hundred and twenty-five to thirty and you could get off a hundred and ninety of the same yarn. They had to know somethin' was happenin', because there's no way a person could hold that speed one night and the next night they could hardly move.

CARRIE: We had twenty minutes off for lunch. In that time, we had to go to the bathroom, eat our food and smoke, and be back to our machine, all in twenty minutes. Your machines didn't stop during this time. You had a girl who relieved you till you got done with your break. And if you didn't get back in twenty minutes, she might walk off and leave your machine. This was my job once, to relieve the other girls while they went to eat. Of course, we'd cheat a lot, let them take a longer break. But if the foreman had a mind to, he'd check and see you had cheated on your machine.

SHIRLEY: We never had a company doctor that worked in the plant. They never put a nurse in there till '73. If you got cut on the job, they'd send you to their doctor in town. When I broke my wrist in '76, it took them three days to decide I needed to see the doctor. It was on the twister's rack where it happened. The top peg in the middle was loose, layin' down over the next one. I loaded from the bottom up. As I pulled the bobbin out it caught on the rim of the next bobbin and jerked it. My hand was on the rails and it caught me on the wrist, knocked a chunk out of my wrist. I went to the office and told 'em my hand was broken. My foreman laughed and said, "It couldn't be . . ."

You see, each department has incentive programs, they try to go a whole year without an accident. And that was the last day of the incentive drive for our department. There's no way I could've broke my wrist on the last day! So the foreman took me into the office and the nurse checked it. They kept ice packs on it that day. The next day it was black. So they put heat on it. They put me to sweepin' floors that day, I didn't have to run my machine. The third day, my thumb was red and the whole wrist was completely black. So then they took me out to Doctor Woodward's. They had it X-rayed. A big chunk of bone had been knocked out of my wrist. So they put it in a cast. And that night soon as I got to work there was a big memo on the board. I got cussed out four times before I even got into the mill. Because I had knocked the whole department out of their free lunch for safety for a year.

If you talked to a woman working there now, she'd tell you what's goin' on, but she'd sure worry about her job. Everybody knows what trouble I got into out there.

Pine Tree has made a lot of changes in families. The wives would go to work, and the husbands didn't have jobs. There wasn't much work for men, and when they had work, they didn't make as much as the wives did working in the mill. Some of the men worked in sawmills, and they were jealous of the wives who made more in the carpet mill. There was a lot of jealousy between families with the wives workin' in the mill with other men. There was a lot of change in family life.

There'd never been work for women around here before Pine Tree came in. Then all of a sudden, the women was out working on rotatin' shifts and handling jobs. A lot of 'em couldn't handle it. That put a lot of strain on marriages. There was a *big* upturn in divorces when the plant first opened, and that reputation's stayed with it even up to today. "If you want to keep your wife, don't let her go to work at Pine Tree."

CARRIE: There was change in children's lives too. They

171

might have had a little more clothing and more money to spend that their mothers would give 'em. But then the mothers aren't home. So the children wasn't bein' guided as well, with their mothers at work and their dads gone. I know a lot of children who were left at home alone at night because their mothers were working and their dads were gone.

There's a new factory opened up here in Dahlonega. Torrington. They make pin bearings. The city council got a lot of special bonds passed to help them come in. Right now, they employ about a hundred and twenty. Pine Tree employs around four hundred.

SHIRLEY: At Torrington, they have a high school you can go to, if you want to get your high school diploma. I've heard people say it's better to work at Torrington than at Pine Tree. Me, I've been working on the highway crew, on the new 400 Highway they're building from Atlanta up into these mountains. But we've been laid off since before Christmas.

This new highway into these mountains, in a way it helps. Because it will take people from up here down to Atlanta where there are more jobs. But in a way it's gonna hurt us too. It'll bring a lot of people from Atlanta up here to buy up our land, take stuff away from us. A lot of them down in Atlanta, they've got their jobs sewed up already, so they can come up here and buy out our land. They're already buying up the land. I was in charge of driveway easements on the highway crew and I know for sure four different real estate companies have bought up land along the new highway. They're gonna come in here and put up developments, housing projects.

CARRIE: Well, one thing's changed. I think moonshiners have about gone out of business since the marijuana's come in. Now, Pine Tree, it's just too dangerous to go in there too awfully high.

SHIRLEY: Most of the workers at Pine Tree drinks more

than smokes pot. The older hands, they like their beer. Now the younger ones, they might prefer pot.

CARRIE: Well, I quit my job at Pine Tree and went to work for this doctor over here. Good benefits, and good wages too. I do everything a nurse does. Now I give shots. And it doesn't hurt me a bit.

Karomat Jakubaeva, the young Uzbek textile worker, lives and works in Tashkent, capital of Uzbekistan. Once a stronghold of Moslem rulers, Tashkent today is an urban center with one foot decked out in ancient Islamic history and the other stepping into a Soviet-designed future. Hit by a strong earthquake in 1966, many of the city's elaborate old Islamic structures, schools and houses of worship, were demolished. So were the homes of thousands of its citizens. Amazingly, Soviet architects were able to rebuild the intricately designed mosques, exactly matching the original designs, down to the last sky blue tile on domed roofs. Yet the less ornamental but more serviceable apartment buildings constructed after the '66 quake were built hastily and with weak materials, and already seem to be falling apart.

Tashkent, with its colorful Central Asian bazaars and its Moslem men's tea houses, has preserved some ancient Islamic customs and rituals, but Soviet Tashkent has done away with more painful reminders of former lifestyles. Moslem women do not wear veils, and, in public anyway, dress Western style like the Russian and Ukrainian population there. Young women like Karomat Jakubaeva do not adhere to some Islamic customs—those which granted Moslem men the right to treat women as slaves.

The afternoon before I visited Karomat Jakubaeva at the Tashkent Textile Plant, a group of Uzbek women who staff the Uzbekistan Friendship Society's office showed me a ten minute film on the mass unveilings of Moslem women

173

which took place in Tashkent in the twenties and thirties. The film was about a young Uzbek actress, popular in that era, who performed before the cameras but always behind a veil. When Soviet Uzbek leaders called for the unveiling of Islam's women, many women feared their husbands and other men, who threatened to stone to death any woman who removed her veil in public. The young actress decided to challenge the men's authority and to be an example to her Moslem sisters. One day, in a public square, she removed her veil before a huge crowd of veiled women.

The film showed actual footage of the unveiling, and of the other Moslem women cheering her bravery. It also showed a photograph taken of her body, found the next morning, her throat slit by her father and husband. A wave of unveilings followed the murder. Gathering in great numbers, Uzbek women removed their veils and threw them into fires. Many women were beaten, stoned to death, or had their throats cut for this simple act of liberation. Today, Islam is still a strong force in Tashkent, but ancient customs that enslaved women have virtually disappeared. Young women like Karomat Jakubaeva were born and raised in a society where, according to the nation's Constitution, women enjoy equal rights.

Textile work, Karomat's occupation, has traditionally been women's work in Uzbekistan. Although some men work in the Tashkent plant, as they do in American textile mills, in the carding room and on equipment repairs, most of the weaving and spinning positions are occupied by women. Their lives are much improved from the days when their mothers and grandmothers wore veils and were stoned to death for baring faces to the sun and wind. Judging from the working conditions in Tashkent's biggest textile mill, though, Uzbekistan's women have struggles to win even in their new society.

After steering me through her workplace, Karomat

174

talked about her life and work. Her young face wore a sunny smile that rarely clouded over, even when she spoke about conditions in the mill. She especially beamed when describing her young son, who, because of cramped living quarters and Karomat's vocational studies, is not living with her at home.

Karomat Jakubaeva

Our family lived here in Tashkent, an Uzbek family. There are lots of nationalities in Uzbekistan, but I'm Uzbek. We were four girls and four boys, and I was born on January 25, 1955. My father was a gardener and my mother was a housewife. I'm the fourth child. We had our house and animals and there was a plot for growing vegetables.

In school, we studied both the Russian and Uzbek languages, from the time I was very small. Back then, I had dreams of being a medic. That is, I wound up here at the textile mill purely accidentally. When I had finished eighth grade, completely by accident I landed in the vocational high school for textile workers. I didn't have any idea of what the profession is. So I ended up studying textile work. It just happened that my girlfriend came to this school and she asked me to go with her, and I decided to.

Before entering the textile school, we were shown around all the shops of this factory, and I liked it. As a matter of fact, there were old machines then and it was very noisy. When we came in, it was so noisy we had to close our ears with our fingers as we went through the shop. And then gradually I got used to it and began really liking the job. They give us paper earplugs, soaked in some liquid that helps cut down the noise. I tried the rubber earplugs but, you see, when I put them in my ears, they're very good for stopping the noise, it's nice and noiseless, but there's an unpleasant feeling of isolation from everything. The paper ones are pleasant too, but when a person gets accustomed . . . one morning you forget, and tomorrow you go to work without them.

I've been working in the weave room almost eleven years. I haven't noticed any loss of hearing. I've never been sick, I've never had any trouble with my health. In general, I'm never ill, except when I was pregnant, I had a touch of poisoning with the child. I never visit a doctor. Through eight years of school, I've never been in a hospital.*

I graduated from the eleventh grade, right here in our factory. And right after, I got married. In 1975, our son was born. We named him Kakhranom, which means hero. His grandfather gave him this name. It's a custom in Uzbekistan that the grandparents name the first child in the family. Sometimes they say, just joking, "The first child is not your child, it's our child."

Now I'm a student in textile technology, in my second year. I want to be a quality control engineer, to coordinate the work of the weavers. But I'm sure I won't be an engineer right away. At first I'll be a Master in this shop, oversee production, keep track of workers at their stations, supervise, assign workers to their stations, sometimes switch them from one to the other machine. We tell the Master when we're short of supplies, so I'd be taking care of that too.

I work a double loom, eighteen machines each. I am working with thirty-six machines. When I get to work, I take the shift over from the other workers. So I check the quality of the warp, how the machines are threaded, the quality of the threads that go into the machine. The threads at the first part of the machine, they need to go smoothly and need to have some distance between them.

*In the U.S.S.R., people tend to spend time in the hospital for just about any illness that keeps them from work or school.

If there are crossed threads, I fix them. Then I check the track links where the cloth is actually woven. We have three teams in our department, and in the first team we have some apprentices working, so I check to make sure they've set up properly. So, after examining all thirty-six machines, when I see that they're all working correctly, I sign a document that everything is all right at the change of shifts. I change the meter that measures the amount of cloth, because each team has its own meter, so I change the meters for our team.* After that, I start the machines.

Right now, my son lives with my mother. Because I am going to take my exams, and because we are supposed to move into a new apartment. But usually he goes to a daycare center. Our new flat will be in the area where textile workers from our factory are living. We have a flat now, two rooms, but we're waiting for a larger one.† It will be a new building, not far from where we're living now. They promised us the flat at the first of May, so it shouldn't be long now.

After taxes, I make three hundred forty rubles a month, so it's a nice salary. I pay very little, eight rubles, ten kopecks, for the flat we have now. For the new flat it will be about ten rubles something, not more. We'll pay electricity separately, about three or four rubles for a four-room flat. Everything else is included in the rent.

My husband is also Uzbek. He operates an excavation machine, working on water supply canals. Because he usually has two days off, on Saturday and Sunday, he tries to take our son to the country, take him out of the apartment somewhere. And when I'm free, I take him out.

Russians have one wedding ceremony, but we Uzbeks have two. Usually, nowadays, young people take the

*These are the same as time clocks on U.S. textile machines.
†A two-room flat in the Soviet Union is like a three-room apartment in the U.S. Soviets don't usually include the kitchen when they count rooms.

wedding car to ZAGS, the registry office, and that's it. But then we have another kind of wedding. We have a ceremony at the bride's house and then at the groom's. At the bride's house, we celebrate the wedding without the groom. And the next day the groom arrives at the bride's home and carries her to his place. Then there is a second ceremony. And when the wedding ceremony is over, the bride and groom, sitting side by side at the table receiving their guests, make toasts. People are playing national instruments and dancing, wearing Uzbek costumes.

I can bake *non*, the Uzbek bread. Mostly everyone can, especially in the countryside, where there are traditional ovens. My mother has such an oven. It's called a *tandir*, it's round in shape and opens from the side. When you heat it, put in the firewood, and when it warms up, it turns black. The wood is underneath and when you first start to heat it, the inside turns black, but as the fire gets going, it turns white. When it turns all white and all the wood has burnt up, and these little coals remain, you put the dough inside. First you throw a little water into the tandir so it won't be too hot when the dough sticks to the sides. Then you wear a sort of glove to throw the shaped pieces of dough against the inside of the tandir, at the top where the heat is even. When they're stuck on, the tandir is hot and the dough bakes a little underneath. Then you break up these coals a little, so the topside of the dough also cooks. So when the *lepeshka* [Russian for *non*] get a little more baked, they turn red, then brown as they bake.

The loaves don't get done at the same time. I don't know how long they take to bake, I just look and know when they're ready. You can bake non every day if you have time. I don't do it every day, living in the city. But I make non on my days off. Made in a tandir, though, non tastes better.

We wear national dress, the *charovar*, Uzbek trousers, and very wide dresses in Uzbek style. I wear them all the time for weddings and when I have guests at home. You wear the trousers under the dress. The traditional shoes are called *kaush,* and *mahts* are sandals. The old women still wear those. They wear a very thin cotton or wool stocking and put on a sort of galosh over it. Scarves, we Uzbeks wear them different than the Russians. We tie them around the back of our head, while Russians tie them under the chin. Uzbek women almost never wear veils now. But you know, there are still very old women, you'll see them in the old city, who still wear veils. In old days, the women used to all wear veils. We call it *paranzha.* And during the Revolution all of them got rid of that paranzha, they burned them in fires.

Well, somehow Uzbeks considered women to be . . . I don't know, somehow it was shameful . . . they'd shame a woman if she went out with her face uncovered; the men and women would throw stones and would drag the woman by the hair. You usually didn't go wandering about with your face uncovered! And they shut in the older people, even killed them if they showed themselves in public. It wasn't allowed for a woman to show her face.

All Uzbeks are Moslems. Yes, all. My father reads the Koran every day. He is a mullah. He prays five times a day, every day. Young people don't do this anymore. My husband and I don't, but it doesn't upset my father. Sometimes he tries to prove that Allah exists, but young people already . . . we knew a little of it, we knew the Koran a little earlier in our childhood. Our father wrote out prayers on paper for us to study, and before that, when we were very young, he would read the Koran out loud to us. We would sit around him and watch him pray. He'd finish his prayers and we'd say, "How do you do?" It's a custom to say "How do you do?" to someone after they are through praying. If you see someone praying, after they're finished, you say, *"A'salaam aleikum."* We were little then, now we don't even pay attention when he prays. Sometimes when

179

we were small we wouldn't see him, because he had his own room, he would close the door.

We simply call our people Moslems. But we don't all practice Islam.

After Irina Leoshkevich graduated from the university in the late forties, she took a job as a production worker in Moscow's Lyubertsy Carpet Factory. Working on a production line was an illuminating experience for a university graduate, and Irina seems to have kept her eyes open ever since. Today, she is director of the factory, but her modestly furnished executive's office bears no signs of high status, nor does this woman, in charge of four thousand employees, seem impressed with her position of authority. A portly, gray haired, energetic person, she was modest about her own career successes the day we met in her office. But her eyes blazed with kindled spirit when asked about working conditions in the factory she was managing. "I was once a worker here myself," she reminded me, punctuating this important point with an index finger raised. "I have personally experienced the improvements in our factory. This factory has come a long way since my days in the weave room." She captured my attention with these remarks, and I listened with interest to a manager's view of her textile plant.

Irina Leoshkevich

This factory was founded in 1947. Since then, a lot of water has passed under the bridge. We've started to put out eleven times more than we used to produce. We've projected our plan for 1990 to double current production. It's important to mention that the number of employees does not increase with the raised production level. So we

180

have four thousand workers, and even with the new plan, we have four thousand workers. This has been determined with the help of psychologists and labor sociologists.

We had, have, and evidently will always have these special objectives to increase the volume of production and to simultaneously reduce the fatigue of the workers. For example, we give our workers an additional break aside from their midday break. This additional break comes between the start of the shift and the lunch break. At that time the workers go to the cafeteria and drink tea and whatever. The second break is between lunch and the end of the shift, about fifteen minutes long. At this time the workers are supposed to do self-massage and physical exercise, but this didn't work out so well here. It worked out well on a trial shift, but in actuality it wasn't so good. The workers didn't want to! It's not convenient for them, standing between the looms, it's too far to go to the corridors. In short, "We don't want to!" So, temporarily we agreed with them. Temporarily, temporarily . . . and now we're building, you'll see it when we go past, a conservatory, a winter garden. When the break comes, you'll see the workers quickly enter those three doors. Inside, you'll see it has special "health zones," lots of greenery, there's a sauna there, specially oxygenated, specially treated air, and all kinds of health treatments. We've already found two doctors who will come to work for us; they'll be arriving May 5.

So now we have two people on a loom with one carpet. And so to alleviate fatigue in the second half of the day, they switch off every hour and a half. The thing is, 70 percent of our staff are women. And of course it is important that they be good wives, the very best brides, and when necessary even good grandmothers. It's important to production that they lead an interesting, socially, ethically full life. The moral strength of our women is very important, very important to us. We have specially elaborated measures to provide entertainment for the women.

We don't have the problem of full employment here, no problem of unemployment, no. To the contrary, we have the problem of a lack of workers. The workers we have, we try to make their work as easy as possible. You understand, against this background of few workers compared to the production level, it's very important for us to work efficiently, productively and mainly to keep working conditions safe. That's the main thing, otherwise what's it all for? The human being, not the machine should come first. That's why we try our best. We try to make daily life easier for our workers and their families.

Our workers live with their families in our factory's own apartment complexes. There are daycare centers, nurseries. We make sure there are laundries, beauty salons. We want everything to be convenient for our workers to work. We have stores, clubs, schools, we're completing construction of a district sports complex with two swimming pools, one for adults, one for children. We have a soccer field not far from here, in Moscow. We have a prophylactorium and sanitoria, clinics for preventive medicine and simple treatments, where workers can be treated without missing work. A voucher to go there is sixteen rubles. This includes five, yes five, meals a day and complete service, all medication. And every fifth voucher is given free of charge. That is, one out of five vouchers, according to need, is given away free. They have all kinds of treatments, water cures, baths, needle treatments [acupuncture], cellophane treatments . . . I don't know what else they have. We have our Pioneer camp and of course, our own youth resort not far from Moscow. But the main thing we have, we have outstanding people who like their work and know how to do it. This is our main treasure.

One of Lyubertsy's jewels is Marina Zhivora, the weaver who burst into Irina Leoshkevich's office while I was there. Marina Zhivora's eyes were vivid traffic light green and her words of admonishment, aimed at her boss, had flowed nonstop with high-speed intensity. Wearing tight blue jeans and a blue denim Western shirt, she looked like a teenager. Yet Marina had already raised her own children, after being widowed, and was a grandmother before she hit forty. Standing before her boss as only a union maid dares, Marina Zhivora might have looked young, but she spoke with a courage and determination that revealed years of struggle, and the durability of one who has overcome hardships.

Later, I visited Marina's home. We sat around her dining room table—Marina, her mother and her brother, Irina Leoshkevich, my Novosti escort, the taxicab driver who drove us to Lyubertsy, and myself, and raised our glasses in a toast to the working women of the world. Marina Zhivora made the toast. "We Soviet women," she said, "have struggled not just for our own rights, but for the rights of every man, woman and child in our Motherland. Women have sacrificed the special privileges of being female, have worked shoulder to shoulder with the men to raise our country from the ruins of war. Women, like my mama, lost their hearts, their loved ones in the war. But instead of dying from broken hearts, what did these women do? They labored, sweating like men, not paying attention to their femininity, to build a society where their children would be secure. Women did these things, and now, what is the state of affairs today?" She looked inquiringly at each woman sitting at her table, then answered the question herself. "I will tell you. Today, women have many struggles they must win. It seems the men have forgotten, sometimes, that the Soviet woman was obliged to be hard instead of soft, to work like a man. Why are we not softer and more feminine? Because our equal role in society has not only granted us equal rights. We have equally shared the burden of responsibility as

183

well. It is not enough for the men to say we Soviet women have equal rights. The men must also listen to our opinions. And we have them. We women have one single demand.

"Women," said Marina Zhivora, "always the women, have been the peacemakers. This is the single demand of the Soviet working woman today. Peace. And I am certain the working woman of the U.S. must feel the same. Peace is more important than the other rights we demand as women, as workers. The working woman sacrifices for her children's future. The world must listen to her message. We bear children not to fight wars. We bear children for love, for the survival of the human race. It is the nature of woman to create life, not destroy it."

With only a few minutes to interview Marina, I asked her to quickly outline her childhood and her experiences as a textile worker. This is what she told me:

Marina Zhivora

I was born in a village, in a terrible* year, a year of war. My father perished in 1941. My mother raised the children. My eldest brother left for Moscow and then I came here. I had heard lots of things about carpet production, and I was interested to see if I could find work in a carpet factory. So when I arrived and walked into the shop for the first time, I knew that my life had begun. Childhood was over.

I told you that my childhood was during war years, but childhood is always childhood. I was my mother's helper, she gave me some of her load. Mama said that I was a very

---

*The Russian word Marina used is *strashnii,* which means terrible, horrible, but has a much stronger meaning than its English equivalent.—Translator's note.

serious child and that I took a serious approach to everything. I was always a helper. We didn't have a real childhood, as other children have, growing up now. We tried to help, to be grown up. We became serious grown-ups very young.

I was born in 1941 without a father. He had four sons, and when he left for the front, he said, "If it's a daughter, bring her to me, no matter what . . ." And I saw him. I saw him. I was six weeks old. That winter, my mother on a sleigh took me. It was December, really freezing, the coldest time, the worst frosts. In spite of this, she took me to him. Because she wanted to show me to him. So she took me on a sleigh. And he saw me and I saw him, the one and only time.

I began working here in 1956. Not everything came easy to me at first. I was in the spinning room where the bobbins are, and I was very frightened by all the machines. The experienced masters taught me to understand everything in this complicated business, but it took a while. Sometimes I even regretted coming here to work, I felt like running away. But the masters were a great help, and now I'm training the younger workers. All those feelings passed with the years.

The icon hanging on my wall, it's generally speaking a whim, for my mother; I allow it, I allow her that. But I like it too; it gives the house a homey feel. And then, its beauty is highly valued. But you know, they say, "Believe in God, but help yourself."

Brave New Town

In September 1981, half a million U.S. workers gathered in their nation's capital to protest government budget cuts that would directly affect the quality of their lives. The Solidarity Day demonstration was so overwhelmingly popular that many union leaders began calling for the organizing of a general strike, an action they say might be necessary to rescue the American rank and file from being crushed by a national economy that favors the wealthy. Strikes have often been an effective tool of the world's workers, whose strongest bargaining point is their ability to withhold labor until their demands are met.

American labor history is full of stunning victories and devastating defeats, violent clashes between workers and their bosses, between workers and government troops called in to bolster corporate security guards in picket line battles with strikers. In spite of the efforts of companies to break them, American unions have remained a vital force, the only organized vehicle representing the united voices of labor. Sometimes corrupt in the upper echelons, unions have always gained their strength from a rank and file leadership that has truly represented members' interests. The recent popularity of a general strike movement indicates that unions have not despaired over the future of organized labor, and have refused to cave in under the intensified efforts of businesses that want to destroy them.

Soviet workers are also represented by unions, but these operate under vastly different conditions. The Soviet factory system provides a picture of organized labor in today's U.S.S.R.

Soviet factories are owned by the state and management is appointed by councils of ministries that represent each industrial category. By law, a factory manager has absolute authority over all personnel and management decisions. Next in authority are administrators and technicians, supervisors and shop foremen, all appointed by the manager. The workers are at the bottom of the totem pole. Hardly the pillar of socialist organization, this arrangement. And not all Soviet factory workers are happy with it.

Workers in the U.S.S.R. claim they are insulted, humiliated and degraded by the upper echelon, particularly factory managers—a common grievance in the U.S. as well. They say that lower-level employees are frequently dismissed because managers took a personal dislike to them, and that they have too little decision-making authority in the workplace. A recent movement, one causing considerable controversy in Soviet trade union circles, indicates workers are pushing for changes in their shops.

The Soviet vehicle for forwarding complaints upstairs is the trade union. These are like American industrial unions; they embrace workers of all trades who are employed at the same plant. About 97 percent of Soviet workers are members. Labor law in the U.S.S.R. does not include a closed shop provision, but workers know it is to their advantage to belong to the union. Management, supervisors and technicians also belong to the factory's trade union, which gives the superficial appearance of one big happy factory family. According to labor laws, trade unions are responsible for "social management" in workplaces, and under the auspices of the trade union, production workers may carry out inspections of the plant and comment on managerial and technical procedures. One Soviet publication claims that in the space of a year, ten thousand factory managers were let go, on demand of trade unions, for failing to observe regulations governing safety and health, for ignoring hiring and firing guidelines, and for mistreatment of employees. Even so, workers have no authority to name management personnel, and replacements are appointed by the ministries.

In 1971, a law was passed giving union members the right to hear official enterprise reports made to ministries, reports similar to those U.S. managers give to their boards of directors and which are rarely seen by lower level employees. The same year, unions were granted authority over "job protection" procedures—no Soviet man or woman may be dismissed without the consent of the worker's trade union. If a person is fired without cause, the union must provide free legal assistance, and if necessary, the employee's case will be heard in a labor arbitration court, similar to, and probably as erratically effective as the National Labor Relations Board in the U.S. Courts may order a factory to reinstate a worker and pay lost wages.

Some factories in the U.S.S.R. operate on a bonus system whereby profits are divided among workers. How bonus monies are divided is a trade union decision.

Soviet trade unions are responsible for securing a place to live for employees, although the factory might actually have built the housing. The unions are also charged with monitoring health and safety conditions in workplaces, with providing vacation facilities and health spas, and with distributing free vouchers that provide access to these rest facilities. Large enterprises with many employees usually have their own union newspaper.

But even in a society that exalts the worker, this system of management and trade unions has been attacked by some workers as undemocratic. There are workers who have become increasingly disenchanted and frustrated with the chain of command in Soviet enterprises, in particular with having no voice in appointing their supervisors.. Although the American media frequently portrays any signs of disenchantment by workers in socialist nations as disillusionment with the ideals of socialism, quite the reverse is usually true. Soviet workers in particular usually view their efforts to democratize their workplaces as their patriotic duty and push for changes they believe will strengthen their socialist systems.

In 1979, a Soviet trade union decided to challenge management's authority and took direct action to increase their control over supervisory personnel. That year, a group of construction workers in Eastern Siberia, at Krasnoyarsk on the Yenisei River, elected their shop foreman by secret ballot. The election was the first time in U.S.S.R. history that supervisors were not appointed by written executive order. The action was neither endorsed nor approved by anyone but the rank and file, who wanted more authority in their workplace. This Soviet action preceded Poland's Gdansk uprising by one year, and secret ballot elections of factory officials would turn out to be one of Solidarity's major demands.

Soviet trade union newspapers spread the Krasnoyarsk story throughout the nation. The construction workers were lauded as heroes by some, labeled as a menace by others. Managers, not surprisingly, considered them troublemakers. Heated disputes filled union halls, workers speaking out for or against the Krasnoyarsk action. In 1980, just weeks before Gdansk boiled over, the Soviet Kommutator factory in Riga—perilously close to Gdansk—carved a new notch in the factory totem pole. They elected team leaders, shop supervisors and section foremen by secret ballot, an action which put them just one short step away from electing the factory manager by secret ballot. Then, a few hundred miles down the Baltic coast, workers in a Gdansk shipyard gave birth to Solidarity, the movement which demanded, among other things, secret ballot elections of factory management personnel.

Soviet executives railed at the idea of workers choosing their own bosses, but in spite of their opposition to the secret ballot elections, and even while workers in Gdansk were writing strike slogans on the shipyard wall, the Soviet Writers' Union decided to present the issue to the public. In hotly worded articles that appeared in the Writers' Union publication, *Literaturnaya Gazeta,* managers cited the dangers of secret ballot elections, principally that workers were approaching the point of collective management. This, the critics agreed, was a preposterous system that would bring about anarchy in the factories and economic chaos in the nation. Soviet socialism, they inferred, was based on government by workers' *mandate,* not on workers' direct rule.

Workers replied to the *Literaturnaya Gazeta,* expressing opinions often as heated as those of management, though some of the letters were carefully diplomatic. A few agreed with their bosses and called for prohibition of the elections, but most workers supported the secret ballot. One tactfully implied that poor administration was responsible for flagging production that failed to meet Five Year Plan quotas and caused shortages of consumer goods. Another worker proposed a system for implementing secret ballot elections within workplaces on a national scale, hinting that labor laws might be revised to include the procedure. Although public debate over the issue has not been exactly encouraged in the media, the controversy has not been totally suppressed and continues to add spice to union meetings.

The best way to understand how Soviet trade unions

function is to talk to rank and file employees. One of the strongest Soviet trade unions is the Volga Automobile Plant's union in Togliatti, a new Soviet city in the southern Volga region of Russia.

The Volga Automobile Plant, VAZ, manufactures the Zhiguli, a compact car, and its Italian export version, the Lada. The Zhiguli is a medium-priced car that costs about 6,500 rubles, equivalent to $9,750 in U.S. currency. It is popular among families who can afford it and among the millions of bureaucrats who shuttle back and forth between government offices and their homes. The Zhiguli and its modified Lada version are based on a Fiat design. VAZ and Fiat are business partners, and Togliatti, by the way, is named after the late Italian Communist Party leader, Palmiro Togliatti. The VAZ produces about 800,000 cars each year.

About half a million people live in Togliatti, a city usually closed to foreigners. Most of Togliatti's workers are employed in the auto industry. Whether they like it or not, these auto workers have earned a reputation as the U.S.S.R.'s most daring trade unionists. They and their city have become legend in the U.S.S.R., and have confounded a Western media that has rare access to the VAZ but nevertheless has speculated that Togliatti's VAZ workers pulled off a militant strike in the spring of 1980.

Togliatti is only fourteen years old, raised to its present status as an idyllic workers' town by Komsomol volunteers who, in 1966, answered their government's call to build an automobile industry. The volunteers raised a model community, designed by sociologists who aimed to ensure the happiness, security and productivity of the city's inhabitants. Young people moved there in droves. Today, the VAZ is a self-sufficient maze of iron and steel works, glass and rubber factories, that embraces an automobile plant and a racetrack for testing cars. The VAZ and its satellite industries were built about two miles outside the city, and workers travel to and from work on a busy and efficient bus system that was planned, like the VAZ, to produce minimum levels of air pollution.

Built on rolling hills along the Volga, residential Togliatti is surrounded by pine forests and birch groves. On the western edge of town, an artificial lake, big as a sea, floats sailboats and small yachts. The city center is a neatly plotted collection of brick and concrete apartment buildings, supermarkets and sleek public buildings, ringed by an "Old City" of carefully restored wooden homes. Togliatti's city planners had a serene, aesthetic eye, and the town blends quietly into its rustic surroundings. As in every Soviet city, streets are clean and litter free, kept that way by responsible citizens and broom brigades. Togliatti is so young that a few years ago the average age of city council members was thirty.

Most of the young people who came to build Togliatti and its VAZ stayed on when the town was completed, took jobs in the auto plant and its supporting industries, settled down and reared families. Today more young men and women are pouring into the city, drawn by its high wages, comfortable living conditions and its reputation as a town where the cream of the working class lives well. To accommodate them, Togliatti has built a youth hostel in town center, men's and women's dormitories linked by arcades to shops and libraries, restaurants, cafeterias and concert halls. Unmarried auto workers live two to a room, and coed visits are allowed till eleven or twelve at night, on a schedule as relaxed as the young folks who admit they break it. The men's dormitory is scrubbed and swept clean by a group of young female housekeepers who did not seem upset about their working conditions the day I spoke with them in the men's dorm.

Togliatti is driven by youthful energy. The Sports Palace has an ice-skating rink, and hockey is one of the most popular local sports, complete with impromptu fisticuffs on the ice. As one local man told me, "Sport is sport." Next door to the auditorium, an Olympic-sized swimming pool is under construction. Cinemas advertise films about romantic love, cosmic journeys and space monsters, and concert halls are gaudy with billboards promoting rock bands. Discos are the most popular form of entertainment, and juke boxes contain a jambalaya of rock forms—Swedish hard rock, German soft rock, Soviet "Jazz," mellow rock, every form of rock but Punk or New Wave. A young man asked me to describe America's contemporary music, and when I began a carefully worded description, my escort whispered under her breath, "Be careful not to corrupt our youth."

Nikolai Ustinov and Alexander Savchuk are the vice director and deputy, respectively, of the Export and Foreign Relations Department of the Volga Auto Works. Like all Soviet factory executives, they are members of their factory's trade union. Ustinov was tall, distinguished, with sensitive eyes and a gentle manner. Savchuk wore a suit and tie with polish, but he had a maverick's daredevil panache and wry sense of humor. He spoke excellent English, although he told me he did not get much practice in the language since English-speaking visitors rarely came to Togliatti.

Ustinov and Savchuk led me through the VAZ production lines and a child-care facility, in and out of a dozen local enterprises and public buildings, through shops and cafeterias, and up and down the main and side streets of Togliatti. "Ask and you shall see," Alexander Savchuk said defensively. "We have nothing to hide." Savchuk had reason for his defensiveness. Previous experience, which he admitted was limited, had taught him that Western journalists were primarily interested in ferreting out "ugly" aspects of Soviet workers' lives. Ustinov and Savchuk wanted an American writer to see everything in Togliatti, and their willingness to discuss tough questions about

Soviet workers was a welcome relief from my escort's constant attempts to evade controversial issues. Two days in Togliatti taught me more about Soviet trade unions than the weeks I had spent elsewhere in the U.S.S.R. Nikolai Ustinov, having anticipated my desire to learn all about this subject, had arranged a visit to the VAZ's preventive health care clinic. "Feel free," he said, "to ask any question about preventive health care measures."

The doctor who oversees the VAZ's health spa is an example to his patients—a robust picture of vigor who in middle age had retained his buoyant, youthful, positive energy. I asked the doctor what kept him so high on life. "Ah," he explained, "it is my work. Every day I see auto workers who come to the clinic, asking me for advice to maintain their health. You see these private bedrooms, these botanical gardens, special treatment rooms, and the concert hall. Everything a person needs to keep in healthy condition is right here. And I am the one who directs this effort. I help people heal. This gives me youth."

I asked the doctor what he considered the major complaint among his patients. "As everywhere," he said, "the chronic illnesses caused by stress. In a society that is geared to rapid industrial expansion, where production quotas must be fulfilled, we have lots of cases of stress. Stress affects a worker's health, a worker's private life and relationships with others. Some tend to drink too much. Some eat poorly balanced meals because they are always in a hurry, in a rush to go to work. And workers under pressure cannot be expected to produce to their full capacity on the job.* Stress is the chief problem we treat, although we treat other problems too, bone injuries, sprains and so on. We have saunas and whirlpools, mud baths and mineral baths for treating muscle injuries and

---

* According to Radio Moscow, worker absenteeism is contributing to the plant's low production rate.

Johnson Stalker

Siberia

Igor Pogodaev

Photographs by Kathy Kahn

Janis Bogdanov

Milt Emerick

Francisca Carrillo

Sultan-Murat Soliev

Sergei Degtiariov

Margarito Martinez

Karomat Jakubaeva

Carrie Bingham

Willie Perry

Lynn Drake

Alexander Kremnev

Afanasii Kulagin

Anna Arinosova

Larissa Vanaga and family

Anya Sleptsova

Lou Williams

Valery Samuylov

skin disorders. We have special diets tailored to each patient's requirements. The patient must live here during treatment, and eat meals here. A patient can continue working, but returns here after each shift. This is such a pleasant environment that many workers don't wait for the union to give them a free voucher, they buy one themselves and come for a week or two. Our biggest problem is trying to accommodate all the people who want to come for a rest."

I said to the doctor, "I still want to know what keeps you bouncing." He smiled and told us to follow him. We walked up a flight of stairs, the landing encrusted with wooden bas-relief plaques, warmly painted serene pastoral scenes of people relaxing. "A gift," the doctor smiled, "handmade by a group of workers from another town who helped build this clinic." We walked along wide corridors where patients in robes and slippers brought from home chatted in soft voices or just sat by themselves in over-stuffed chairs, reading paperback books or gazing out windows at Togliatti's latest construction projects and the choppy artificial sea beyond. "Here we are," said the doctor, leading us into a room off the corridor. A small, cozy room. Two nurses in white uniforms stood next to a long, narrow table that had a copper pipe running down its center. Slim plastic tubes protruded from the pipe, about a dozen of them, each resting on the table before an empty chair. The apparatus looked like some sort of modern peacepipe setup. "This," explained the doctor, "is where patients receive their oxygen cocktails."

A nurse stepped forward, holding a glass vial, about one cup size, filled with clear liquid. She attached it to the pipe and the tube apparatus. "Would you like the nurse to demonstrate?" the doctor asked me.

"No," I said, "I think I'll try it myself." The nurse gave me the vial, assuring me it contained an herbal liquid concoction, totally safe, healthy and beneficial. She turned a valve on the pipe and instructed me to start swallowing when the liquid began to bubble. It bubbled, frothing, as oxygen, pumped through the pipe into the tube, entered the herbal tonic. I swallowed and swallowed, more bubbles formed and frothed, and the vial seemed never to empty. The bubbles had a sweet, grassy taste. I felt a little giddy. Somewhere in the distance, the doctor's voice echoed, "Have you had enough?" I shook my head and kept swallowing, my body on the verge of floating. Levitation must feel like this. Every negative thought I had harbored since childhood fled, leaving a brain enveloped in mellow euphoric bliss. The nurse turned off the valve and the doctor said, "I think one treatment is enough."

As we were leaving the VAZ health spa, I floating on Nikolai Ustinov's arm, the doctor handed Nikolai Ustinov a vial of medicine. He had noticed comrade Ustinov was evidencing hay fever symptoms. The doctor presented me with a small bottle of nose drops. He had observed some slight nasal congestion in the American guest. I had not. All I could think about was applying for a job at the VAZ.

Back at the plant, in an elaborate meeting hall with deeply cushioned red lounge chairs, under the gaze of a mammoth rendering of Lenin's face, I met with about fifty rank and file VAZ workers and took the opportunity to ask them about Western media reports of a Togliatti auto workers' strike.

In June 1980, the Western press reported that the previous May, Togliatti was the scene of the first labor strike in Soviet history. Reporting from Moscow, correspondents said that according to their sources two hundred and fifty thousand Togliatti and Gorky auto workers had walked off their jobs to protest food shortages. (Gorky is a few hundred kilometers north of Togliatti. Trucks are manufactured there.) The reporters also conjectured that a dispute between Togliatti's bus drivers and transportation officials contributed to the unrest that caused the walkout of the auto workers. Preceding Poland's Solidarity uprisings by just a few weeks, the Togliatti story was buried after only a handful of vague, unsubstantiated articles appeared in the Western press. U.S. workers who read reports of a Soviet auto workers' strike were left wondering what really happened in Togliatti in May 1980. One correspondent implied that the strike had been suppressed by militia, leading American readers to wonder if the workers had been forced at gunpoint to return to the production lines.

I asked the VAZ workers what really occurred that May. They told me that there was indeed a disagreement between citizens and city officials in Togliatti. Meat and dairy product shortages, combined with a dispute over bus drivers' wages and work schedules, were the sources of the citizens' anger. After exhausting all over the table negotiating efforts, the bus drivers appealed to the city council to resolve their differences with transportation management. Meanwhile, citizens irate over food shortages publicly demonstrated, demanding that quick action be taken to do something about this problem as well as about the drivers' discontentment. The demonstration was large and no doubt spirited, judging from the generally high level of energy exuded by Togliatti's youth. The VAZ workers told me that the citizens were exercising their democratic right to protest official action, or inaction, that affected their lives. While the men and women I spoke with strongly denied that the demonstration had reached the stage of a workers' walkout, they insisted that Soviet labor laws do not prohibit such strikes. The Togliatti and Gorky demonstrations—Gorky was also protesting food shortages—never reached strike proportions, the VAZ workers said, because the issues were quickly resolved to the citizens' satisfaction. "What Americans should learn from this experience," one man told me, "is that the Soviet state listens to workers' demands. We do not usually have to make much fuss before we get results. We have the right to strike—we just never have had to go that far."

Although the Western correspondents reported some of the Togliatti facts correctly, if the VAZ workers' version is true, they confused a citizens' protest demonstration with a labor strike.

It is true that Soviet labor laws do not prohibit strikes. Neither do they explicitly grant that right.

Soviet workers, including the VAZ's rank and file, can be strongly opinionated when asked about Poland's Solidarity movement. "Polish workers are being selfish," one man said to me. "They have fewer shortages than Soviet workers. Why? Because the Soviet Union keeps them supplied. We make sacrifices in our own lives to keep them fed. That is our socialist duty, to help less self-sufficient countries. Polish workers are being selfish." Another said, "Poland is not the Soviet Union. Maybe their government is not responding to workers' needs. But we do not have that problem here." A bureaucrat commented to me, rather hotly, "The Polish people have a habit of warring. They always seem to want a fight. That is why Poland has problems." A factory engineer en route to the United States for a vacation told me "I am watching Polish television. I have a good antenna." And he smiled.

Another Soviet worker with whom I spoke had a strong and well thought-out position on Solidarity. "First of all," he said, "Poland has unique problems, and not being a Polish citizen, I cannot be the judge of them. Polish workers must solve their own problems, like we Soviet workers, like workers everywhere solve their problems internally. It is the only way. Otherwise, you will have foreign governments interfering, using workers' struggles for their political purposes. Do you honestly think the U.S.

government supports Poland's workers? How can they say they support them when they send their own troops against U.S. workers who strike? What do I think about Poland's Solidarity? I will tell you. I think Polish workers must be very careful to know who their true allies are. I think they must not confuse anarchy with democracy. For democracy, there must be order. Anarchy is chaos, and democracy cannot survive in an anarchist state. But Poland is not my concern, you see, I am a Soviet worker, and I must be concerned with Soviet issues. What should happen in Poland? No intervention. Peace, of course. Peace."

In all the talks I had with Soviet citizens about Poland's Solidarity movement, the only time workers spoke in support of it was during private conversations with me. Considering the similarities between the Krasnoyarsk and Kommutator actions and the Solidarity movement, one might have expected more outspoken support of Poland's workers, if not of outside agitators who many believe have used Solidarity as a vehicle to sabotage Poland's socialist system. Soviet citizens seemed well informed about the Polish crisis, but reluctant to offer their opinions publicly. There is no question that fear of official reprimand figures in their reluctance to speak out. Polish workers are too close, both geographically and politically, to the Soviet trade union controversy. Perhaps when Togliatti heated up in May 1980, a more stringent censorship policy was enacted in Togliatti. But Soviet workers seemed most frequently just plain cautious. They seemed to say with their eyes, and on rare occasion with their lips, that they wished Americans would recognize the hypocrisy of their own President who on the one hand has supported Poland's Solidarity, while on the other hand, fired U.S. air traffic controllers who struck after President Reagan broke his campaign promise to improve their working conditions. Soviets, workers especially, seem bewildered at Reagan's

199

double-speak, and seem to fear American intervention in Eastern Europe. As one young woman said to me, in a low but determined voice, "There are patriots and then there are patriots. These false patriots, they wear two disguises. They follow the Party line without thinking for themselves. And they are smug. Others are the dissidents, the ones who are just out to get something for themselves. In the name of our Motherland they conspire with the West. But the real patriot is one who wants to make socialism really work for everyone. This is possible by trusting only those who have her interests at heart. And President Reagan is not a patriot of the Motherland."

I asked her if Poland's Solidarity, in her opinion, represented the struggles of Soviet workers as well. "The ideals of Polish workers, maybe they are similar," she said. "But the anti-socialist elements do not."

The VAZ workers had given up their lunch hour to meet with me. As the meeting moved into its third hour, I asked them to describe their working conditions. Several persons began speaking at once, but one voice boomed out over the others, and my attention was drawn to it. He was a handsome Russian with the posture of a military man and one of those daring Togliatti smiles that flash proudly. "If you please, Katya Kahn," he said, "I have given up my lunch hour, like my fellow unionists, to meet with you. We have been discussing many subjects related to workers' lives. We have talked about U.S. workers and even about Polish workers. Now I must return to my job. The least you can do is to visit my workplace and take time to understand *my* working conditions. See them for yourself, and then tell me if you think we VAZ workers have it rough."

I did visit Alexander Kremnev's workplace on the VAZ production line, after his fellow unionists bade me farewell, one after the other plucking *znachki*, little badges, from their jacket lapels and pinning them to my jacket. Badges that signify membership in the VAZ trade union, that depicted the VAZ's vacation resort and yacht club. Badges of friendship and union solidarity.

In the living room of his high-rise apartment overlooking Togliatti's artificial sea, Alexander Kremnev talked about his life.

Alexander Kremnev

Well, it's probably no secret to anyone that we all came from different cities of Russia, for the construction of the VAZ. As for me personally, I came here from a city called Michurinsk. This is the birthplace of nature's reorganizer, Ivan Michurin.* So that's where we lived until 1968. In 1968, when the construction of the Volga Automobile Factory began, I came here alone. My family—my wife and daughter—stayed in Michurinsk. After a year, I received an apartment, two rooms. And then my family came to me here. Of course, I was happy.

You probably rode through the so-called Old City as you were on your way into town. This—where we live now—is the new district. We lived there before, and we went to the VAZ on the city transit system. In 1973, my little son was born, and after three years, in 1976, the trade union gave me this larger apartment. That is, the size of my family increased.

When my wife came here to me in 1970, she also started working at the VAZ. We work side by side. You've seen my workplace. Literally ten steps away is her position. So we're together, both at home and at work, though we work in different shops.

---

* Michurin was a horticulturist and geneticist who conducted grafting experiments with fruit trees. Based on his experiments, Michurin concluded that grafting can induce hereditary changes and that acquired characteristics can be inherited. Thus, Michurin is dubbed "Nature's reorganizer."

My father is a lathe operator and works in a plant in Michurinsk. My mother worked in the administrative offices there. I have a brother, and he lives with my mother. He works as a grinder of the sixth grade. He is younger than me, by eleven years. And a sister. She works in Kazan.

Now let's return to my ancestors. Well, just on the twenty-eighth of March, my maternal grandfather turned ninety-two years old. We all thought it was his ninetieth birthday, and sent him congratulatory messages. But a few days later, he sent us a letter and corrected our error. Well, it may be that my gramps is an historical figure. You probably know the world famous writer, Leo Nikolayevich Tolstoy. Well, my gramps, he had a personal meeting with him. My grandad's letters are published in the eleventh volume of Tolstoy's letters, from everyone he corresponded with. They wrote about this in our newspaper, *The Volga Auto Builder*. I have a copy somewhere around here. When we asked him, "Grandfather, how did all this happen?", he said, "We were just accidentally riding in the same train from Petersburg to Moscow, and we became acquainted, and since then we kept up a correspondence." Many of the letters haven't been preserved, but if they all had, there would have been very many.

Granddad says that our line is long-lived, and that's why we should live a long time. But he wasn't like Lev Tolstoy. Lev Tolstoy only ate vegetable cutlets, he didn't use meat. But my granddad, even at ninety-two I'm sure he drinks his share. And every morning he runs three kilometers. He has his own vegetable garden. He dug the earth himself. He chops firewood, stokes the oven, and he repairs the house. They have their own house, a small one. That's why he has to get his hands into everything. And when we come to visit him, he looks at us and says, "You probably don't do any physical labor. That's why you'll get weak when you get older."

So there you have it.

I'm forty-five years old. My father was a cavalryman under Davatov. Not far from Moscow. Oh, you remember the war. When the living come back after war, there are lots of tears, lots of memories . . . there was only one thought, that this should never be repeated.

This is all I can say; it's burned into me for life. I will always remember how we came by bread. I was the oldest, and my sister was small, just born when the war started. In school, we were given rations, a small piece of bread sprinkled with sugar. My sister was always waiting for me to come from school, waiting for me to bring her that little piece of bread. I had to divide this piece of bread and share it with her. And that will always remain in my memory.

Well, we had no toys like our children have now. Everything was homemade, homemade dolls. Because, you know yourself, during the war there was no industry to make such toys and other things like that. The best game was . . . they don't play this game here, because there's a house, then another house, a school, there's no space . . . we had a big meadow and we played this Russian game called *lapta*. We'd throw a ball. It was simply a dense rubber ball. We lived at the edge of the town, that's why we had a meadow right by our place. And when we had our spring vacation in April, the river would overflow and our house was completely surrounded by water. We had a boat right from the door—into the boat, and let's go! When the ice begins breaking up, it would bump up against our house. Then the favorite game was to ride the pieces of ice. They broke often, and we would come home up to our ears soaking wet with cold water, and our mother would give it to us.

I was in the army three years. Till 1959. I served in Ukraine. I was the first rank after private, private first class. But I was exemplary there, so they gave me ten days' leave to visit my parents. I had to display exemplary behavior, observing all the regulations. So, they didn't give you leave for nothing. In a word, you had to earn it.

Yes, children play at war games. We played them, and our children play them. It's a peaceful war. Our children play only at that kind of war.

I worked in artillery. The most memorable event was in 1959, I joined our Party. That is, first I was a candidate member. Well, at the very beginning of my Party life, as they say, was, namely, serving in the army. That is, the army helps us realize everything, train ourselves. If we go into the army as, how would you say it, not-so-disciplined boys, it's in that very army that they train us to serve our country, to be more conscientious, more aware. Simply, a young fellow's consciousness so developed as a result of all the things we learned, the work that our commanders carried out with us, all of that leaves its stamp. But I wouldn't say, for example, that each of the enlisted men would join the Party afterwards. I'm talking only about those who understand correctly, who realize things for what they are, who see things, each at his own level. Whether as a Pioneer, a Komsomol member, a Party member. Someone who understands everything correctly could only follow that path, and must go though these stages, from Pioneer to Komsomol to Party member.

To be a communist, I would say, in my granddad's words, he always says to me, "Sashka, do only good things for people. Don't answer evil with evil, answer with good, with kindness. Then people will treat you with understanding."

And that's what I'm trying to do now.

Well, to begin with, the word "communist," it doesn't carry any boons, any built-in rewards. He should be where it's difficult, where he can apply his knowledge and experience. And to be only at the forefront. That is the duty of any Party member. But he doesn't have any special benefits, we're the same rank and file like everybody.

I can give you lots of examples of the benefits of working at the VAZ. You have probably visited our dispensary, our health spa. We also have the same kind of dispensary at the site of our children's Pioneer summer camps. It's called Scarlet Sails. A voucher to go there costs only fifteen rubles. I vacationed there, I went for a cure. It costs our state ten times more, so I paid fifteen rubles out of one hundred fifty rubles. While working we can take cures to improve our health. In the morning they take us to work; at four o'clock they bring us back. We go for our treatments, whatever we need.

My workday begins at seven o'clock. We get up at five thirty together, the two of us. My spouse takes care of getting the children off to school clean and neat, thoroughly looked over. And I, correspondingly, shave, get myself in order. Then I have breakfast, a light breakfast, a cup of tea and a sandwich, a small piece of bread with a slice of cheese or sausage. The same is available at work on special carts, so if I don't have time to eat breakfast at home, I have it there. We go outside at six fifteen, after having listened to the latest news. Our bus stop is nearby, a three-minute walk in either direction. At twenty to, or a quarter to seven, we are at work. So that's that. And then at eleven o'clock, we have lunch.

I am a polisher. Of *course* we have a daily production goal!

So, we work until eleven. Then we work for fifteen minutes at the table. We have a planned full-course meal. At one time, there are one thousand people eating lunch for fifteen minutes. The food is all prepared and hot, waiting for us at the table. And then, thirty minutes are left, to think, to play chess, tennis, to read the papers. And, at a quarter to twelve, I'm back at my machine until four o'clock. At four, the buses are waiting, we go out the exit, board, and at four twenty, we're home. Twenty minutes after finishing work. Then, accordingly, household chores.

Women have women's work, and men have men's work. But we don't chop firewood, we don't have a wood burning oven here. Then comes a visit to the movies, or to the Sports Palace. My son and I are hockey fans. The trade union committee encourages us with season tickets. Free entry to the Sports Palace. So, if we've seen a hockey game, we come home at nine o'clock and watch TV. At ten o'clock, we watch "Time," the news program, and we go to bed at fifteen till eleven. And then we do it all over again.

The trade unions, you could say, are everything. It's apartments, it's daycare centers, it's vouchers to the spa, it's Pioneer camps. In a word, it is a school of rule by the workers. Well, if some kind of conflict arises, we always go to our trade union committee. Either it's switching vacation times from winter to summer, or something in our working conditions changed, and the administration didn't react properly.

Well, it's clear that we go to work to *work*. But if some questions arise . . . you see, there are many considerations here. There are many jobs on the production line, starting with the part itself, and ending with its manufacture. That is, questions can come up for the rate setter, for the technologist . . . but all these questions are decided during the course of the day. We see to it that our problems are solved. That is, if a part needs to be produced that day, it is produced.

Well, there are eight people of the same occupation in my team. We understand our task to be that all eight people should produce what has been assigned. If there are only five of us, then five of us have to do the work of eight. If we're four, then the foursome has to do the work of eight. We have to carry out any program they've given us. It is a matter of honor for our team to fulfill the monthly plan. And so we've been working together since '69. No new comrades. We celebrated the fiftieth birthday of one team member, then another turned fifty, and I feel that I'm not going to escape this honor either, in five years.

How do I perceive the role of a woman? Well, if you take a family, a wife and a husband, here they have to make all decisions together. I think it's wrong to think of the kitchen as being for women and hammering a nail for men. We must divide our housework equally. In contemporary conditions, women are working, they are under the same conditions as men. So we must divide up all our housework equally. For example, let me tell you about myself. Our kitchen is both hers and mine. That is, I may do the cooking and washing—well, the machine does the wash. Earlier, women did the wash. Now anyone available throws the clothes into the machine. Even my little Maxim can do it sometimes. Whoever has time, shops for food.

Vacations, there are summer and winter vacations. While you were riding here you noticed that we are in an area of large tracts of forest. There is nothing more pleasant than winter skiing in the forest. Even if the wind is blowing here and it is really freezing, then in the forest, it's only half as strong. So in winter, the best way to spend your leisure time is to go on ski outings. Sometimes my son and I leave for the forest at ten A.M. and return back at five in the evening. We have ski lodges there. There are skiing competitions. We hold these "health days," but it's all related to competitions. Downhill skiing. Children ski to win a prize, with responsible dads and moms. It's well organized here. So, we arrive at the forest ski lodge in winter, and for sure, every Sunday some enterprise is holding a health day. And at the close of the season, they set up this skiing competition:

The first to come to the starting line is the shop superintendent. He passes the baton to the Party organizer, and the Party organizer gives it to the trade union. They pass it to the Komsomol and then to a good skier. And that's the close of our winter ski season.

In the summer . . . you can see the artificial sea from our window. It's ten kilometers from shore to shore. Width. And our rest area is located on the far side. It's called "Free

Will." So we relax there. We swim, sunbathe, pick berries and mushrooms. We can them for winter. The housewives cook jam. That's how we pass our summer leisure. We have days when after work . . . we have a very good beach. Come, the sun is blinding, lie down . . . baaaask! The water isn't salty. Bathe. That's the way we spend our free time in summer.

At Free Will, we have a sailing club. Only I'm not a member.

Alexander Savchuk, who was a member of the VAZ yacht club, politely interrupted Kremnev to offer a few words on the VAZ sailing club.

We have several sailing clubs, one of which belongs to VAZ, and there is a whole string of sailing clubs that belong to other plants in the area. All of them are part of the system of sports facilities of these factories, and all of them, to one degree or another, belong to the trade unions. Since it's a type of sport, anyone who wants to take it up can. Well, you need to have certain physical characteristics to do it. But the main thing is the desire.

"If, say, I have no physical abilities and have no experience sailing, but I have a great desire, I still have the opportunity to go to the club and sign up as a member. And there, in that sailing club, I can gain the necessary skills. And after that, I have to pass an exam. If I pass the sailing exam, I get a special sailing license. Since, as you know, on both the river and the sea there are official traffic regulations. If I've mastered all these skills, I'll receive the right to sail. If I get a license, then the sailing club will assign me a particular sailboat and I can use it however I want.

"I can own a private sailboat if I can afford it. The cost depends on the class of boat. Boats vary greatly. I can buy a brand new boat, deluxe class. I can buy a secondhand boat. Nevertheless, I will be a member of a club. I can go

by boat from the Upper Don, down the Volga. I can go into the open sea, into the Baltic for example. I can use my boat however I want to. If I want, I can participate in competitions. So forth and so on. . . ."

Before Alexander Kremnev could take up his story again, Nikolai Ustinov politely reminded us the hour was getting late, and that Kremnev and his wife, since they worked the early shift, probably needed their sleep. That night I fell asleep in my bed at the Zhiguli Hotel and dreamed about a place called Free Will

As Ustinov said farewell to me at the airport, he wore a sad expression. Not because I was leaving Togliatti, but perhaps because he had fears, left over from the days of the 1980 Togliatti protest, that a Western writer might misrepresent his town, his fellow workers, his society. His gloved hand shook mine firmly. "Please," he said, "write about our town from your heart."

Togliatti, the brave new Soviet town, is an interesting 20th century experiment. The state has created an environment that combines optimal laboring conditions with carefully ordered work and recreation schedules, special health cures, and vacation areas. It is altogether a compelling place, mostly because its citizens are so warmly human, but it is so comfortable that it tends to lull one to sleep with its aura of security. When Togliatti's citizens publicly protested food shortages and bus drivers' overloaded work schedules in May 1980, they demonstrated that even a brave new town's carefully designed systems can malfunction. And when such a breakdown occurred, the citizens of Free Will resorted to their own spirited cures, reminding the sociologists that those who supply society will probably always demand a fair share of the goods. Not even an oxygen cocktail can subdue an angry worker's spirit. Not even in a brave new town.

The Mavericks

Hey cabbie, drivin' deep for a no-go
Hey, hey cabbie, drivin' deep for a no-go
You jumped the wrong bell, baby
And the devil ran the radio.

—Cabbie Blues

America's bootstrap legend created, polished and en-
shrined one of the nation's most popular heroes, the
maverick. Mavericks prefer working alone, without bosses
breathing down their neck, dependent only upon themselves for survival. They tend to be independent-minded
folk who form opinions through their own intellectual
efforts rather than succumbing to peer pressure or social
propaganda. Since they are individualists, mavericks do
not necessarily agree with one another, politically or
philosophically. But even a maverick knows that a thousand free spirits united carry more weight than one
stubborn hombre. What happens when a thousand American mavericks gather together under one roof to analyze

the benefits and liabilities of the system that spawned them: American free enterprise?

No United States citizen is more of a maverick than the taxicab driver. The imagination reels at the idea of one thousand independent, often single-minded and stubborn, rough and tumble cabdrivers discussing free enterprise in a smoky barroom where hard liquor and draft beer flow as freely as ideas. But the event is not fantasy. In 1978, Denver, Colorado's, Yellow Cab drivers collected together in their union hall/barroom around a single point of unity. They were weary of being at the mercy of the whims and fancies of a single man who owned controlling stock in the company that employed them. Some of the men and women were planning a unique sort of rebellion against an adversary they believed had done the free enterprise system wrong. The essential theme under discussion in the mavericks' union hall was, does free enterprise mean the right to barter and trade one's own labor *or* does it also sanction one man's right to reap huge personal profits by underpaying and overworking his employees? A flammable subject in American labor union circles.

When the smoke finally cleared, the Independent Drivers' Association, IDA, had voted nearly unanimously to take their collective future into their own hands. Here is what happened as IDA devised a scheme to combine the bootstrap legend, the work ethic, and a unique version of collectivism, when Denver's Finest decided to look out for one thousand Number Ones. . . .

Willie Perry has been driving a taxicab in Denver for over twenty-five years. Raised in a black neighborhood in Dallas, Texas, he received an athletic scholarship and became a track star for Louisiana's Southern University in the fifties. After an army stint, he moved to Denver, where his brother worked as a cabdriver. Willie decided to take up the occupation and has been driving a cab ever since.

In IDA's union hall/barroom, Willie Perry is a peace-maker. I know, because I used to be the bartender there. On many occasions when heated arguments threatened to escalate into fistfights, Willie's cool, gentle persuasion intervened. Once, when a white driver, twice Willie's size, scribbled racist graffiti on the men's room wall, an angry black driver called me in to view the obscenities. From the height of the wall scribblings, it was a good bet the tallest white cabdriver, now sitting at the bar, was the culprit. The angry black driver began spouting threats. But nothing came of them, because by then, Willie Perry was sitting at the bar, with his arm around the man who had scribbled the racist remarks, admonishing him in a gentle voice. The big white driver was crying.

Though he never aspired to union leadership, Perry's opinions, quietly voiced in loud meetings, usually figure strongly in IDA's policy decisions. Ranking high on IDA's seniority list, he has seen a lot of action as a cabdriver, both in his union hall and on the streets. His comments begin the story of the mavericks' unique and thought-provoking victory over management.

Willie Perry, Tom Hanlon and Ed Cassidy

WILLIE PERRY: I started driving a cab in 1955. I think it was August. Driving part-time at first, and working as a mail handler too. I drove Yellow the whole time. I've got over five thousand shifts now. We had the Teamsters back then, and they weren't worth a damn in my sight. I'm not saying the Teamsters Union isn't good. It was the people we would elect as our local leaders. They sold us down the river all the time.

Driving a cab in those days, well, the rules were a lot stricter than what they are now. You had to apply more courtesy than what you do now. And you had to take whatever they gave you over there to drive, because you were brand new. The company never gave you any new equipment. I can remember trips from downtown to the airport ran about a dollar seventy, a dollar eighty, and you were glad to get two bucks. From the train depot to uptown, it was only like forty or fifty cents. The flag drop was thirty cents. You could be sitting at the Cosmopolitan Hotel and five old ladies would get in. Yellow used to advertise that five could ride for the price of one. And these five old ladies would ride from the Cosmo to the Denver Dry for tea in the afternoon, a five-block ride, and it'd be fifty cents. All five of 'em would get out and one old lady would hand you a fifty cent piece.

Back in them days payoff was like five fifty or six dollars, rental fee for the cab. You got your first hundred miles free, and if you drove over a hundred miles you'd pay a penny a mile after that. So if you drove a hundred and ten miles, you'd owe the company an extra dime. The company bought the gas then too. So, if you went home with like, oh, fifteen, eighteen dollars . . . what we used to push for was a twenty-dollar day . . . wow. I could go to work maybe one week out of the month and make enough money to pay the rent. Course, the rent was only forty-five dollars a month. So I'd go to work and make enough to pay the rent and the phone bill and go to the grocery store with twelve or fifteen bucks. That would buy you enough to last all week. That was easy.

But we never got any benefits until IDA took over.* There was some crime on the streets back then, but not like now. Back in those days, black guys would never hold up another black guy. Nowadays even black guys would just as soon knock me off as anybody else. These young punks, white or black, they don't care, they'll knock your head off for four or five bucks. Nowadays they couldn't pay me enough to drive nights. I used to. I was lucky.

*In 1969, the union local voted to separate from the Teamsters, and formed their own unaffiliated independent union.

It was the old company in those days, and you had to drive nights if you was new. They had these old '52 Plymouths, they had yellow bodies and black tops, and you could damn near drive the things in one gear—just push it up in second and drive 'em all over town. But you should've seen the cab. It looked like Rhodan. I was new, I got it because nobody wanted it. That cab was the worst goddamned thing you'd ever want to look at, it'd scare you to death comin' down the street at night. But I finally got on days, after I gained a little seniority, I got a four A.M. shift, then four thirty. Then when I got the five o'clock shift, seemed like I stayed there for years till I could finally move up to six A.M. But now, after twenty-five years, I can get just about any shift I want.

There was a period of about five years that I worked seven days a week. But my kids were growing up and leaving home and I didn't need to work so hard. I finally said what's wrong with me, I don't have to work this hard. I lived in a cab, I smelled like a cab. I even started lookin' like one. So after the younger two finished high school, I figured, hell, I don't have to work this hard anymore, and even still I can save some money. Well about that time inflation hit. I was just thinkin', man, the sixty-five and seventy dollars a week I used to make back in the late fifties, now it takes like three hundred a week for just me and my wife. Three hundred a week for just two people. Sixty-five, seventy bucks back then, oh man, even with four kids that was good. We used to pay a babysitter and go out and party all night. We'd go out and party like three, four times a week. Then I'd just drop my wife off at home, change clothes in my car and go down and pick up the cab and go to work. I've changed clothes in my car many a time. But you can't do that now, you can't afford to party three or four times a week, not even if you're single.

I used to go out and make the bar breaks a couple times a week. But I got scared off that. I picked up a guy one morning around three o'clock. On the West Side. He was a big brown skinned guy. He was huge. And I brought him over to Curtis Park projects over there right off Champa and about 30th. It was in the summertime. He says, "I want you to wait for me." He says, "I want to go in this place here and see if this broad's home." I said, "Sure." The light was on, you could see the light in the house. You could even hear music playin'. I could hear it from the cab. And the porch light was on too. So he went and banged on the door. All the lights went off. So he started banging on the windows, but nobody'd let him in. So he came back and got in the cab. He said, "Take me back over on the West Side." I says, "Fine." All the way back over there, he didn't say nothin'. I crossed the 8th Avenue viaduct and I was going to make a right turn on Decatur, and he says, "Hey, hold it!" And he starts cursing. He says, "Pull it over, pull it over right now!" And his eyes were like cat's eyes. He hadn't been drinkin' but he was high on somethin'. And he's got this knife, like a hunting knife. He's sittin' in the back, so he reaches over and grabs me, puts this knife up at my neck. So I says, "Hey man, look, I only got about six bucks." He says, "I don't want your damn money." He says, "The goddamned broad messed me over. Everybody's messed me over since I've been in this town." I says, "Well, look man, I haven't done anything to you. Why don't you just leave me go?" I started pleading with him. I says, "Look man, I got a wife and kids. Why don't you just leave me go, man?" He was shaking, the knife was shaking in his hand. He says, "How much do I owe you?" I says, "Nothin' man, just forget it." He says, "No, I'm gonna pay you." And he threw a roll of one dollar bills on the front seat. Somethin' like three dollars and forty cents. And he still had hold of me with one hand. I says, "Can I go in my pocket and get your change?" He says, "No, you keep it." And he took the knife and put it right up here in my face and says, "Consider yourself a lucky man. I was

gonna kill your ass." And he got out. I cranked that baby
up and took off.

I don't make the bar break no more.

Tom Hanlon grew up in a working class Irish neighborhood in New York. He rose to an executive position in the
banking industry and was a vice president of the First
National Bank of Denver for many years. The world of
finance and commerce fascinated him, but the politics and
social pressures of banking conflicted with Tom Hanlon's
inherited working class sympathies. The last bank job he
held was in Anchorage, Alaska. After arranging financing
for the first school built and operated by Eskimos, Hanlon
had a dispute with his boss, who had just lost a political
campaign. He told his boss what he could do with the job,
quit the world of banking, returned to Denver, and began
driving a taxicab. His experience as a banker proved
invaluable to his union.

TOM HANLON: The single element that attracted me to
cabdriving is the lack of having to become involved in the
organizational structure of a company. You go in and pick
up your taxicab and you go out and you don't have to
answer to anybody, eh? And the relative lack of supervi-
sion. If you have difficulty getting along with people, it's a
perfect job because you're not with anybody for any length
of time, maybe fifteen, twenty minutes at most. Almost
everybody can get along with people for fifteen minutes.

I didn't understand at first the economics of this
business. There's a lot going on underneath. While we
were working on the union pension plan, we discovered
the technique that later led to financing the Co-op. We
worked the pension plan so that every driver who'd been
working over twenty-five years without any benefits would
get to retire immediately the day we opened the pension
fund. They'd get credit for twenty-five years of driving a

cab. We started the pension in '74 and immediately twenty-five people retired. What we did, without going into all the technicalities, the union was the employer, which is one of the unique things about IDA.

The former owner of Denver Yellow Cab, Danburg, was from Houston. He had a chain of auto parts stores, owned Houston Yellow Cab and other investments. Danburg had a particularly brutal, crude kind of nineteenth century version of capitalism, attempting to disguise it as a benevolent system. When he bought Denver Yellow Cab, we said, "We better get ourselves a strike fund." He'd broken a Teamster's local in Houston.

In order to accumulate a strike fund, we raised the union dues by a dollar a day. Then the strike happened, and an hour after the strike was called, we passed out a check to everybody in the union. The confidence this built helped when we wanted to buy the company.

Typically, in a union there are members who only want the union when they've got a crisis, right? And so if you're not in a crisis, some will vote—if your employer calls a decertification election—against the union. The inevitable discontent is, "Well, what do we get for our union dues? What is the union doing?" And the union tries to justify itself and is only really successful in justifying itself when there's a very direct attack and everybody feels threatened. Over the long run, there's a discontent directed at the union that should be directed at the philosophy of unions that accept the system. But there's very few people who have that consciousness about the limitations of a union. By no means am I saying a union is a bad thing. It's just that people must understand you can only do a certain amount through unions. People often say, "If we only had a good union, a tough union, we could solve all these problems . . ." Well, a good tough union is better than a weak patsy union, but they both operate with the same fundamental limitation. They accept the system.

So whatever discontent and disillusionment there was in the union completely disappeared as soon as Danburg attacked. When danger came, union members knew they had to stick together, and their basic loyalty is to each other as workers. They'll fight like hell among each other and disagree and get in each other's way, but they have the good sense to know the difference between "them" and "us." The net effect of attack is to weld the union and its members closer and closer together. The harder Danburg attacked, the more unified we became. The issues were very clear, very direct, and therefore much easier to deal with. When Danburg called a decertification election, we voted in a union shop with 93 percent majority affirmative vote. I don't know what the other 7 percent was thinking about . . .

When Ed Cassidy was elected IDA's president, the bearded Irishman changed few of his old habits. He continued driving his taxicab. And every evening, about six o'clock, he could still be found on the barstool nearest to the pool table in IDA's bar. Swilling his usual after hours mug of draft beer, anything but Coors, Cassidy continued his role as barroom Father Confessor, soft-spoken spiritual leader of Denver's Finest mavericks. Setting a much needed example for the nation's union leadership, Ed Cassidy remained faithful to the rank and file and to their cause. As IDA's president, he refused to adopt the too familiar sweetheart position with company management. Even though IDA and Denver Yellow Cab moved beyond that stage, forming a marriage of sorts, Cassidy remains staunchly faithful to the union cause. He recalls the strike that led his union into a new era of labor-management relations.

ED CASSIDY: The strike started as a lockout. The company locked out the inside people, the telephone operators and dispatchers and machinists. They locked them out. The inside employees didn't belong to IDA, but they had unions and had come to an impasse on their negotiations. The company locked them out and shut the company down. The company fully expected the drivers to capitulate and go back to work. We went out in a show of support for the inside employees. We prevailed upon the company to let the inside workers go back to work under the old contract and continue negotiations with everything negotiated being retroactive. We thought that was the most reasonable way.

The company balked, there was a lot of bitterness there. The drivers decided not to go to work as a group. We had only one or two, three at the outside, who chose to go back when the company reopened with substitute people. They were going to farm the mechanical work out and recruited management to run the radio and telephone rooms. They told us they'd like us to go back to work too, said the inside people were making unreasonable demands. We told them we wouldn't go back to work unless they negotiated a contract with the inside people.

I think they fully expected a bunch of people to cross the picket lines. But only two or three did, and then only for about a day and a half, then we shut 'em down completely. We put pressure on the two or three who kept driving. We had people out informing them that they were facing not only union charges but they were betraying the rest of the groups that we had pledged to support. You're talking in terms of perhaps a hundred to a hundred and twenty people on the inside, all the support workers, mechanics, dispatchers, telephone operators, etc., as opposed to a thousand drivers. It was a very small group that we were supporting. I was very impressed with the support the drivers gave them. We just all thought the company was being particularly stubborn in this case, and that if they could do it to the inside workers, they could do it with us.

Later on, after the strike was over, what we found out by

virtue of literally going through the company's trash and coming up with correspondence—notes taken and whatnot—that there was indeed a concerted antilabor movement, but within the law. Later our own labor lawyers said it possibly constituted a conspiracy and probably was against the law. We found some notes in the company's trash that looked suspiciously like threats. There were threats against Steve Johnson and Art Gross, who were involved in the union.* This was in the handwriting of one of the company's officials. It said something like, "Steve Johnson and Art Gross . . ." and then there was a curious little thing that said "accidents will happen" underneath their names. Of course everyone in management denied it.

We ran a courtesy car operation out of the union hall. We recruited everybody's cars and rented a bunch of cars, got the telephone company to install ten telephones. We charged each driver a rental fee, just like the company did, only quite a bit less, paid everybody for their work, and kept the thing going for thirty-seven days. Even then, the two sides, the inside unions and management, were far apart, so it was up to us to go in there and force a settlement upon management. Management was trying desperately to get the Public Utilities Commission to shut us down, they had served several subpoenas on drivers, but we could have kept it tied up in court for another month or two and meanwhile the company was losing money.

What was in our favor, the public loved it. We couldn't charge money and if people wanted to donate, that's fine. Sometimes passengers would ask, "Well, how much do you want?", and we'd have to say, "Well, we can't accept money . . ." They'd say, "Well, what would the trip run if I were in a cab?" And the driver could tell them and they'd either pay that fare or more, as a donation. Drivers were

---

* Steve Johnson and Art Gross were union leaders during the strike.

making more money than they normally did driving for Yellow Cab. 'The rental fee was less and people were paying more because they were glad to get service. It was an interesting time, and one of the more heartwarming times I've ever experienced in the cab business—to see that support for the inside people and the support for the drivers from the public. It was the best of all possible worlds because we kept the public served and continued our support of the inside workers. Nobody got hurt over this, except the company.

TOM HANLON: In the fall of '78, Danburg, having failed to bust the union, he got interested in real estate development over on the Western Slope. We heard some rumors he was actively trying to sell the company. Steve Johnson was union president at the time and he checked them out and indeed the company was up for sale.

Back in 1975, we attempted to form a co-op, Steve and I were involved in that. That was before the pension fund, and before dues on a daily basis, before that whole technique had been invented. The original architects of a co-op plan then based their idea on everybody coming up with twenty-five hundred dollars cash. That was the fundamental flaw, anytime you had a plan based on cabdrivers coming up with a whole lot of money on short notice, it was absolutely doomed to failure. And it was also based on the assumption that some people were going to be members of the co-op and some weren't. It was a share buying plan, little distinction from a stockholders' company. So the effort to build a co-op was taken away from the architects and given to a Co-op Steering Committee which consisted of Hanlon and Johnson and Henry Feldman and Dave Flores and Joe Hardigree, Walt Smith, Tiny Maiselson and a number of other people.

We did an awful lot of work and learned a lot. It was an educational experience and that's all it was because it didn't go any further. But even with that, we raised about forty thousand dollars. But we had to come up with about a quarter of a million. We wrote the bylaws, articles of incorporation, all that, but it all fell through, the basic reason was money. But it was a good foundation for the next time, we didn't make the same mistakes the second time. In addition we had the strike fund, so we had a big chunk of cash, we had two hundred thousand dollars cash. So we said okay, he's got it up for sale and we have half the downpayment . . . so Danburg unloaded the company on us for more than it was worth. He had only paid nine hundred thousand for it in '76 and here two years later he's selling it to us for two million, so in less than two years, Danburg made a gross profit of a million and one hundred thousand dollars. And we were going around, "Well, we sure beat him, didn't we?" We knew we were paying way too much for it, but it was . . . no matter who buys it we're going to pay for it, it was a once in a lifetime opportunity so we got screwed on the price. We probably paid twice as much for it as it was worth. But we bought it.

Well, this is where some of my background in banking came in handy. Danburg banked at First National of Denver. How convenient, right? The loan officer happened to be in a training program while I was working in the bank and, "Oh, Bob Pulcipher! How good to see you again!" So it was "good old Bob" and "good old Tom," it was a little bit of a connection with the "good old boys," you see. Steve did most of the political organizing and the smooth talking to the membership. Steve's background and general reputation gave credence to the effort.* And

---

* Steve Johnson, a Denver native and a graduate of Harvard University, drove a taxicab in his hometown for several years before being elected IDA's president in 1977. Although he openly expressed pro-socialist views, he made a campaign promise to keep his political opinions separate from his job as IDA's leader. One union cabdriver, formerly a member of the right-wing John Birch Society, later said of Johnson, "I voted for him because, even though I disagreed with his politics, he was the best man for the job. And he kept his campaign promise. He was a

additionally my reputation and experience gave credence to dealing with the company's bank. I don't know what the bank expected when Danburg told them he was thinking of selling the company to cabdrivers, they probably had visions of some wild people coming in. Steve and I both hunted through our wardrobes and got out our three-piece suits and went down with our attorney and talked to the bankers, we didn't let them come near any of our union meetings, kept them out of the bar at IDA, we gave them the impression that we were very responsible and highly articulate businessmen, and it *"just happens"* it was a co-op. I'm sure if we'd tried it twenty years ago it wouldn't've worked. Pulcipher is a pretty decent guy and it was a good loan for the bank, a good account. The nature of the business is a lot of cash, like we deposit fifteen thousand dollars in currency every day and build up pretty good cash balances from all the cash flow that's generated, so it's a very attractive account for the bank. And they had all the collateral on us anyway. So Pulcipher went to the First National Bank of Dallas and arranged for a three hundred thousand dollar loan for us there. With that and our strike fund we bought Denver Yellow Cab.

Actually, IDA doesn't own the company. We formed another corporation called Yellow Cab Co-operative Association. † Now, all the members of IDA belong to the Co-op. So we abolished the strike fund, reduced the dues to two dollars from three and a half, and put the dollar and a half a day into Co-op dues. So the drivers didn't have to pay anything more. Painless. And everybody had to pay a one-time fee of forty bucks to cover the organizational part. And you know, that was the hardest part of the thing to sell

---

good leader." As IDA's president, Johnson led the drive to purchase Denver Yellow Cab. Johnson is presently in graduate school at Stanford University, studying economics. Ed Cassidy succeeded Johnson as IDA's president in 1980.

† Tom Hanlon is presently serving as the Co-op's manager.

to the membership, that forty bucks cash. "You mean I gotta come up with *forty* bucks?!" Shouting, screaming, "Are you gonna give us interest?" The dollar and a half you get back when you quit. But this one-time payment of forty dollars was nonrefundable.

There was an idealism, we told ourselves, "This is the next step beyond unionism." The potential for getting people out of their attitudes . . . the whole problem of getting people to cooperate and injecting a democratic process going is still at a primitive level. While we may be beyond unionism, we still have the inherent difficulties that unionism has, it's one microcosm of worker-ownership and control and we're still at the mercy of the system as a whole. Not as much as we were before, but just by forming a co-op hasn't made all the problems go away. And now we're smart enough to buy the company, now let's see if we're smart enough to run it. My personal opinion is that creating the owner driver program, letting that program in here created a fundamental economic conflict—we have a two-class system, owner drivers and lease drivers. Many of these people who own cabs are very conservative-minded people who see themselves as different than day-lease drivers. "My cab is all nice and clean . . ." And it's all mixed up in the ideology, "Well, if you own it, it's much better, you take care of it and you don't abuse it." Naturally that virtue now suffuses their whole personality and they feel they're much more worthwhile people because they're in "business for themselves." One of these guys, he's kind of a Bircher, all of a sudden got interested in the union, began coming to union meetings. Where he used to have an opposite driver, now he's got an "employee" working for him. He gets up in a meeting and starts expressing discontent about the "terrible slovenly work habits" of this guy. He said, "Well now, I depend on the income I get from this cab, and this guy didn't even have the courtesy to come to work yesterday. Now," he says, "I couldn't arrange on such short notice for another driver so I lost that income. Now, what's the union going to do about this? I think we ought to charge that guy a ten- or fifteen-dollar penalty to compensate me!"

It took us ten years to get rid of the no-show penalty at Yellow Cab, we'd just gotten rid of it in the previous contract, and here's a union member behaving like a boss.

I opposed the owner driver program very vehemently. I anticipated it as a divisive tactic. One of the structural things about the cab business is there's practically three drivers for every cab. We have four hundred cabs, we have a thousand drivers, right? With single ownership of a cab, you gotta have one guy drive it day shift and another drive it night shift. So one has to own it and one has to be a nonowner. So it's built in. A minority of the drivers are going to own their cabs. They've got a greater financial interest than another driver who for one reason or another doesn't want to own a cab. So he's going to be the one that ends up being the employee. Ironic.

ED CASSIDY: One of the lessons we've learned from the Co-op Board is that just the proximity of being over there at the motor, they tend to think more like management. When I go over there, coming from the union hall, I'm still a visitor. If we moved the union hall over to the motor, I'd be considered one of the boys, going out to lunch with management. Although it wouldn't necessarily be capitulation, it might lead to suspicion. I think the union hall needs to keep its own building separate from management, from the Co-op. If we're involved in a situation where one of our drivers is fired by Co-op management and requires union representation . . . we need an arm's-length relationship with the Co-op, if we defaulted on our loans, we'd still have the union hall to come back to. The bar at IDA still loses money, but it's still the center of activity.

The Co-op Board has indeed become management.

Negotiations the last time were as bitter as any I've been involved in. We anticipate the next negotiations to be the same way. It's going to be a battle.

The biggest problem with the Co-op has been the "us and them" relationship that exists between the drivers and the inside unions. If anything it's become more bitter since the drivers bought the company. We thought they would be as excited about it as we were. But if anything the exact opposite has occurred; they probably distrust the drivers more than they distrusted Danburg. Back when we came up with the idea to buy the company, we invited their participation immediately, but they were immediately suspicious of it. And I'll tell you what, their contracts expire next September and they're going to go to the Co-op with some pretty stiff demands. And the drivers will be faced once again with the question, will we support the inside workers if they go out on strike?

The way we set it up, was we've said that the first organized inside group that chooses to go along with the Co-op is guaranteed one seat on the board, and if all the inside unions join the Co-op then they're guaranteed two seats on the board. Two out of nine, which is more than fair. Now the Co-op is dismayed that the inside workers have chosen not to go along with it, so there's a movement to write that out of the bylaws.

I look forward to the next negotiations with foreboding and anticipation. What would happen if the inside workers chose to go out on strike? The reality is the Co-op couldn't operate for more than about a week at the present debt level without being in default. So we could be repossessed. I don't know in good conscience if I or any of the drivers could recommend that the Co-op go into default. So we're faced with the horrendous prospect of possibly having to cross a picket line in order to save the Co-op. But my goodness, in these days of inflationary rates, almost anything the inside workers ask will be justifiable. I hope the Co-op finds the money to meet their demands.

The inside people are obviously low paid compared to industry standards. But within the cab industry they're the highest paid in the country. But still they are not paid as high as they would be working the same jobs in other industries. That's another thing we inherited from Danburg, the low pay for inside workers. The money to solve that problem has got to come from the drivers through payoff. Can we reasonably ask our customers to start paying a lot more for cabs?

The drivers once again have to make the decision whose demands are right—the management's or the inside workers'. But we are a union, and union considerations have to come first. But balance that against the fact that we can't operate the Co-op without money. So that's where we are.

WILLIE PERRY: Trips, I take them as they come. I like deliveries. On deliveries, you get paid the same as if you had a passenger, by the mile, and a fifty cent delivery charge. Tips vary. Some days you might get ten bucks, other days you might get less, and other days you might get twenty bucks. This one old lady that rides, she's been riding for years, and no matter what the meter reads, she always makes it double. But, if she gets a driver who's nasty to her, she'll pay just exactly what's on the meter. No tip. Once I took her around town, she had a lot of stops, and when the trip was over the meter read eighteen dollars. She paid thirty-six. It pays to be nice. I used to have a "personal." She was a millionaire, but she's passed away. She used to call out to my house and tell me the night before that she'd need a cab in the morning. I'd get out to her house about seven in the morning and wait maybe two hours till she was ready to go, and I'd get paid for all that time. Sometimes, she'd use me all day, I'd come into the motor, and I'd have just one trip for the whole day. And she always tipped real good.

Not everybody's cut out for cabdriving. A lot of guys come down and they have dreams of making a fortune, but they don't want to drive more than four or five hours, and you can't do it that way. You have to learn the whole city. As long as I've been driving, I can still have trouble finding a place. Denver, they're building so many new areas on the outskirts. There's whole new territories you gotta learn. And the younger guys, they don't like the seniority, some of them. They don't understand. I've seen union meetings where some young guy gets up and he's only been driving like three or four months and he'll make a motion. "Why can't we do away with seniority? Why can't we all be equal?"

You stop and think. The money that went into buying the Co-op came directly from the union. The strike fund.

Nyet, Nyet

"It is the duty of, and a matter of honor for, every able-bodied citizen of the U.S.S.R. to work conscientiously in his chosen occupation, and strictly to observe labour discipline. Evasion of socially useful work is incompatible with the principles of socialist society."
—Article 60
U.S.S.R. Constitution

"Work and praise the day."
—Anglo-American proverb

America has its Protestant work ethic which holds that every responsible person should work for a living. But no article in the Constitution requires a citizen to perform labor that is compatible with society, and American workers are absolutely free *not* to work when they choose. The Soviets Constitution requires that every citizen perform a "socially useful" task, and Article 209 of their Criminal Code gives the government the authority to prosecute violators. Known in some circles as the "parasitism law," Article 209 is aimed at individuals who "freeload" off society: "beggars, vagrants," and what Soviets term "parasites." While many American workers express a desire to rid U.S. society of freeloaders, the Soviet law is probably not the model they would opt for.

With its inclusion of the word parasitism, Article 209 is vague enough to apply to persons who might refuse job assignments and who stay out of work while looking for something to their liking. It also might be applied to those who live off contributions from family and friends while working on their own projects or tending to personal problems. Although many Soviet workers say, quite accurately, that 209 is rarely enforced, the existence of such a nebulously worded law might be questionable from the point of view of civil rights. Like so many American criminal laws, 209 could be applied discriminately.

If a Soviet citizen appears to be leading a "parasitic" existence on a continual basis, that is, repeating a pattern of laying out of work, a warning can be issued requiring him or her to find employment within four weeks' time. "Toilers' deputies," employment offices, are obligated to help men and women who have been thus cautioned to find a socially useful position, and factories and other enterprises are obligated to train them for this. Anyone who refuses to accept work after receiving a warning, who fails to take a medical examination to determine ability to work, may be subject to legal sanctions.

American workers who are laid off, or persons without occupational skills, face unofficial sanctions brought to bear on them by federal and state employment office officials. For while the American unemployed are not actually prosecuted for their condition, they are frequently denied financial assistance. Many U.S. workers accept jobs they do not like because the idea of sponging is repugnant to them and they cannot find anything in their chosen trade. Only the man or woman who has searched in vain for a position in an ever-shrinking job market can appreciate the fine line that exists between freeloaders and those who genuinely need financial aid. Americans fortunate enough to stay employed in jobs they enjoy might conceivably promote a law similar to Article 209, in spite of its dangerously open-ended wording. Meanwhile, no U.S. law prohibits corporations from laying off workers to suit their profit goals.

Panhandlers are not popular in either country. But, as Americans face degrading job layoffs and Soviets confront the prospect of "socially useful" but disagreeable toil, work ethics are undergoing tremendous changes. Millions of Americans, forced into idleness, no longer regard welfare programs as pork-barrel projects, and complain with justification that when they are fired, they are often denied compensation either from the government or from their former employer. Soviets do not have layoff problems, but the opposite dilemma of too much work for too few hands. Their disenchantment with labor is the result of too little free time and lack of job satisfaction. As the imbalance of the distribution of labor's rewards becomes more obvious in the United States—the rich getting richer, the poor getting poorer—the "work is honorable" principle has become a bad joke to many. As Soviet workers become better educated, the demand for more self-fulfilling jobs and a better lifestyle increases, even though the idea of doing socially useful work may appeal to them. Workers in both societies want more, materially and spiritually, out of life. On the brink of the 21st century, job dissatisfaction has thus become a serious concern both for workers and for the societies they sustain.

A new worker is emerging—better educated, healthier, with a more balanced perspective on life's priorities. While keeping in mind the general good of society, this new worker also wants society to respect the happiness of the individual. But society has not kept pace with these men and women, who still face the prospect of taking jobs they

231

do not like or standing in unemployment lines. A work ethic cannot survive where jobs do not exist or are degrading or unrewarding. Today's worker is tired of clumsy excuses for the dismal state of the employment market, and is aware that governments are spending more time and money on military hardware than on industrial health, safety and welfare. The old "work is a patriotic duty" bromide is no longer acceptable unless the officials who preach it are willing to provide suitable rewards for faithful service. Contemporary industrial societies, which still depend on human labor, will either meet the new, justified demands, or will go under.

Sometimes material rewards are not enough to keep an employee happy, and many American and Soviet workers share an ambition to improve their rank. Prestige positions that pay higher wages are in short supply in both countries. American corporations and Soviet enterprises usually select a few fortunate men or women for advancement and begin preparing them well ahead of promotion day. Many American companies pay for vocational training, and Soviet management also provides free education for these people. Usually two or three years before they are about to assume the new position, the chosen worker and Soviet management sign a nonbinding contract which stipulates that the worker will complete all necessary training. However, not every worker is promoted in either system. While both U.S. and Soviet enterprises benefit from this procedure—trained workers can always float around in the labor pool—in the process of final selection and management's mood changes, many wings are clipped. Usually a worker's.

Workers who do not earn enough to support their families and lifestyles often find second jobs to supplement incomes. Second jobs are usually some form of legal employment, but in both countries black markets operate, some directly out of workplaces. Most black market factory operations are run by management-level personnel, for example, executives who have easy access to locked storage rooms and warehouses. But production workers have also been known to engage in pillaging. Almost any item made in a factory can be appropriated by an enterprising employee who knows the layout of the plant and the habits of its security guards. Any streetwise person knows where to sell the loot.

Why do workers steal? Usually because they feel that wages and benefits do not adequately compensate them for their efforts. Since theft in both societies is patently illegal, workers who pilfer are frequently prosecuted as criminals. But employers who commit a form of grand larceny by profiting from the labor of others without paying a fair wage are rarely brought to trial. A criminal law that allows the prosecution of "parasites" might be better applied to the country club and dacha set.

Sometimes a worker becomes so fed up with hard toil and no rewards that the "grass is greener on the other side" syndrome takes hold, and the despairing laborer begins drifting from one job to another in search of a better deal. In both the U.S. and U.S.S.R., it is fairly easy to quit a job. In the Soviet Union, all one must do is give two weeks' notice. In the United States one can simply walk out the door. But sometimes going from job to job only raises new frustrations. Disillusioned, perhaps seeking some intangible spiritual lift, and still clinging to the belief that somewhere the grass must be greener, a worker might decide that another country offers a better shake. Or at least want to find out.

Prior to World War II, boatloads of disillusioned American workers sailed to Eastern European ports and began new lives in the Soviet Union. Today, relatively few U.S. citizens seek residence in the U.S.S.R., partly because they have been given a distorted and somber picture of life there, and also because the Soviet Union accepts very few

233

immigrants. Nikolai Ustinov, the foreign relations official at the VAZ, half jokingly told me, "Send the laid-off auto workers over here to Togliatti. We'll give them jobs and pay them good wages too." But his government might stop such would-be immigrants at the border. Some American workers who have spent a few years in the Soviet Union report positive experiences, but not many have had the opportunity to try this experiment.

In recent decades, a number of Soviet professional men and women and a handful of workers have emigrated to the West. The United States government has encouraged them to speak out against the communist system in exchange for special privileges such as quick access to work permits, guaranteed employment, and sympathetic media coverage arranged through the press contacts of hawks in Washington. Usually scientists or artists, these men and women know that cooperating with the authorities here helps them further their careers and boosts their egos through media notoriety. Hoping to obtain American citizenship, many speak out publicly against the Soviet way of life, unfairly emphasizing its negative aspects. But alert U.S. media consumers quickly spot personal and political bias behind the barrage of reports about these dissidents, and would like to hear from Soviet workers who have come here but who rarely have the opportunity or even the desire to draw attention to themselves. These men and women have to be ferreted out in working class neighborhoods, where a very few now live.

Soviets who have recently arrived in America are usually starry-eyed and, like Americans who first visit the more spectacular cities of the U.S.S.R., lack clear perspective on the realities of life in their new environs. Soviet immigrants who have been in the United States for a while, who have walked enough mean streets to know that none of America's boulevards are paved with gold, usually have a more seasoned outlook and a more balanced picture of the good and bad sides of life in both countries, whether they are dissidents or patriots who regret having left their homeland. An immigrant whose opinions are all positive or all negative rouses suspicion and loses credibility with the public.

Tamara and Ivan are Soviet immigrants, workers, now living in New York. Their stories are as different as their life experiences, and suggest that the search for greener pastures is most often an illusion that results from the wall of hostility dividing two nations. They live in separate neighborhoods and do not know each other. If they met, they would disagree on many issues. Back home, most of their fellow workers would not share their opinions and would be appalled by their decisions to try to solve personal problems by leaving their Motherland. The experience of Tamara and Ivan do not represent those of all Soviet citizens, because life in the U.S.S.R. is as diversified as in the United States. The lives of this man and woman represent the unhappy position of today's Soviet working class immigrants to America. Their precarious and un-privileged position "on the fence" makes them targets for smug attacks against their patriotism, and the cunning games of anti-Soviets who think of them only as cannon fodder that might conveniently be used to discredit the nation they left behind. Political hawks who would use citizens of no country like Tamara and Ivan as pawns in a dangerous game are the promoters of the greener pastures myth. A fence always serves someone's purpose. Often with cruel and tragic results.

Tamara is a pseudonym. Her interview was conducted partly in English, partly in Russian and Ukrainian. A Ukrainian-American friend of hers interpreted. Tamara is in her mid-twenties, an attractive Ukrainian woman who was permitted to emigrate because her husband is a Jew. When she arrived in the United States, she had three dollars and some change in her pocket. Aided by an

Orthodox Jewish organization, Tamara quickly received a Green Card and within one month was employed as a tailor. She has lived in the U.S. for two years.

Tamara

I was born in Ukraine, in Kharkiv, in the fifties. I was born into a family . . . oh, not so well to do. My parents, my mother and stepfather worked in a factory. I had a sister, younger than me. We lived from day to day, maybe from week to week. Childhood, well, there was nothing out of the ordinary about my childhood. Religious? Of course not. It was the Soviet system.

Now, my stepfather's mother, she lived outside the city, in the countryside. She was religious. In the country, people keep religion. In the city, I don't know. Not so much.

Every summer, maybe from eight years old, I went to Pioneer Camp. The Pioneer Camp was connected to the factory where my mother and stepfather worked, so it was possible for me to go. Pioneer Camp was a very good time in my childhood. We did all the things you do at camp, we played sports, we had dances and singing. We made things out of paper, did embroidery, you know, crafts. It was a good time.

I went to public school. The very first day of school, our teacher asked us to name the occupations we would choose for ourselves. We were very young. I answered, "I would like to be a teacher." The first feeling, you know. After that, I don't remember being encouraged to choose a particular occupation. We more or less decided for ourselves.

From fourteen years old, I was working with my mother and stepfather in the factory. I went to school in the evening. In the factory, we were making some electrical parts. Well, I asked special permission from the authorities, to work at fourteen years old. If you are not

236

sixteen, you must ask for permission to work. My family was fairly poor, and we needed the money. So I told the authorities that my parents didn't get along so well, and that if I went to work, it would help relieve some of the stress in the family. It wasn't true, but I told them this so I could go to work.

I made sixty or seventy rubles a month. This was money for my family. There were the four of us, and we didn't live extravagantly, you know. We used the money for food, for some clothes, rent and, well, electricity. Not restaurants, no. Oh, once in a while some movies . . .

My parents belonged to the trade union in the factory. Everyone belongs to the trade union. It is not a law, but, you know, in order to receive privileges you should belong. You paid 7 percent, or maybe just one ruble, I can't remember exactly, of your monthly income for union dues. From sixteen years old, I also belonged to the trade union. It is better to belong, because even if you are from the lowest class, if you knew someone in the trade union, some leaders connected with the authorities, then you could draw some benefits. If you are close to the factory director, say, then you can get special benefits. Vouchers to the health spa, maybe. The trade union is connected to the Party. And to the factory management, certainly.

The factory had its own Pioneer Camp, but it didn't have its own health spa, no. You could buy vouchers to go to the health spa in the city, but it is very difficult to get in. Many people are trying to get in. The trade union gives out vouchers to the health spa, but not very often. Each month, the trade union received maybe three or five vouchers for the health spa, and would distribute these among, oh, about five thousand workers. It was not easy to get a voucher for free. Once in a while, they would single out a worker, somebody who really needed a voucher, and give them one. They would say, "See how we help our workers."

I believed in the Soviet system all through my childhood.

And even when I was working in the factory, I believed. But I changed my mind, maybe from seventeen or eighteen years old. I changed my job . . . I will tell you what happened to me.

I was attending Technicum, the technical institute, studying for, like a business school, studying to be a buyer. When I arrived at the institute, this was the situation. I did my studies in the library, and I wrote my papers in an honest kind of way. But I always received the same kind of marks, always average grades. But other students, they were receiving better grades, even without reading the required material. The teacher would give them good grades, or she would allow them to rewrite a lesson, she would help them. These students were bringing gifts to the teacher, something in deficit, say shoes, or a jacket or a dress. Among this, I had an incident where I got sick right before an exam. I missed three exams in all, and had to make them up. The make up exam was on a one-to-one basis with the teacher. So that was a difficult position for me.

When other students are taking exams around the same time you are, you can maybe get help from them, study together. You know, help each other with the answers. But when you go to face the teacher, on a one-to-one basis for the exam, if you can't answer the question, that means you don't know the material. So with no other students to study with me, I was worried about my exams. A girl suggested to me, "Bring the teacher some cologne!" I asked her, "Who told you this will work?" She said, "Everybody does it!" So I did it. I bought her perfume. She didn't ask me anything, and she gave me a very good grade. I got my diploma.

It seems to me very young children learn this from knee high.

While I was studying at business college, I worked as a cashier. I was waiting for a better job to open up, a job as a buyer in a store. But because I was not active in Komsomol, a good job was not available to me. If I would become a Komsomol Youth, follow the Party line and progress along that path, I would probably have got a better job.

Every youth must belong to Komsomol. Only a few avoided it. You must belong to Komsomol until you are twenty-eight. * Then you decide if you want to become a Party member. Only by changing jobs all the time can you avoid Komsomol. They can't keep track of you so well if you are changing jobs all the time.

I was twenty when I got married. The girls realize that it is better to marry when you are young, because by the time you get your own flat, you'll be thirty or thirty-five. If you get married at thirty, by the time you have two or three children and receive a flat, you might be dead! This is why women have only one or two children. Not enough income and not enough living space.

We lived in a flat with my husband's parents. It was very small. The kitchen and toilet, it was half ours and half for the neighbors. If guests came to visit me, I couldn't have them in the kitchen, because it wasn't really ours. Well, if you have a friendly neighbor, it's okay, you can invite your guest and your neighbor won't mind. But in general, people aren't so friendly, because nobody likes living in such cramped conditions.

We had our wedding in our flat. Twenty-five people in that small space. We extended the table into the balcony.

My family also lived in very small quarters. Being married, I couldn't bring my husband there, to live like married people and maybe start a family. My parents had twenty-five square meters of space, and four people were living there. For each person, you are required to have five

* No law requires young people to join Komsomol. Tamara is implying that social pressures are exerted, however.

square meters of living space. This is considered sanitarily permissible. If you have over five persons living in one flat, then you must have seven square meters for each person. So this was the situation: if I brought my husband to live at my parents' flat, that would be five persons in twenty-five square meters of space. This would be sanitarily permissible. But very crowded, and not so good for a young couple just married. But, because it was sanitarily permissible, we would not be eligible to apply for a larger flat. So, when my husband's brother got married and moved out of his parents' flat, we moved in. And those quarters were very small. We applied for a flat of our own, but didn't receive one. So we lived with his parents.

I was not happy. I wanted more out of life than my husband did. I began confiding my feelings to my parents. I always talked to them about everything. I talked to them about the idea of emigrating, and I mentioned this to my mother-in-law also. But when we were first married, we didn't think about this. We were just working, making a living, and trying to get by.

You have a work book that you take when you apply for a job. This is required. Without it, you can't get a job. Like, when you are looking for a job just after finishing school, you take along your diploma. Same with the work book. But say you've been out of school two or three years, and you don't have a work book. Then you go somewhere to apply for a job. They would want to know how you subsisted in those two or three years. If I said my family supported me, they would want to know where my family got the money to support me. If I can't show evidence that my family supported me, or that I worked somewhere, then it must have been black market. I would get a year and a half in prison, or in a labor camp. Then it would be marked in my work book. Then nobody would want to hire me.

Black market? I would say 90 percent of the people worked on the black market.

We also had passports, internal passports. And like in the work book, your nationality was listed. If you are a Tatar, or a Jew, if you are a minority nationality, then you can't receive so easily a good position. If it shows in your work book that you are a minority nationality, it is very difficult to raise your status. Now myself, being Ukrainian, and if I had also been active in Komsomol, then I could have received a very good job. As it was, I could not get a job as a buyer, although I had studied and received a diploma.

If I wanted to travel by train, say to visit a friend in another city far away, I would not have to show my passport. But if I went by airplane, then I would have to show my passport. Why, I don't know. Maybe because air travel is so expensive, and they want to know who you are, how did you receive the money to buy airfare. You must show your passport when you travel by air, but not when you take the train. I don't know why. To me, it's just a guess. I can't rationalize it. Everything possible is being supervised.

We had a friend who was a communist. He was a very close friend. Because of him, we were able to do things, to receive certain advantages. We could get tickets to go places, because he could help us. This was lucky for us, it made things a little better. We could go places we couldn't otherwise go.

Even though I had criticisms of the system, I could not raise them. If I were to criticize the system, the politics, or something I did not like, I might get into trouble. Another person might decide to take advantage of this, to show his "patriotism" by writing a letter exposing me. Such a person might receive special privileges. At work or at school, I would never make criticisms of the system. But among my close friends, maybe at my birthday party, we would talk about these things. If I had a nosy neighbor, then I would ask my friends to talk quieter.

My husband and I began collecting letters and photographs from people who had emigrated. From outside the Soviet Union. Describing life outside the Soviet Union. We could not believe it. I was very skeptical, I didn't believe it was better in other places, in other countries. I spoke to my mother-in-law about it. She said, "Even if you have to wash toilets, to take the lowest position in society, what do you have to lose?" I was not firmly convinced that we would be better off in another country. But I thought to myself, "If I am going to end here, then I can just as well end there." There was nothing to lose. When we couldn't get an apartment of our own, my husband and I decided together that we would emigrate.

We waited one year after we applied. Being Ukrainian, I was not allowed to leave. But because my husband is a Jew, he was allowed to leave, and since we were married, I could go also. The only way he could emigrate was going through Israel. Outside of Germans and Jews, Poles and Polish Jews, no one can leave. My idea was, that after I emigrated—we had decided to go to the U.S.—I would send for my mother.

But she died. One year after we left. She was forty-seven. She died of heart disease. Then my stepfather became ill right after that, with cancer, and he might be dead by now. I don't know. My sister was all alone, so she got married, and she had two children. Her husband became a drunkard. It's been over a year now since I've heard from her. She never had anything good to write about. Maybe not all her letters were censored. We had so much tragedy in the family, we never had much political to write about. We just wrote about our hardships. Before my mother died, she wrote me a letter. She had read all my letters and looked at the photographs I had sent her from here. She wrote me a letter and said, "Now I believe it's better for you. It's like in a fairy tale." This was the last letter before she died.

It was heart disease. She was only forty-seven, and she had been ill for maybe seven, eight years. She was being treated in a hospital, but by then it really didn't matter anymore. I received a letter that she was preparing for an operation, but she died before she received admission to the cardiovascular unit of the hospital. My stepfather finally got the admission card, and was coming to the hospital with it, but by then she was already transferred to intensive care. He called the hospital that morning, and was told that my mother's condition was stable, that her blood pressure, everything was stable. He was going to come the next evening, but transportation was difficult, so he telephoned the hospital to say he would come the following day. They told him, "She's already dead."

She was walking around the ward, seeming quite normal, and she sat down on the bed to rest. She sighed and said, "How I would like to see my grandchild." And she died then.

I got a telegram after they buried her. It was not possible for me to return. Automatically you lose your citizenship when you leave. So now, only if I become a U.S. citizen could I go back as a tourist. Even then, I think it would be dangerous. It seems to me, I'm not a citizen . . . no, not of the Soviet Union, and not yet of the U.S.

We went to Austria first. There we were greeted by representatives of Israel. We said, "Thank you very much, but we are going to America. We have friends there who are helping us, who are willing to sponsor us there." We sent a request to be allowed into the U.S., and we waited in Europe. We saw several countries.

After we came here, our friend who is a communist was writing to us. We corresponded. America, my first impression—crazy! So we wrote back and forth, how we were living, how things were for us getting settled here. Then a friend of ours went from the U.S., as a tourist, to visit the Soviet Union. She looked up our friend. And this is what he told her. The authorities, the KGB, had called on him. They asked him, "Why do you want to correspond outside the Soviet Union?" He said, "Because they are my friends. I care for them. And so I will keep writing to them and receiving their letters." But we have not heard from him since then, for many months now.

My sister's husband became a drunkard. Before that, he was a complacent, nice person. When we asked him, in letters, "Why did you start drinking?", he answered, "What else could I do? There's nothing for me to be happy about. When I drink, I receive two hundred grams of happiness. Then I don't have to think about tomorrow."

Now I am working here in the U.S. We had to get Green Cards. I have a job, I work as a fitter, a tailor, for a good company. And I am studying in the evening, like I was doing when I was fourteen and working in the factory. Working in the day and studying in the evenings. For me, speaking for myself, it is better for me here. But sometimes it is difficult, like when I heard that some people back home said something not so good about me. They were close friends, very close. And they wrote a letter saying that I was not a patriot. That I was a traitor. They say the system is for workers, but the system did not work for me. There are members of the Party, the Party rules the system, and there are some who do not care about workers. And I am afraid if I talk about this that something might happen to our relatives back home. I hope one day to bring my sister over here. She is having a hard time, being divorced and with two children.

Women—in the Soviet Union it is the same as in the U.S. Women have equal opportunity. If a woman conducts herself well, she can advance in her job, she can become a supervisor or a director. There is equal opportunity for women.

Abortion? Some are legal, some not legal. Birth control pills are not common, almost no one uses them. The most common way of not having children is abortion. Like my mama. She had abortions. Many women have them. During her childbearing years, a woman has maybe five, ten, twenty-five abortions. I know that my mama had at least three abortions, the legal maximum. But the abortions a woman has that are not reviewed, that are through illegal means, is another thing. Many young women die in infirmaries because they got illegal abortions and became infected. Bad abortions.

Right after I was married, I became a little sick, just with the flu. My boss had done some favors for authorities at the hospital, so I was able to stay in the hospital for a few days. Of course, later I repaid my boss with some gifts. While I was in the hospital, I noticed in the ward that there was a great turnover of women and girls, married and unmarried, who would come in for one or two days or a few hours to have an abortion. They would take a leave of absence from work, give some excuse, and come have an abortion. Off the records. The hospital cleaning staff would come in and clean up after them. The doctors would take the money under the table. Black market abortions.

Only now have I begun to understand about this. I remember an incident when I was a young child. My mama took me with her to this apartment complex and left me outside. She said, "You play out here for a little while. Later, your father will come and pick us up." And my mother went inside. Later, my father came, and I saw my mother was in a very weak condition. We took a taxi home. Then my mother was sick for a while after that. Now I've come to a realization that quite probably my mama went for an abortion.

There's a saying, "You better shape the metal while it's hot." It's easier to do abortions in the first three months when it's legal. But if you've waited, and it's too late to get into a hospital for a legal abortion, you go to a midwife or a doctor on the black market. Sometimes you have to wait, and it costs money to have abortions in this primitive fashion. But you can get one.

Everywhere, *everywhere,* in all forms of media, it is written that the Soviet woman should have more children. For new generations. And yet they support abortions. It's a dilemma. I am speaking for myself, just for myself. Now that I have become a woman, I can't understand this reasoning.

Many Soviet women cannot understand their government's policy of promoting abortions as a "preventive" birth control measure. Soviet medicine has generally rejected oral contraceptives, saying long before American medical experts would admit it that they can be extremely damaging to a woman's health. However, Soviet science has failed to invent and distribute a safe, convenient method of birth control. In the United States, some 33 percent of women practicing birth control still use oral contraceptives. For every 1,000 pregnancies in the U.S., about 25 abortions are performed. In the U.S.S.R., oral contraceptives are rarely used, diaphragms and IUDs are not easily acquired (U.S. and other foreign manufactured diaphragms and IUDs are popular black market items), and most importantly, a Soviet woman usually has several abortions during her childbearing years. For every 1,000 Soviet pregnancies, about 115 abortions are performed. In spite of claims that the government's abortion clinics are safe and comfortable, practicing abortion as "contraceptive" must have negative effects. Vasectomies, I am told by women who know, are "unheard of," and couples are not fond of using prophylactics.

Contrary to Tamara's statement that a Soviet woman is allowed only three abortions, the law in fact contains no such stipulation. However, each abortion is supposed to be recorded by her physician, and after three or four, the doctor may decide she should have no more. In that case, there is no recourse other than the rhythm method of preventive contraception, or black market doctors who perform abortions that are not "reviewed," or recorded in the medical records. For these operations, the woman pays a high price—in rubles and in her physical and emotional health.

Tamara told me that she suspects her mother's poor health was caused by multiple abortions she had during childbearing years; that she does not accept the official diagnosis of the illness that caused her mother's death.

Two days after I interviewed Tamara, she received a letter from her sister. Her stepfather had died.

Seven years ago, Ivan, a Russian Jew, gave up a good job and a comfortable lifestyle in Leningrad, packed a few belongings and left his homeland. Unlike Soviet dissidents who say they emigrate because of religious persecution, anti-Semitism, or other violations of human rights, Ivan was happy with his lot in Leningrad. He left neither for political reasons nor as a dissident—Ivan wanted to "learn the truth," to get a glimpse of other pastures and see for himself what the grass looked like. In order to embark on a journey without time limits and other visa restrictions, he was told by Soviet authorities that he had to give up his citizenship. Because one of his parents was a Jew, he was allowed to emigrate.

Ivan visited many Western European countries before deciding to go to America. He told me he has had "probably a hundred" jobs in his lifetime. He is in his late forties and has lived in the U.S. for about seven years. His interview was conducted in English.

Ivan

I live in United States. *Da,* right here. But I am Soviet citizen, *da.* Why am I here in U.S.? I will tell you.

Look, in Soviet Union, what does a worker have? First of

all, he pays only small rent, say on average, twelve rubles a month. His health care—for free. His vacation, if he is good worker, if he does good job for a year—everything paid. Bread costs very little. He can live comfortably, eat well. Food, well, it only depends on your stomach, everyone has different appetite. Theater, cinema, his union gives him vouchers, he can see films and fine concerts for free. Censored? *Konechno, konechno!* Of course! Who could stand these American movies? And on the job, look how different Soviet worker is from U.S. worker!

Look, here is Soviet worker, he feels like sitting down on his job, he feels like resting. Here comes the boss, and what does Soviet worker do? He does nothing. Boss says, "Hey, why you aren't working? Get up and go to work!" Soviet worker says, *"Nyet, nyet.* Go away, leave me alone. I am resting." Now you take American worker. If the boss sees American worker not working, maybe talking to other workers, boss thinks it's conspiracy. "Get back to work!" And what does American worker do? He tiptoes back to his job! So you see, for the worker, it is better in Soviet Union.

Me, I grew up in Soviet Union. At fifteen years old, I was a tramp. You know what a tramp is? Like a vagabond. I traveled all over U.S.S.R. Not stealing. If I needed food, I went to communal kitchen. I say, "Please, give me piece of bread, a few potatoes." They give me. No problem.

I live for many years in Leningrad. I have good job, very good job, and I work as a hustler too. You know what hustler is? Just like here in the U.S. I work on the black market. See, everybody in Soviet Union uses black market? Why is that? Look, average Soviet worker makes maybe one hundred twenty rubles a month. Every few months he has opportunity for raise in his pay. Maybe fifty rubles each time. That is enough, enough to live because everything costs so little. Rent . . . nothing. Even poorest workers, they make seventy rubles a month. On seventy rubles you can live in Soviet Union. Because rent is so low, you see? But yes, everybody tries to find other work, other ways to make money. Why? I will tell you.

You see how well Soviet people dress. A pair of Soviet-made boots might cost only twenty-five rubles. Not expensive. But people don't like them. But a pair of Swedish boots or Finnish boots, very good boots, very beautiful, might cost ninety. And you can't get these in stores. On black market, best Swedish boots cost one hundred fifty. You see these nice boots on people. Soviet people are well dressed, but see, they don't like Soviet-made clothes. So they buy imported clothes on black market.

There are other ways to make money. Stealing, *da*. Stealing from where you work. The guy who works in a paper mill, he'll steal some paper. Later he can sell it somewhere. Waiters, they can fool customers. Customer orders bottle of very fine old cognac. The waiter, he brings cheap bottle, keeps fine old cognac, hides it in his coat. Later, he sells it. Many workers steal from their jobs, and I have seen this is also true in United States. Everywhere, everywhere in New York, I see people stealing. But who steals? I see bosses stealing, *da*, here in U.S. I have many jobs, many jobs in U.S., and this I have seen. And the worker steals too, American worker. But why? Don't you know? Because he need to. Soviet worker, he maybe steal, *da*, from job, he maybe steal to have nice things. But not for, how you say, surviving.

Work book? *Da*, Soviet worker has this. What for is this book? Look, say worker want to change job, go from one job to another job. This is record, worker takes book to new boss. Worker says, "Here is my work record, here is what work I can do." Boss reads this book, maybe book says many good things about worker. Boss knows this is good worker, gives him good job. And when he retires, this book helps worker get pension. Work book is good for Soviet worker.

When you travel in Soviet Union, internal travel, you

don't need special papers. *Nyet, nyet.* You can go anywhere, anywhere you want to go. And if you want to take little vacation, go maybe to fishing, you can take train a very long way for only two rubles. To beautiful, beautiful places. Try to do this here in U.S. You can't do it. *Da,* every Soviet citizen has internal passport. This is never used. Only when you move from one city to another city to live. Then you must have passport stamped. Say you live in Moscow, you want to move to Leningrad. Okay, when you go to Leningrad, they stamp a new mark on passport. But for no other reason this passport is used. It is true, you must sometimes show passport for travel near border republics, *da,* also sometimes for airplane travel. But in Soviet Union, everyone is free to go where they want, and I know because I have done this during my life.

Have you seen the places for rich people? We have them. Take Estonia. The whole northern half of Estonia, it is rich people. The southern half, below the lake, that is all poor people. And the rich people, they are wearing jewels, they all have *dachas* in countryside. Outside Moscow and the big cities you can see these *dachas.* They have it better than workers in these things. A bureaucrat, he makes maybe lower wage than a worker, this happens often. But a bureaucrat, he might have opportunity to enjoy some things, maybe he manages factory and he steals from it, maybe from black market sales . . . but not all bureaucrats, only some. It is another thing like in U.S., some people take, how you say, advantage of their job, their position. *Da,* we have poor people, not so rich people. But do you see poor, poor people like in New York streets? *Nyet.* Do you see criminals, drug addicts, people with guns? Crime? *Nyet.* Not in Soviet Union. And the streets, they are clean, always clean, not filthy like in U.S.

Anyone who wants can work in Soviet Union. Anyone. Here in U.S., look at me. I have been here many years, and look at me now. In Soviet Union, I lived like playboy. I had fine clothes, very fine clothes. Now look what I wear!

I am a traveler. I have to see places, I want to learn the truth. So I travel. When I leave Soviet Union, they tell me, "Please, sign this paper. You agree to no more be citizen of Soviet Union." Everybody signs this paper now if they leave. If you want to leave, "Please go. But don't take any money, you can't take any money. Here is your luggage and take a few gifts if you want. Please, if you want to leave, go." I wanted to see the world, not just sit and think how good the price of bread is in Leningrad. So I travel, many countries. And I come here to U.S. I do not live well here. *Nyet,* Soviet Union does not allow me to go home. So I am here, see, now I am Russian-American worker.

Today things are good in Soviet Union. Maybe not before, maybe not under Stalin. But how do you say, you can't generalize. I was just a small child in late thirties. I remember only what I have learned in books and heard. It was very bad in some places with Stalin. *Da,* there were camps in Siberia, and many people were killed. But look, today is today, things are better. Khrushchev got pensions for workers. And now today when a person is arrested, he goes to labor camp. He can walk around, free to come and go. Maybe they move him from Moscow to labor camp in Siberia. But look, he can eat three meals a day, he can even have health food if he wants! He can go where he wants to. Political prisoners, *da.* Also criminals. But in U.S. you also have criminals and political prisoners. And how do they live? In little holes, little iron cubicles. No food. Cruelty. Terrible. It is better even for prisoner in Siberia. I have friends, they tell me they like to live in Soviet labor camps, they are comfortable places to live.

Jews, if they want to leave Soviet Union, "Please go." But not everybody can go. You see, many people work for defense, for military. There are secret bases—you have them in U.S. too—technology institutes. If you work there, the government gives you papers to sign. There are three levels. Depending on your work. Government says, "Please, sign this paper." This paper says you will never be a tourist, never leave country again. They don't want military secrets to get out. They say, "Please, sign this paper if you want to work here." And if they sign, and two years later, say they want to travel. "Please, look at this paper. Isn't this your signature?" So you see, to protect military secrets, they can't go. These are the people who can't leave Soviet Union. Other kinds of people leave all the time. Yes, there is a quota, you might have to wait. But if you want to leave, "Please, go."*

It is impossible to generalize about Soviet Union. There are so many different people, so many Ukrainians, Russians, Siberians, Azerbaijani, Uzbek, Latvian . . . so many, how you say, cultures. Different things in different places. And you can't say everything is just equal for everybody. Take the worker, for example. You can't say every Soviet worker has it good, every Soviet worker has it bad. Ridiculous. It is just like in U.S. Say you have a husband, he is drinker, heavy drinker. He don't feel like going to work, he lay around the house all the time. It is hard life for you. Or say you have very good husband, very good provider, he love you very much and take care of you. Then you have good life. *Nyet, nyet,* you can't generalize about the worker. Not even in U.S.

Today, what is most important is not where a person lives. Not in what country. World is too small for that. Ideology is what is important. If you have same ideology, then okay. Maybe Soviet Union and China will be allies soon. Against Western aggression. It is very simple, the ideologies are very similar. And you know yourself how governments, they change friends. But I think sometimes that Russia will be destroyed. I am very sad about this.

* This statement is somewhat inaccurate. Today, non-Jews are rarely allowed to leave the Soviet Union, unless, like Tamara, they are married to Jews.

I hear American people say Soviet Union is controlled society. Ha! If Americans only look very close, they will see control, right here in U.S. Who runs America? You ask me, an immigrant, this question? I will tell you what I think. The very rich. Everything here is controlled by the very rich, but you see what happens? Rich Americans are very clever. They use propaganda to make people think they are free. How much freedom does American worker have? Tell me that. Here, look at me. Now I am American worker. Can I afford just nice, simple, decent life? *Nyet*. Because to live in, how you say, dignity . . . this is bought with dollars.

I have a father, but I never saw him. He went away in the war and never came back. It was hard for our people, the war. I was just young boy then, but I know. I have been married, *da*. Now I am not married. Just trying to make a living. If I could, if Soviet Union would let me, I'd go back home. Before the cataclysm. I feel it is coming.

Moscow Sous-Chef

Twenty-first-century woman will owe her improved job status to the working women of today. But this future gratitude is not what motivates contemporary women, American or Soviet, in their struggle for equality both on the job and in society. Today's women are driven by a spirited refusal to accept a minor role in societies where women constitute the majority of the population.

The United States Constitution contains no specific guarantee of equal rights for women; the Soviet Constitution has this provision. Both countries have laws prohibiting job discrimination—laws that are supposed to protect women, minority nationalities and ethnic minority groups. Yet both in the U.S. and U.S.S.R., women, particularly women of minority nationalities, remain in the passenger seat of the vehicles that carry society along Progress Road.

In the U.S.S.R., there are over twelve hundred basic trades. Two hundred of them are closed to women. The official explanation is that they involve physical strain harmful to a woman's health. This concern is refreshing, but unfortunately it does not carry over into ruble figures.

Most of the occupations on the "no women allowed" list are the highest paying ones, "hero occupations" that are generally speaking considered men's work. Textile work, which ranks among the most dangerous occupations in terms of health and safety, is not considered a "hero occupation," is poorly remunerated, and is dominated by female workers. No constitutional clause, it seems, guarantees equality.

Soviets lead the world in the training and employment of women airline pilots and even sent women cosmonauts into orbit. The government encourages women to take up professional occupations, especially in science and medicine. A high percentage of Soviet factory managers are women. As workers, Soviet women receive wages equal to those men earn in the same job category—equal pay for equal work is a reality in the U.S.S.R. As citizens, Soviet women enjoy equal status except in some areas such as health, where the question of safe birth control measures has been seriously neglected by the state. In a male-dominated society, Soviet women are treated much like their American sisters; they are expected to maintain the household and usually an outside job too.

Today's U.S. labor laws allow a woman to apply for work in any occupation that suits her fancy. But even though the regulations prohibit racial or sexual discrimination in hiring, women are often turned away from jobs simply because they are female. A strong rebellion has been waged against the pillars of male-oriented society, and working women are gradually winning the struggle for equal pay for equal work. They are also gaining entry into trades previously reserved for men. Still, American working women, like Soviet women, are not always treated equally on the job, either by their supervisors or their male co-workers. Women have made gains on the homefront too, and it is no longer uncommon to hear a husband admitting he cleaned the house, washed the dishes or vacuumed the carpet. As in the Soviet Union, single mothers probably face more obstacles in their day-to-day lives than other women, and since child care is more expensive in the U.S., an American single mother might have more financial worries than her Soviet counterpart.

Working women have spoken out against the stereotypes of them portrayed on television sit-coms, and have always seemed to have perfect vision when targeting those responsible for their unequal status in society. The working woman has always known, both in the U.S. and U.S.S.R., that her toughest adversary is not her fellow workingmen, but the men, and in rare cases the women, who control the workplaces, wages, goods and services, and the governments that are leading workers into the 21st century. Or taking them for a ride.

Some women have managed to find employment in occupations once reserved for men, in jobs that allow, even demand, that a worker be creative. The mysterious world of the sous-chef, behind the swinging kitchen doors in top restaurants, has been a jealously guarded male domain. In an era plagued with uninteresting, uncreative, tedious positions, a good job is hard to find. In a town called Moscow, one courageous woman has managed to get her foot in the kitchen door. Lynn Drake is Moscow's sous-chef, and she likes her work.

The first time I saw Lynn, she was sitting next to me on a train. She was a pretty woman, with light brown hair that framed high cheekbones and a fair, clear complexion. She had no discernible accent. I asked her what she did for work.

"I'm a sous-chef," she said.

"What's a sous-chef do?"

"A sous-chef works in haute cuisine."

I thought that over for a while and wished the woman would speak to me in English. I asked Lynn Drake where she lived.

"Moscow," she told me. "I moved to Moscow to accept this position as sous-chef."

"Really?" I said, getting more interested. "What can you tell me about Moscow?"

Lynn Drake was surprised. "You mean you've never been there?" Then she told me about Moscow.

Lynn Drake

Moscow borders on the edge of Appaloosa [horse] country. Moscow, Idaho, that is. It's a region of rolling hills. All in farming. It's dry land farming, there's no irrigation in our area. Our rainfall is sufficient to survive. Most of the crops are wheat and lentils. Some peas. Within about a mile there is hill country which sports pine trees. There's a small mountain range called the Moscow Mountains. And there is the Coeur d' Alene Mountain range, where logging takes over. It's about twenty miles away from Moscow, but you'll see a few logging trucks. But it's not your typical logging community—those are back in the mountains. Moscow is right in between flatland farming and rolling hills with different colored fields. Then the mountains start up.

From most of Moscow, you can see the mountain range. It's one of those nice gentle ones. There's a large mountain and three smaller ones, just nicely in proportion, tailed down. It makes a very nice view. The apartment where I live is up on the ridge of a hill and I have a beautiful layout, right out my windows, of the Moscow Mountains. I can see a bit of sunset, and lightning storms out in the mountains. I'm much happier where I can see the mountains, because that's what I'm used to. I grew up around mountains.

I live alone. With two cats. Nobody else will put up with me. With all my hours of work.

Moscow, as the story goes, was settled by immigrants. The largest faction were from Russia. They called the area

257

after their home, Moscow. Instead of Moscow, we pronounce it Mos*go,* which makes it different in people's minds. Somehow Moscow became the official name, it got put down on the maps. Now there aren't any pure Russians here. There might be some of Russian descent mixed in with the population. About twenty thousand people live in Moscow.

We have two universities in this area, really small, ivyleague colleges. People are considered conservative. We did not get into the protest marches, we did not have a lot of that going on when there were problems elsewhere. The Pacific Northwest is somewhat isolated in many ways. We don't get the recessions other parts of the country get. We don't get inflation rates and a lot of things like this. We also don't get a lot of the positive things, name performers and interesting things going on, but in its own way, it's well trafficked. Because of the universities, you have a large international community. It's very common to see people in saris walking down the street. The mixture of many languages is nothing to blink your eyes at. You never really had the idea of a small town. You have three different factions in the area around Moscow, Idaho and Pullman, Washington—which is right over the border. You have the business community, the university community, and the farming community. The university figures the farmers don't know what they are doing out there. But a lot of the farmers have college degrees tucked away in the bottom drawer. They farm because it's far more lucrative than whatever else they could do with their degrees. They are the ones with homes in Palm Springs, they are the ones who go to Hawaii and Acapulco, not the college professors. These are the big wheat farmers in the Moscow area.

Probably the only faction not represented in the area is Native Americans. Although there's a tribal reservation within sixty or so miles. There are several reservations in

the district, and many of the towns have Indian names—
Spokane, Walla Walla. But Native Americans were never
much involved in the community. All the nationalities
have been accepted very well in the college communities.
When I was in high school in Pullman, there were two
students, one from Pakistan, the other from India. This
was when the war about Kashmir was going on. These two
walked down the hall talking about it. Arguing a little, but
it was part of our state of life, pretty much.

We moved in far more of an intellectual level of things
than most everybody we socialized with. My friends had
professors for fathers, like I did. Talk often got very
technical within their own little fields. That's what we
grew up around. I went two years to Eastern Washington
State, and took a few courses at Washington State University. But to my father's displeasure, I haven't bothered to
finish. It wasn't, I felt, a very good education I was getting,
and I wasn't particularly interested . . . I was in Home
Economics, which wasn't all that good. But you were
expected to go to a four year college. You couldn't go to a
trade school, which is what I should have done. There was
an excellent baking school at Spokane Community College
and I wish I had gone there now.

I've always been in food service. I started when I was
fourteen, I went to work in a drive-in, a hamburger stand.
The owners promoted me, and when they went into the
restaurant business, I worked in the restaurant as assistant manager. I worked for them fifteen years, but a lot of
things changed and the relationship was sort of strained. I
kind of went out and began looking for another job. I
worked three years for another restaurant, but when they
went to serving fast food, Mexican style, I left the job. It
was good Mexican food, but . . .

I had a nice résumé made out, the first one I ever had to
do. I went to a job interview, the first formal job interview
in my life, and I had been working eighteen years. I was

about thirty-one at the time. This was American Management Company, their Western Frontiers Incorporated chain. It's a food service and lodging chambers, headquartered in Coeur d' Alene. I got a job as a banquet chef at their Moscow convention center. I work for an executive chef, who is of the old school of thinking. Women don't really belong in the kitchen. They can't be sous-chefs. Only problem is, there are not many people out there who can qualify for this job. So he just gets around it by calling me a banquet chef instead of a sous-chef. A banquet chef means actually a full chef who is working banquet, where a sous-chef means assistant chef. So even though he gets around it in his own mind, it's giving me technically more of an elevation in position, and the rest of us all know the difference. As a banquet chef, I'm responsible for the coordination and preparation of all banquet foods that go through our facility. As a sous-chef, I'm responsible for the day management of my shift, management of our kitchen facilities. Then I'm in charge of the cooks.

I have a crew that prepares food with me, and I do take an active part in the preparation, because I prefer to. In the executive chef's thinking, a sous-chef does not really prepare food. But that's the part I enjoy, therefore I do it. Our executive chef does not prepare food. He will show us a few things, or tell us, but his position, in his way of thinking, is more of an adviser. He used to say that in his other operation he knew the names of his sous-chefs, but not the rest of the kitchen staff.

We have a twenty-four-hour restaurant. Family dining. We also have a haute cuisine dining room that is open only for lunch and dinner. The menu features Scampi, Veal Oscar, and, of course, steak. Can't get away without steak and potatoes no matter where you go. Oyster cocktails, things like this. Then we have a banquet room, and the menu is a little more exclusive. We have roast beef, always served with a baked potato and full garnish. We do a lot of prime rib, and plated dinners for our steaks. And we do buffets.

All of us, including the executive chef, work for a corporation, They set a great number of the rules and regulations that we work by. Their operations are the same in every restaurant in their chain, at least in the family dining area. So a person could go to one restaurant, find something they like, and be able to find it in the other twelve, exactly the same. The haute cuisine dining room is much more the executive chef's free choice. We do a great deal of sauté work and fancier type items. The banquet work is a mixture of both. This is where we can be creative and let our staff have some fun. You can carve a watermelon in the shape of a whale or Viking ship, or you can take mashed potatoes—it sounds very odd, but it works well—and you tint them. Using a spoon, you curl them around an orange, and they turn into a rose. Only problem is, people try playing with them. They can't figure out what it is and play with them. There's another process, and it sounds equally odd; you take very thin slices of raw potatoes, drop them into a solution of vinegar and food coloring, and let them sit for about six hours until they turn rubbery. They won't discolor then, they're a little bit preserved. Then you curl these up into roses, dip them in clear gelatin, and you have this beautiful rose for decorative work. But I don't use these very often because people tell me they "taste very good." Can you imagine, people eat them? So I would rather not put them out because people who try eating them might get a very odd idea of what constitutes the food we serve.

I would probably make a fool of myself if I cooked for people at home. My ideas and my timing, which are important in cooking, are set for large quantity work. It's a very easy matter to prepare vegetables for two hundred people, if you have the equipment. But fixing them at home for one or for four, everything is changed. At home, I don't have the convection ovens, tilt skillets, and all the big equipment to work with. I'm more comfortable with mass work.

For a banquet of two hundred people, I'd probably put on a crew of three, maybe four, depending on what other business is going on in the building that night, and myself. I would take an active part, so you would have let's say four people working for four hours on the kitchen side. Serving time, we pull other people from other areas for those eight minutes, and they help to serve the meal, and usually a convention center staff, with their manager on duty, for two hundred people, would run somewhere in the neighborhood of five or six people. So you've got, with your dishwashers included, you've got twelve people, let's say. And about what an individual is paying for that meal, with the prime rib dinner, which is a seven ounce serving of meat, and all the other items, at current prices is ten dollars and ninety-five cents. That includes their beverage, dessert and salad, and their entree meal.

The eruption of Mt. St. Helens caused a rather drastic event. We could not run our overhead fan systems, because the intake that feeds your fan system was drawing in the volcanic ash. Therefore we had to shut them down. That meant that all gas units in the building had to be shut down, and all our cooking facilities are gas, it's the most efficient and best cooking fuel. We have two electric ovens, and those were the only units we could use. Therefore the menu had to go cold, but then as soon as the wind died, the volcanic ash would settle, you could turn back on your gas systems, back on your fans. When the ash started swirling around again, then you went back to a cold menu. So for days we would go back and forth between cold and hot menus, as the weather conditions existed.

There are always instances of problems that you have to cope with. If the delivery truck breaks down with the roast beef, which takes approximately ten hours to cook, and they are thirty miles in the country—we cook at very low temperatures, that's why it takes so long. The beef is usually a forty-five-pound piece of meat that will feed about seventy to eighty people, and when the truck breaks down, you must get that meat in the oven. Say it's thirty miles in the country, that means you jump in the car and you go get the meat out of the truck, and get it into town, and get it cooking. Otherwise your banquet will fall apart.

I have heard about an incident, luckily we've never had it here, six hundred people turned up for a dinner, but the kitchen didn't know about them. But this hasn't ever happened to us, thank goodness.

One of the things about being a sous-chef is that there are always—you answer questions. That is almost your main job, being sous-chef. You are there to make decisions if the executive chef is not. You make the decisions, answer the questions, give the directions. There's always something coming up. The dishwasher coming in, he's fairly new, telling you there's something wrong with the dish machine. The soap indicator is going off constantly, it just isn't getting its soap. That's because he forgot to fill the machine with water after he cleaned it out. There's no water in there for the sensor to see if there's soap or not. So you have to explain to him, if he's new on the job. You have to deal always with—luckily there have never been any serious injuries, but there are minor ones you have to take care of, watch over.

Coordination between staff is important. We are very much departmentalized. We do not have jurisdiction over the waitresses, and yet of course there is interaction between the waitresses and the cook. And sometimes there's the need to mediate relations and try to keep it settled down and the operation running smoothly. Once, the waitresses demanded that their order was never put up, and the cook says they have put it up, somebody else took it. Both of them are under a great deal of pressure, and your job is to try to keep the staff smoothed out and functioning. There's a great deal of pressure on each side. There's a time factor they must meet. I would figure though, my philosophy is that the mistakes are not important, the corrections are. Everybody does make mistakes. We don't want people just constantly making mistakes they have to correct. But if they make one, what counts is how easily they get it corrected without causing a domino factor. If you make one error, sometimes it gets you flustered, and you tend to make several errors in a row. So the corrections are far more important than the mistakes that they make. I make mistakes, they make mistakes, what we do about them is important.

Job security, I suppose it goes through phases. Relationships are always changing. You must please several people at all times to keep a secure job. But because I am willing to put up with a vast amount of hours, skip days off if need be, that makes me, I believe, a sincerely valuable worker to them. I think they definitely get their money's worth from me. So I think I'm quite secure in my work for them. You can never be totally secure. Maybe that's what keeps you improving. I can see at times vast improvements of myself. The wage scale is not necessarily very high in the industry we work in. However, I am being paid a good wage for my work, I believe. It could always be better. It is improving, but it does take time to do that sort of thing. Since I am on the management team, my health insurance is paid for by the corporation. Yes, there is that. There is no retirement plan, though. I have my own setup for that, and of course they don't cover dental or anything like that, just straight health insurance. I have Social Security.

Soviet kitchens, I think I'd probably gain more from seeing their facilities than anything. What they have to work with, what equipment is what interests me. You can guess a great deal from what kind of equipment they have,

264

as to what they do. I'd like to see a representation of their work, but I suspect their problems managing kitchens are very similar to ours. What kind of facilities, how advanced their technology is . . . like we have all stainless steel surfaces to work with, that are very nice. If they have equivalent. It would be more of a comparison. I would be interested in seeing . . . I'd like to see a representation of their work, and I suspect it's going to be very parallel, the problems they face and we face.

Computer technology can help us a great deal. It can be used in your inventory and ordering systems, to cut a lot of manual labor out and improve your system. We get ordering gaps where either the supplier's salesman didn't get it written down, or whoever was placing the order thought he said it but didn't. Or it got missed on inventory and so on. And the computer could probably smooth that out. I would not want to see the day when a computer would decide how to cook the roast, you know, if you put a sensor into it and put it in there, and the computer would turn on the oven to the temperature and turn it off. I'm sure they could do those things easily enough, and probably call you when it's ready, whatever they want to do. The only thing they couldn't do is slice it for you, and I don't want to see getting that much automation. I don't really believe in that. I like nice handy equipment that helps us in our jobs, but on the other hand, I think there's a point . . . now they have electric egg scramblers and vegetable peelers. That's going a little too far. Way too far.

I work about sixty hours a week. We try and bring it lower so it averages out. The work load during the busy times can get pretty high, but then you lose your efficiency, so we are attempting to cut this down to normal hours. It just doesn't pay to be working that long, you overdose on the work. On my time off, I sleep, and use television as a tranquilizer. I used to own horses, but I didn't use them that much, so I sold them off when I moved to Moscow. Now I collect miniatures, and I'm attempting to build a one to one scale Victorian mansion to put the miniature collection in. I'm not much of a builder, less of an architect.

We built an ice carving once, the staff and I. We needed an ice carving for the Idaho Symphony. We needed a violin. We couldn't find a picture of a violin, so we finally had to go to the dictionary. We found this little tiny picture. We said, "Okay, this is what we're supposed to build. With strings and a bow." Three of us were working. We used a chain saw and little pronged ice picks, four- or five-pronged carving tools for when you get down to the finer details of the work. You work quickly, and if the ice gets too soft, you put it back in the freezer for a while. We worked quickly. I'd be chipping on the ice and it would be falling down on the others, down their necks, in their hair, but we had a very short time to get it done. We managed it. In about three hours we had carved a violin out of a two hundred pound block of ice. The way we did it, we did it in relief form, and I guess we had about sixty pounds of ice in the final product. So we did it in relief. It was a good, heavy, nicely substantial ice violin.

Children's World

Alexander Yemeljanov is a dead ringer for Johnny Carson. When I told him this, the Latvian journalist said, "Tell me please, who is this John Carson?" Yemeljanov poured me a glass of Latvian liqueur, smooth distilled fruit of Latvia's orchards. We were sitting in his Novosti office near the Daugava River in Riga, waiting for Larissa Vanaga, a department store salesclerk, to meet us for an interview. "While we're waiting," said Alexander in crisp English, "I shall tell you a few important facts about my Latvia. First, you must understand that we Latvians enjoy the fine things in life. If you hear our music, you will hear chorales of spirited voices, singing as only a liberated people know how—voices in love with life. If you drink our Latvian liqueurs, you will taste the perfume of bitter fruits that have ripened to full-bodied sweetness. Listen and drink. You will discover how we Latvians have risen out of the Nazi concentration camps and ghettos into the glorious moment that is Latvia today. Drink up!"

We toasted Latvia, and Alexander refilled the glasses. We toasted an American's visit and a few other things, and

Alexander shook his head and frowned. "I don't know," he said, "how this salesclerk interview will turn out. When I heard you were coming, I made a few telephone calls around the city. You see, I don't know any department store clerks, sorry to say. So I called up Children's World— that's our children's department store—and asked the store's manager to suggest someone. I know nothing about the girl who was selected. She might not be your girl."

In the street outside Alexander Yemeljanov's office, a group of teenagers were unfurling a red banner, preparing to tack it up on a building. The banner advertised *Subbotnik*, the all-citizen volunteer work day, which was only two days away. Soviet railroad workers invented Subbotnik in the early 1900s, when they volunteered overtime hours at the Sortirovochnaya freight yard that serviced the Moscow-Kazan line. Today, every Soviet citizen is encouraged to honor the Subbotnik by giving one day of volunteer labor to the state. Subbotniks are scheduled on the Saturday that falls nearest to the anniversary of Lenin's birth, April 9. Subbotnik frequently falls on Easter eve, the most celebrated religious holiday in Soviet European republics. Every adult and child capable of performing any sort of labor is asked to volunteer Subbotnik "wages" to the state. The government says the money accrued by not paying this day's wage, is used to construct facilities that serve needy segments of the population. For example, a recent Subbotnik earned several billion rubles that went to construct a hospital which treats children who have cancer, and for other health facilities. On a Subbotnik day, every street and roadside, every park lane is lined with brigades of citizens who plant new trees or flower gardens, or just sweep and pick up trash. Factory workers put in extra hours on the job. Even the intelligentsia labors, some exercising muscles that rarely get flexed in the normal routines of "brain workers," as they are referred to in Soviet statistical data. Every able bodied citizen seems to honor the Subbotnik.

Alexander Yemeljanov consulted his watch. "We have a little time," he said. "I'd like to show you around my native city."

Riga rises out of Yurmala Forest, lofty pillars and domes of Lutheran cathedrals, Russian Orthodox and Catholic churches, and high-rise Soviet modern housing projects. Riga is an ancient Western European town, its cobblestone backstreets winding past buildings a thousand years old. Narrow alleys lead to secret courtyards, where Priditis, the legendary Finger-Sized Boy, enacted some of his good deeds. Downtown, near Dome Cathedral, a hydrofoil pleasure boat skiffs up against the Daugava docks, toylike next to a mammoth freighter unloading supplies for Riga's electronics industries. On the main boulevard, a dusty Czechoslovakian trolleybus scoots around the corner, children's noses pressed against windows, feeling the cold from outside. Men on Riga's streets wear berets; women in dark stockings, snug skirts, with flambé hennaed hairdos, seem Parisian. The town is a smorgasbord of gargoyled and turreted architects' whims, serving up Old Europe the way it was, preserved with loving care by citizens who are proud to be Rigans. From its ancient nooks and crannies to its brand new high-rise multimedia building, the city is as intricate and confusing as Latvia's history. Latvia's government has changed hands six times during the 20th century, between German, Latvian and Soviet rulers. Today, the Soviet republic exudes a peaceful and prosperous energy. Riga's once war-torn neighborhoods, many formerly Nazi-ruled ghettos, have been restored to prewar elegance. At night, the main streets of Latvia's capital city glow under string crowns of pink, green and blue neon lights, as if each sunset marked the opening of a new holiday.

The old Dome Cathedral, once a house of worship, is now a public museum and concert hall administered by the state. Active churches hold services in smaller, less elaborate buildings that were refurbished after the war with funds raised from workers' wages. The government provided some rubles as well, because Riga is one of twenty-four Soviet cities selected for historical preservation. Soviet laws prohibit public display of theological beliefs, and you will never be solicited by a Hare Krishna devotee at Riga's train depot, nor will you find a single treatise supporting theology in Riga's bookstores or public libraries.

This afternoon, Riga's turrets and gargoyles are draped in huge red banners with yellow lettering, announcing Subbotnik, which this year falls on Easter eve.

Midsummer, Riga is bathed in White Light, a lower-latitude version of the Arctic's Midnight Sun, and Rigans adjust sleeping schedules to fit in nocturnal strolls along the boulevards and through the city parks. As in every Soviet city, streetlights are dimmed or completely doused before midnight, and moving vehicles navigate with parking lights because the nation is trying to conserve energy. This makes night travel dark passage, and at midnight in Riga only the neon string lights illuminate the byways. Still, like all Soviet towns, Riga is almost totally free from street crime, even in the darkest hours before dawn. It is illegal for citizens to own handguns in the Soviet Union, and penalties for violating the peace and security of the streets are strictly enforced. Law and order prevails in public places, and even children need not fear for their safety. When they are victims of violent crimes, their assailants are most likely young "hooligans," other children picking a petty gang fight. Soviet children stand a far better chance of reaching adulthood than children in America.

Latvian parents are fond of the Soviet axiom "Everything for the children." Families are small but parents have a tendency to treat children like precious jewels. The average Latvian family includes one or two children. Because of a shortage of workers, the government says,

270

Soviet families should produce more progeny. This campaign is particularly encouraged in European regions of the country, because European Soviets tend to have smaller families than Central Asian Soviets. Non-Soviet critics in the West charge that the Soviet government is concerned that soon Central Asian nationalities will outnumber European nationalities. But Soviet citizens told me their government is simply encouraging the highly industrialized European sector to share the burden of rearing future generations. For whatever reason, the campaign that encourages families to have more children is not very successful. Young Soviet couples have little time to raise large families, and few can afford the expense both in time and rubles, matching a pattern occurring in today's U.S. workforce. Married couples who do want to raise large families often must delay their plans because workers' flats are rarely large enough to contain armies of children. Still, a trend toward early marriages is sweeping the U.S.S.R., partly because married couples have a better shot at receiving a flat than singles, who must live with their parents or in dormitories.

Soviet parents seem to combine deep love and strict discipline in child rearing. It is a rare child in the U.S.S.R. who is not dressed well, and the children usually show a great deal of respect for their elders. Soviet children seem to have a discipline, both in their schoolwork and their personal lives, that many American parents complain their children lack. Soviet parents do not necessarily spare the rod, but they also spoil their children. At least among workers' families, children are their parents' pride.

Soviet boys and girls are encouraged to plan early for their future occupation. Although they may decide what they will take up after completing school, like children in America, their dreams are not always fulfilled. As workers' children become better educated than their parents were, young people in both countries show increasing signs of

271

disenchantment with the job market. Fewer young Soviets are willing to work in today's unskilled labor positions, especially in service jobs like restaurant work and house-keeping. The literacy level among Soviet children is phenomenally high, nearly one hundred percent, compared to as low as fifty percent in some major American cities, and they are not satisfied with jobs their parents would have once coveted. As one busy female bureaucrat said to me, "I have two children at home and need somebody to care for them. But it's awfully hard to find a good woman these days."

Even if a young Soviet has trained for a prestigious profession, an opening might not be available. The new Siberian cities promise the best opportunities for young workers; they are moving there in droves.

Soviet sociologists say that young workers tend to job hop so frequently that industries have a hard time keeping their payroll records straight. Entering the job market can be confusing and even frightening for a young person in any society, so it always helps to know an experienced adult who is willing to give you a few tips on how to take the first crucial steps into an alien and all too cynical adult working world. Teenagers who begin their working careers in Riga's Children's World breathe a lot easier after they meet their co-worker, Larissa Vanaga, a compassionate grown-up who remembers her own struggles as a junior clerk. Now a seasoned employee, Larissa Vanaga is helping teenage trainees adjust to life behind the cash register.

Children's World, in downtown Riga, is the child consumer's dream realized, a store devoted to children, where floor after floor of merchandise dazzles even the most jaded adult eye. Every material item a young Soviet dares dream of is available there, and on the day I visited, blue jeans were the hottest selling item. They were piled row after row in stacks high as the ceiling, good imitations of

Wrangler's, manufactured in the U.S.S.R., and they were selling like hotcakes. A few steps away, pint-sized consumers and their parents were packed three deep at another popular counter, waiting to buy children's toiletries, toothpaste, colognes and soaps made to fit a child's hand. Larissa Vanaga stood behind this counter with two young female trainees and listened to a mother describe her daughter's favorite cologne. She couldn't recall the name, but she could remember the scent, and Larissa listened patiently to a flowery description.

The trainees stood beside Larissa Vanaga, watching how she handled customers. They obviously admired her skill. And the senior clerk's well-groomed, sophisticated appearance seemed to impress them as well.

Larissa Vanaga is a knockout brunette with flashing black eyes and full sensuous lips which she bites when she is under pressure, as she was constantly the day I saw her in her workplace. She is tall, slender, long-legged, and somebody has taught her how to dress like a model. Her dark brown hair is stylishly short with bangs that hang like an apostrophe over her forehead. She is a woman men stare at in the street, yet she hardly seems aware of her attractiveness. She is self-confident on the job, and the teenage trainees seemed to regard her with awe and respect. Her suave, almost flashy manner has carried her a long way in her career. Her teenage trainees might think of Larissa Vanaga as a "career woman." But I talked to her one evening, for several hours, and discovered that beneath the sophisticated polish, Larissa Vanaga holds quite a different image of herself. When she talked about her life, beginning with childhood, Larissa's priorities turned out not to be so flashy after all.

Larissa Vanaga

I was born in 1946; I'm an old lady. I was born in Riga,

so I'm a Rigan. I'm kind of proud of that because my husband is from Dauvopolis, you know this city?* But I'm a Rigan. My father died ten, twelve years ago. He was a driver. My mother worked in a daycare center, and she retired three years ago, although it's hard to believe she's retired, she looks so good, so young and attractive. All her life she worked in a daycare center. I have a sister too. She has two children and needs more help than I. My mother lives with her. She is really needed there, they're all little ones.

My mother began working when she was very young. We girls were still very little, and we went to the daycare center where my mother worked. It wasn't a bad setup for us there. Mother worked there all her life without changing jobs. It was a daycare center run by the railroad, for the children of the railroad workers. So now my mother's retired.

When I was small, in my early childhood, I didn't understand how beautiful this city was. We are great fans of old Riga. It was only once I was grown, not as a little girl . . . as a matter of fact, I lived right in the area of Children's World. The ten-year school I went to was across the street from Children's World. They were building it while I was in school. Children's World is where I've been working for fifteen years. So all in that one neighborhood.

We had a flat on the second floor, the four of us; my mother, my father, my sister and I. Then my mother received a new flat from the railroad that ran the daycare center. So she got an apartment from the railroad.

We had lots of books, both in Latvian and Russian, and also in Lithuanian—collections of fairy tales. Now I tell these fairy tales to my daughter, Elizaveta. Oh, there's a Latvian fairy tale about the little boy, "Priditis." We call it

---

* Dauvopolis is a small town in Latvia. Larissa is implying that she is a sophisticate and her husband is a country boy.

in Latvian "The Finger-Sized Boy." Well, the basis is . . . all the children's tales are adventurous. So is the Finger-Sized Boy. He goes about the world in his little national cap. So, in this little national cap, and with a little bag like wanderers carry. And he carries *lapti* [traditional Baltic straw shoes] over his shoulder on the end of a little stick. It's kind of a symbol, a symbol. And then he has lots of adventures, helping out with all kinds of good deeds, overcoming evil. His name was Priditis, and, by the way, he is the symbol of our Children's World, the emblem.

So Priditis goes about the world doing various good deeds. "Priditis and the Marvelous Souvenir," that's one of the tales. He carries his shoes over his shoulder. It's a kind of a symbol that he goes along the road. Maybe he can go faster with bare feet. He's faster and lighter probably without his shoes. He goes about the world, not in vain, not just wandering, but doing good deeds. He conquers evil. I should tell you who he did battle with. As little as he was. He would conquer, oh, these kinds of giants like Lutautis. But he would always win. There is no "ogre," no. That is in the Russian version of "The Finger-Sized Boy."* In the Latvian version, there is no ogre. It's more plainly in a national vein. In the Latvian version, there are these trials, like, well, in Latvian, once he was hired for a time by a manor lord and this lord gave him endurance tests, ordeals. This tiny little fellow had to tend a big herd of pigs. But before this, you see, Priditis had done some good deed for an old man, and the old man had given him a magic flute. So Priditis plays on this magic flute and the herds belonging to the manor lord scattered . . . Priditis would always win.

Honestly speaking, I think there are so many beautiful children's books in the world now. Not beautiful, won-

---

* Larissa makes this comment in response to a question asked by the interpreter, a connoisseur of Russian fairy tales.

drous. When I was a child, we used the library more. Then there wasn't anything like this. And now it's the greatest delight for me to buy them for my child. And we have many books. To tell the truth, we buy our daughter books in Russian and Latvian. She reads them equally well. It's easier for her in Latvian, but all the same, school is very easy for her. At least she can pay more attention to her English because her Russian is fine. She picks up languages instantly. Only straight A's. And so she can pay more attention to English.

From my early childhood, even earlier than Elizaveta's age, from the first grade up till now, I've thought of myself as a homebody. I like to stay home. And then maybe, I'd think about what kind of a little child I'd have, and I thought I'd like to have a little daughter. In particular it was always clear to me that I wanted a good family and children. I will tell you a secret. All my dreams of a husband, my husband has fulfilled two hundred percent. Because he balances my character a little, which is so quick and hot tempered. My husband could not be like that. He should be even-tempered, understanding, and that's just how he is. Because of his character everything is good in our house, and everyone around envies us. Because of his character.

I was twenty-three years old when we met, and he was thirty, or thirty-one. Oh, you want to know all my secrets, all my secrets, huh? That's okay. There were other boys, there were. I had acquaintances* from my school years. I

* In Russian, which Larissa is speaking, there are three words that can be translated as friend. *Drug* is the most intimate of these, and when used for the opposite sex, often implies romantic involvement. Next comes *pri'atel,* which is more than a casual acquaintance, but not one of the closest circle. Least intimate, most commonly used and the term that Larissa uses here, is *znakomii,* which is often translated as acquaintance. Everyone in your class, everyone you work with, is in this category. The implication of Larissa's statement is that she had platonic friendships with boys.—Translator's note.

had my school friends there, then when I started at the Institute of Trade, I also had friends there. But my husband was my first love, my source. And I am very lucky to receive this love. At first, it's so difficult to recognize the kind of feeling. He was so attentive. Unfortunately it doesn't always turn out that way for everyone. Very romantic, how we met, and a very funny story.

I was returning home from work. In the summer season, there was nothing to do, so I'd work, not "work" but go and help out. It was seasonal kind of work, to organize a shop and sell some goods in a small shop. I was traveling, like on a business trip. I remember everything very well. After work I was tired but nevertheless I didn't look bad. My mother is a very good seamstress, she sews lots of fashionable clothes for me. That day I wore a corduroy coat of dark red, the color of cherries. On the one hand maybe I looked very tired, but on the other I looked very nice.

Larissa's husband, a tall, slender, fair-haired man with quiet blue eyes, watched his wife describe their first meeting. His total adoration of this gypsylike woman was obvious. He could not resist commenting on the fateful train ride that brought Larissa into his life. "I went with my friends to Yurmala," he said, blushing, "and we went there in the same train. And I noticed her while I was already in my place. When she was getting off, I gave her my hand, helping her to go down the stairs . . ." Larissa picked up the thread of the story.

And he looked at me with such eyes, I knew something else was going on. In any case, fate is fate, the die is cast. It was my fate. I believe in fate. For me maybe not from the very, very first sight, but it was true love.

In those years it was very difficult for me to think about

it, because there was an age difference. Now we don't feel it; it even helps in our family.

I told my mother everything. She was my dearest friend, and I told her everything. And when I brought him home to my mother and father, they said, "With such a nice, good smile, he must be a very good person."

We met not far from Yurmala in Bugur. It was in 1968. Looking through contemporary eyes, we were old-fashioned. We were conservatives. Maybe nothing was allowed before our marriage. All my girlfriends, we all agreed, we had pretty much the same view. From the point of view of today's young people, we were conservative, but in those days . . . very many of my girlfriends from school, they all felt the same.

I understand young people a little, they talk with me, they explain themselves. Maybe I am a teacher for youngsters in our store now, and that's why I know lots of stories about the premarital period of our youth. I'd say that today's young people are very, very well balanced. Because in my team, I have unmarried girls,* though one of them recently got married and had a little girl. They're very modern. Our whole collective in Children's World sometimes discusses moral questions, questions of appearance with our director, so that the salesgirls present a similar image. She gives them advice on how to dress; some should wear a little makeup . . . our girls are very modest. I think it's maybe because here and there in discussion we have heard of certain instances . . . we carry on a great deal of educational work. And then we have girls, lots of girls who enter our store right after school . . . very young girls. It's very important how you approach them. What role should we play? We have to be an example for them.

*The Russian word for girl, *devushka*, is a standard form of address for females up through middle age. If anything, using the term *zhenshchina*, meaning woman, can sometimes be insulting. It implies age or sexual experience.—Translator's note.

There's nothing like the example of a good family, no method is better than a good example. As soon as a young girl comes to work we give her as a supervisor an older, well, more experienced woman. She takes an interest in what boys the girl goes out with. If she doesn't go out, why doesn't she? "Meet someone." "Get a dress." So everything comes out as it should be.

I think that any girl, regardless of her situation or time, that when you ask a girl her thoughts for the future, it's a future mother and a future wife. And the main thing, of course, is to start a good family. But it doesn't always work out, unfortunately. But every girl dreams of a good child, a career, a good husband. So I think that there is really no difference how we felt when we were their age and how they feel now.

I say that maybe the women of our society, maybe we take too many duties for our own good, in our country. We must be an excellent worker, and an excellent housewife, and excellent mother. There's lots of work for us, professional work, physical work and public work [i.e., volunteer work]. The state does a lot for us now; it's easier to be with the children, the family, more time to spend with our families, raising our children. My husband shouldn't have to wait for me to come home. He's also at work. I'd like to spend more time at home myself. But it's impossible to stay at home all your life.

I remember very well when I first started working at Children's World. I remember what I wore. My mother and I had sewn a skirt for me of tweed. I had a fashionable hairdo for those days. It was fourteen years ago, I was almost twenty years old by then. After technical school, I had a choice whether to go to work as a salesperson in a store or go to a warehouse as a control master. I chose the store. I completed the institute while I was working. I went on for two more years at the institute. The other day, I was in a meeting of women department store clerks. We were remembering the many sins of the young of those days: too many were much too heavily made up. The older sales-women criticized me. Back then, I used black pencil for my eyes, it was very fashionable then, and some women criticized me. But some of the girls defended me, saying that I was very fashionable and had good taste, and that I only used as much as necessary. So, to my youngsters I tell them, "Well see, we had our difficulties in those days, and you have yours." One issue of our workers' in-house paper, they made a caricature of me with these eyes. It's a pity that I couldn't keep that paper, it was very well done, better than I was. But on the other part, some girls were defending me and that's why we just made jokes about this paper. Then, being an editor of our Komsomol paper in our store, I also myself drew other girls, the conservatives, criticizing them. It was lots of fun.

In those days, we couldn't do things as our salespeople do them today. We were very responsible, very responsible. It's not that they're worse now, but then everything was so exact, everything was put just in the right place.

I got into the job fairly quickly. We had our practical courses, we had practical experience in different stores, with various types of goods, so we came to our jobs prepared. We knew how to do the work already. Right after technical school they take you on as a salesperson. These days, you come on as an apprentice and then as a junior salesperson. I guess I made something around ninety rubles a month. Now they receive much more. Now a junior salesgirl receives one hundred twenty rubles, one hundred thirty rubles a month. We receive a little more in Children's World because ours is considered a department store, so we get additional pay for difficult service here. Rightly so, because we have more shoppers.

When I first came to the store, I worked as a salesperson in the underclothes section. At the time, they were just introducing NOT(SOL), the Scientific Organization of

Labor, to the department in Children's World. They offered me a position as NOT engineer.* My very, very first steps in the system didn't have to do with sales particularly. A little bit maybe; it was mostly pure mechanical work. I had to make a schedule for the workday, do time studies, what are the buying patterns of the shoppers as a group, at what time should there be the heaviest staff concentration, who should be assigned to work at the busiest times and where. We had to open a new section, a toy department, children's toys serving the daycare centers, schools. They offered me a job in that new department that had just been organized, as a promotion. Then I worked there for a while as a team leader, and in the perfume section. And we decided purely on a physical basis that this was the right place for me, that I had the right look to work in the perfume section. There were a lot of young people in that department. I've been working there for six years now.

We have the necessary children's wares: soap, special children's colognes, special boxes for children with soap, cologne, toothbrushes, toothpaste. They come in various combinations. They vary. We receive from Estonia little figure bottles of cologne for girls, little figured soaps made in Latvia, in different colors so that they should be more pleasant for the children. There is a huge demand for children's goods. We consider our main priority, you know, to increase the quantity of children's goods. We love our children and always will. We don't skimp on money or anything else where they're concerned. So children's goods are increasing.

Across the street, in the perfume shop, I also work there. We have some women's toiletries there and the same assortment of children's goods as we have in Children's

---

*In the U.S.S.R., anyone who has responsibility for anything mechanical is called an engineer.

World. The demand, as they say, for children's goods is growing, and there's a sharp increase in goods. Our department store is the only large children's one, and it's solving this problem. But the same trend is spreading into all the little nearby shops. We act as kind of a service bureau for tots.* That's our store. Handling purely children's goods is difficult. Our goods are purely for teens and children. Further down the street there's a women's perfumery and a men's haberdashery.

I am a team leader. There are eight people in my team. All girls. We all do pretty much the same work. Maybe I do a little bit more. I'm paid for greater responsibility. I lock up the department. According to our schedule and according to the shift, one day from the morning until two o'clock, and the next day from two till eight. And that's why I have an opportunity to keep my house. Sunday is our common day off, plus one weekday, depending on the schedule. Two days off.

When I had my baby, I stayed home for a year. I didn't lose any benefits. They reserved my job, and I didn't lose any position. There was a great hope . . . My husband works at the Institute for Statistical Planning, in the cooperative computer center.

(LARISSA'S HUSBAND: The Department of Statistics, the institute for planning computer centers.)

In fact, on his job, he would do translations. He could help Elizaveta with her English. I, of course, couldn't help her, although I studied English the first year she was in school. I used to know more than him, now I've forgotten everything. So my husband could help her with her English studies.

Elizaveta is now in a special school for studying English. She was not studying English before this special school.

---

* Children's World advises and often supplies smaller shops that carry children's goods.

On the whole there were many children entering this school who had been either studying English at home or in the daycare center—we have one that teaches English—in special kinds of linguistic daycare centers. We just decided to send her. The second reason is because this school is very famous not only for its English language but for its other teachers. It's got a very strong staff of teachers of other subjects too. An enormous percentage from this school get into the [foreign language] institute. It's a good school. We ourselves made the decision to send her.

There was a small selection made. They were able to accept thirty-six children, and there were approximately sixty applying for admission. For a half year they went to this school, they were still going to daycare centers too. Aside from this, they went to the school once a week. It either works out or it doesn't work out. So she went through this selection, this little kind of competition, and got in. It's purely voluntary, so to speak, and free. She lives at home. She's on the first shift at school, which gets out around two o'clock, and then she goes home. Sometimes she comes to my job, and I feed her there, give her a snack. A very good children's café just opened there. She's a spoiled eater, she won't eat just anything, but the food's very tasty there.

I'm a homemaker by nature. For me, the family is something great. And now that I have my little one beside me, my life seems so beautiful, worth living. . . . We thought it would be a boy. We even had a carriage, a blue carriage and a blue blanket. They predicted that I would have a boy, but now I am very satisfied. And we love her very much.

Arctic Boomtowns: The Last Frontier

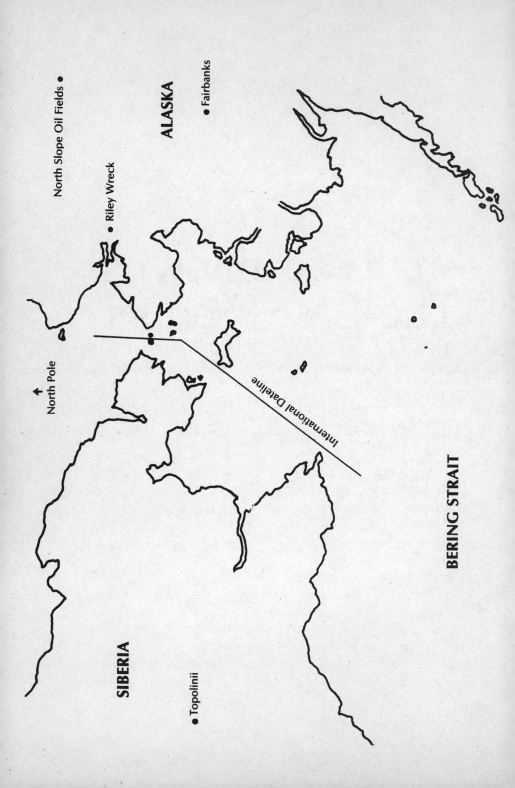

Denali

"Protect the Alaskan way of life."
> —Secessionists' credo

Before governments existed, about ten thousand years ago, the lands now called Alaska and Siberia may have been joined by a natural land bridge, a footpath for Mongol Asian nomads who followed eastward-migrating ice age mammal herds. As Nature struggled with her northern masterpiece, powerful glaciers could have driven a channel through the tundra bridge, carving out the narrow and shallow strait that now separates Asia from North America. However it happened, the lands were already divided in the 18th century, when the nomads decided to settle down on both sides of what is now called the Bering Strait. Their lands were called Siber and alaxsxag, and northern peoples shared similar language and customs. As kinfolk will, families maintained contact across the strait.

Alaxsxag, which means "the land toward which water flows," is an Aleut word, from the language of settlers on little islands, tips of severely doused volcanoes in the sea below the strait. The Aleutian Islands stretched from alaxsxag, in a necklace chain of stepping stones, one link short of clasping Siber's shoreline. Above the necklace islands, two broad peninsulas faced each other. A maverick wolf, today's Alaska, and a bold bear, today's Siberia, were profiled on the Bering Strait, mouths agape as if to swallow up the dividing waters.

Midnight Sun and aurora borealis fused enchantment into the landscape as nomads settled down in the North Country. Coastal sea hunters lived off whales, seals and walrus, salmon and lowbush tundra berries, and dug subterranean homes out of permafrost or constructed domed, animal skin *yarangas*. Inland hunters stalked dense *taiga* forests and fished clearwater streams. All northern peoples lived subsistence lives, killing only the number of sea and land creatures they needed to survive, treating land and its resources as sacred gifts from Bayanai, spirit of the taiga, and the Great Woman beneath the sea. Guns were unknown, though killing in self-defense with simple weapons was accepted custom. Life among Arctic societies combined violent struggle with the forces of Nature and harmonious distribution of her bounty. As northern peoples divided into separate societies, different dialects evolved, but language always retained a common feature: a respect for the spoken word that combined sincere brevity and eloquence. Ask an Inupiat Eskimo when hunting season begins. The answer: "Not long." Ask how far to the next village, and the Inupiat might answer: "Not far." Ask a Siberian Even the word for snow, and the Even will ask: "Which kind?" Among the many dialects of the region, Siberian Yupik is the common language of Eskimos on both sides of the Bering Strait today.

Before governments existed, life beneath the Midnight Sun was uncomplicated and usually harmonious. When winter paved the Bering Strait in ice ribbon highway, snowshoed kinfolk scurried across to family reunions, arms laden with the Great Woman's gifts.

The sea otter, with its fine fur coat, lolled in thick communities along the Aleutian Island beaches. But its endearing face, wide smile and vulnerable brown eyes failed to capture the hearts of the Arctic's first Caucasian hunters. The sea otter's hide was worth more than a smile to a fur trader, and one quick swipe with a heavy club put out its lights long enough to rob the stunned otter of its luxurious fur coat and life itself. Baby otters' soft supple hides brought top prices for Imperial Russian and Anglo-American fur traders, who spread over the Northland in the 18th and 19th centuries, ravaging natural resources and enslaving the inhabitants. After conquering the Siberians, Russian fur traders moved into alaxsxag and forced its peoples into subjugation. When the sea otter and every other fur-bearing animal approached extinction because of the white man's slaughters, Russia lost interest in the American half of her northern possessions and lack-adaisically sold alaxsxag to the United States government for seven million two hundred thousand dollars.

The avowed American imperialist William H. Seward kept Russia's emissary, Baron Edouard de Stoeckel up all night on March 20, 1867, working out fine details of the sale. "Seward's folly" brought alaxsxag under U.S. control, and the federal government promptly anglicized the territory's name, calling it Alaska. Nothing changed for Alaska's natives, though—they were not granted U.S. citizenship and were still subjected to the rapacious exactions of Caucasian fur traders, who brought "civilization" north at gunpoint.

Washington took little interest in its new territory, and apart from banning the manufacture and sale of alcohol, passed few laws affecting it. Russia, having slipped one icy albatross from its imperial shoulders, continued to oppress Siberia's peoples, forcing them to pay the *yasak*, a tax to the Russian Empire, on their hunts. Siberians who agreed to be baptized by Russian Orthodox missionaries and take Russian names were granted dispensations from the yasak. Meanwhile, Christian missionaries from Canada and the United States began moving in on Alaska's peoples, Bibles in hand, hoping to convince Eskimos and Indians that the white man's way was more sacred than theirs, though Alaska's missionaries often spoke out against the white man's violent treatment of natives.

Occupations changed for Alaskans and Siberians after the white man arrived. Northern peoples were forced to hunt for Russian and Anglo-American fur trading companies, and the only wage they received for their toil was the right to go on living. Some Russian and Anglo settlers were different, though, and did not travel to the Far North to profit from the land, but rather to escape from humdrum lives in industrial centers or to hide from the white man's law. Some came north in exile, prisoners of Imperial Russia, whose politics did not accord with the tsars'. A gradual change came over the region as Asian, Eskimo and Caucasian peoples intermarried, and while northern peoples adopted some of the white man's ways, some Caucasians learned to live and work like native northerners. Harmony existed there, alongside terrible cruelty. The power of the white man's technology ruled the area as the Russian and American governments and their corporations prepared for one of the greatest heists in the history of Planet Earth.

Earth's precious jewels—pockets and veins of gold, diamonds, coal and other fuels—had been locked for thousands of years beneath eternal frost. Northern peoples never raided the treasure chests, believing in the sacred rights of the ground and its permanently frozen condition. Then, for a century, the Northland would be subjected to sporadic forays into Earth's treasure chests.

In the 20th century, the Soviet state and a few individual

Americans under the auspices of private corporations began laying open the eternal frost and extracting the hidden jewels. The mining operations were on a grand scale, and new job opportunities opened up in the Northlands. Some natives found jobs servicing coal and oil boomtowns, as construction workers or waiters or housekeepers. Most of the high-wage jobs, and virtually all the jobs as foreman or supervisor, were reserved for Caucasian outsiders who were paid handsomely to move to the harsh north and work there. The cost of transporting companies' supplies and consumer goods was great. The price of food, clothing, housing and other essentials rose in the boomtowns built largely on natives' labor with the white man's tools. Natives' wages did not rise, though, and thus these workers faced a hard choice: either accept the new economic order and try to assimilate in spite of the difficulties posed by the racist attitudes of many company bosses, or be plunged into poverty worse than before the boomtowns existed. In Siberia, natives had accepted Soviet rule, which was far superior to life under the tsars, and most began to assimilate into the Europeans' boomtowns. In Alaska, some natives, now full-fledged United States citizens—on paper anyway—joined hands with major oil corporations, participating in the mine and drill work. While many natives acquiesced to the white man's ways, others kept a distance and watched in despair as boomtowns came and went, moving about like pieces on a Monopoly board, throwing the economy into chaos. Today, jobs, their wages and rewards, come and go in the continuing boomtown shuffle, but job security is nothing more than a bad joke mentioned in crowded barrooms where workers with the layoff blues gather to drown their misery. The Northland is changing, and so are peoples' lives and work.

In Siberia, the Soviets go after gold, diamonds, coal, natural gas, oil and other precious resources in such haste that they are tearing up eternal frost before learning how to repair the damage. Although they have developed highly advanced methods to preserve *untouched* eternal frost, strip mining and drilling operations are taking place in Siberia before they understand how to repair the eternal frost they are damaging. In Alaska, America's most powerful oil corporations, with the federal government in their tow, are in such a hurry to take oil that they also have not bothered to wait until they understand permafrost. Neither the Soviet state nor U.S. oil companies are placing Earth's ice blanket on their priority list. Power has become the motivation for the grand robberies of the North. Meanwhile, in the boomtowns, even Anglo-American workers have little job security.

In the gentle shadow of the mountain Denali, a laid-off Alaskan oil worker wonders what is happening on his icy little acre of the world. Rex (a pseudonym) is twenty-six years old, an Anglo-American Alaska native who has worked on oil rigs since he graduated from high school.

Rex

All the oil companies up here are staying separate. Because there's still a chance of hitting a bonanza. Down in the States, they've been drilling for a hundred years, they know exactly what they're going to hit every time. But up here, there's still a good chance of hitting a bonanza. So they all stay separate.

Prudhoe Bay has hit big, and now there's rigs on the Beaufort Sea. And it's all moving to offshore drilling. Right now, they're going about fifteen thousand feet. They're finding some of the highest grades. Most of the drills at Prudhoe are eight thousand feet max. They're hitting good, shallow holes there, a big pool. But down deep, it's still pretty high grade.

When you drill and hit oil, you always get a higher pressure gas coming up with it. You go out to where the shaker boxes are, they pump mud down the hole to keep the bit cleaned off. When it comes back over on the shakers, you've got sensors set up there, so you take the percentage of the oil flow and the mud. Like, maybe you have five hundred gallons of mud, and say you pump back one hundred gallons an hour of mud and oil. It's a lot of chemicals. So many pounds per gallon, to hold the pressure back. The pressure in the ground, you've got to balance it. If you go under it, you start squeezing and you're stuck. If you go over it, you break the formation down, and that's when it kicks.

There's a diesel based mud, but it's not used too much. Too flammable, too risky. You drill faster, though. Up here you think about safety. It's about like the Gulf of Mexico, you're so close together that if a fire ever started you could wipe the field out. You could have an underground fire by one going off. Once it starts, there's no stopping it, it goes until it burns out. They've had one that I know of. But they keep it quiet. Stuff like that's not heard of. We had a small one, nothing spectacular. That was in 1977.

You don't use water pressure to drill, because up here you got to deal with the permafrost. Like you may have eighteen hundred feet of permafrost, where the ground is permanently frozen underneath. This is the on shore jobs. Prudhoe Bay is mostly on shore. Offshore rigs, most of them are on Beaufort Sea. Right now, there's about a hundred twenty-eight rigs up at Prudhoe. They all use mud, organic mud to pump.

Most offshore in Alaska has been natural gas. The onshore rigs are hitting the oil, hitting I'd say ten to one, and that's fairly good odds for an oil field. Every hole the oil companies drill is great. If they hit, they've got oil. If they don't hit, Uncle Sam reimburses them. They claim it as a loss, see. That's where the monopoly comes in for the oil companies. That's why they've got their hands in everything. There's no way to stop them in this country. An oil company could take over this country if it wanted. They're that strong.

You've got your big ones, Exxon, Conoco, Phillips, Chevron, I'd say your big five are up here. Arco (Atlantic Richfield) and British Petroleum-Sohio. BP owns the Prudhoe side, Arco owns the Beaufort side. Then they lease to other companies to drill. Everybody's got their own pump stations. They're leasing land, the smaller oil companies, from BP-Sohio and Arco. When the State had a land bid for oil rights, they were the two biggest, they had the money and they bought it all. State put it up to the highest bidder and they won. We got rights, the State, but as far as who's in control, BP and Arco are.

Like, the State has certain environmental rights. All the samples from rocks and stuff where they drill, the State gets a copy of them. And there's a certain percentage of the profits that goes to the State. But not like the profits the two big companies are making. The State would be rich if it made those profits.

A lot of the oil goes to Japan. Out of the country. That's the American way. Export ours and import theirs. It's a pretty well known fact that the United States could supply itself. We've got the oil. We could surpass the Soviet Union ten times with what we've got, if it came down to every country supplying itself with its own oil. Yet we're selling to Japan and importing from Iran. The big American companies, they're stockpiling oil, they've got it in reserve. What they're doing is going out and getting another country's oil till it goes dry. Then there's going to be all this reserve here. The big oil companies, they could maybe just hold enough in reserve to supply the military, I could see that, that's just covering us. But they hold most of it in reserve. It's the oil companies in control when it comes right down to it.

It's the oil companies and the federal government. And the oil companies are running everything. The federal government knows what kind of riches are up here. That's why they're doing so many land closures. Not to protect the environment, but to protect the riches—for the oil companies. Who holds the oil in reserve? The oil companies. And if we need it, the people need it, or if the military needs it, they've got to get it from the oil companies. So you tell me who makes the decisions in this country.

The people of Alaska, come right down to it, they'd secede. If there was a vote put on it, they'd vote to secede, I'd have to put my money on that. Only thing, the military would be sent in. We'd probably get the shit kicked out of us. The State would own the oil. Then Alaska becomes a power. No shipments anywhere else. Give us ten years, we could hold our own. The corporations are certainly not doing a very good job of running things. Neither is the federal government.

Look what the federal government's doing up here now. They get these land closures, they say for environmental purposes. They take these lands away from the State, and what for? So they can sell them off to the corporations. Because the land is rich. Once the federal government gets control, they keep the land for a few years, put it up for bids for some company to buy, and there's no way the people are going to get it back, that's for sure. Already they've got a good foot in here, it's going to be hard to shut them down.

The State of Alaska, there's no state in the union that's fought harder to protect the environment. Up here, they'll fine an oil company fifteen thousand dollars for spilling a gallon of diesel on the pad where they're drilling. People in the Lower 48, they don't understand, they don't know what the hell is going on up here. I don't think people understand how vast Alaska is, how much virgin country there is up here. Maybe this will explain. The federal government took all this land in Carter's Land Act, and now Reagan is holding it in reserve for the corporations. Meanwhile, they put a lot of people out of work, old guys who've been fishing and hunting guides up here. Sure it's somewhat of a drawback, you lose some wildlife, but you got to understand how big Alaska is. And now the land's no use to anybody but the corporations, it's all closed off to the people. The guides were responsible, most of them. They used to be issued a spot of land, and that's theirs forever, not to own it, but to be a guide on it. If they go in and wipe out the wildlife, that wipes them out too. The State's controlled it before, and if the federal government would let the State run itself, it would remain that way.

There's hatred up here. Like if you get up around Galena, the smaller places away from the big cities, they've got signs up there. Federal agents are shot on sight. They refuse them gas, they wouldn't sell them a hamburger if they were starving. That's the general feeling of most people up here. Okay, you passed your Act, your Bills, but we don't have to live with them. That's how the gun wars started. There's been quite a few people shot and trucks blown up. They've had protests and campouts in the national monuments now. It's like a small civil war between the government and the Alaskan people. Comes down to it, a lot of people are putting it all on the line, that's for sure. Everything the federal government does up here, they do it the same as they did in the Lower 48. And it don't work. It's too different up here. Like population-wise. We've got land that equals about a third the size of the United States—that's close enough—and a very small population. Most people up here are barely making it. They go fishing and hunting, it's the way it's always been and they'd like to keep it that way. But the federal government coming in, that's when a lot of hostility came in.

The federal government actually told our Fish and Game

Department it wasn't doing its job. They said we've got five years to pull it together or they would come in and take over. They keep making threats up here. The people up here see what it's done to the Lower 48, with the federal regs, the controls and all. They're trying to stop what's happened to the Lower 48 from happening in Alaska.

Denali. When Carter passed the bill taking the land, people camped out on Denali* that weekend. The federal agents came in, blocked off the roads, tried to stop it. They brought in wreckers to haul out the people's trucks, to get them off the land. Gunplay broke out. I don't think anybody was killed, but about five or six people were wounded. That was in '79. All the people were doing was just fighting for the Alaskan way of life. It really wasn't the federal agents' fault, they were just doing what they were told. One of the signs that went up, that you saw around, said, PROTECT THE ALASKAN WAY OF LIFE. The local law enforcement was laying low. Too many friends involved, and there's deep enough hatred; they would've been on the peoples' side. Probably if they called in the National Guard, even some of them would've been on the peoples' side. It's that strong. I'd have to join in for sure, if they called in the Guard. But we're not that close yet.

No, we wouldn't let the corporations in here if we seceded. They'd be run out, I'm sure. They'd be gone.

Look at the federal government, they make a Five Year Plan. They say if Alaska can't prove so much in five years, they're going to come in and take complete control. Once they've got control, they can keep the land a few years, then put it up for bids for some company. Then it's gone forever, the land. Now the people are starting to see it, they're trying to stop it before it's too late.

The Russians made a mistake when they sold Alaska. That was her back door straight into Canada and the

---

* Denali is the mountain sometimes called Mt. McKinley.

United States. And they shut it themselves. The world would have worked out different if they hadn't, that's for sure. In fact, I bet Russia is sorry now. But Russia was here for a different purpose. They were here for furs, furs only. That's all they came for. They did trap out a lot of areas, and when they saw that happen, they thought the land was worthless. Back then there wasn't no big battles with the oil companies. It hadn't come up yet. Now all of a sudden, boom, it's critical.

The Soviet Union, they can do things like have permafrost institutes, stuff like that . . . they're willing to put out the money because they haven't got the costs. They've got their cheap labor force, and people have got no say-so there. Over here, we'd never . . . over here we've got pushed to the point where we need to try it. Over there, they're trying it out of necessity. I've got to hand it to them, some of the stuff they've done. In oil, for instance. They've got more modern rigs, they can outdrill us as far as distance. I think our deepest well in the United States is like thirty-five thousand feet. I think the Soviets did a test hole of fifty thousand. There's no way the American oil companies could ever do that. We're pushing thirty hard, and that's pushing it. It took them almost two years to do it. I think the Soviets did theirs in eleven months. The Soviets go to the big oil conventions where our companies go. It's kind of like a "show and tell." They just kind of compare powers.

We could do what the Soviets do with their drills. Only thing is, the companies aren't willing to give up the profits, to invest. Most of the equipment for drilling the holes now, we're using the same stuff since they started the drilling, except they're using steel derricks instead of building them out of wood. But we're still using . . . it's so out of date compared to what the Soviets are using. Like, a typical U.S. rig, it takes at least a minimum six man crew to run a rig, just on the floor, keeping the drill pipe going through. And the Soviets, they can do it with two. They've got so much better equipment. They've got, like for picking up the pipe, they've got regular longarms that go down and pick it up and set it in. We're still bringing them up with ropes and shit.

Up there on the Slope, they've got a lot of books comparing what's going on in different countries. Also journals. When you're up there on the Slope, there's not much to do on your time off. I do a lot of reading. That's where I learned about Soviet oil work.

Up on the Slope, the working conditions really, they're unsafe. You go out on the floor, we're using all out-of-date equipment, still using regular old tongs, where the Soviets have rotating tongs that clamp around a drill pipe. Ours are still manual. And the Soviets, they've got most everything electric. Quiet. Ours, you got four big diesels sitting out back roaring away. The stuff makes a lot of difference, for safety especially.

I make at least fifteen dollars an hour. When I'm working, I work twelve hours a day, seven days a week. For as long as you're out. It depends on what outfit you're working for. The outfit I came in from last, they worked eight weeks on, two weeks off. One guy will rotate every eight weeks. You sit there and mark the calendar. "Oh boy, my day coming up." You're covered by Blue Cross, and some of the drilling companies, they've got additional insurance that you can take out. But pretty much it falls back on Workman's Comp if you get hurt. They've got a medic up there.

They had a union, but it got busted. They were doing good, they weren't getting better equipment or nothing, but they were getting policies for work safety, stuff like that. They kept the wages up too. They called it Arctic Slope Roughnecks' Association. But they got voted out. What they did was, they tried to go on strike, they were asking for about five dollars an hour raise. They went out on strike and the oil companies locked them out. Told them to go to hell. Hired new crews.

On a drill, there are no covered walkways. Like, if you're on a drill all the time washing the mud off, and you trip . . . and it's below sixty outside, it's slick. There's all kinds of people broke their legs and arms, busted heads open. It's an everyday occurrence up there, it doesn't faze people anymore. The frostbite in wintertime, that's the major safety thing. I've had it a couple times, fairly good, nothing serious. There's nothing you can do. Take an aspirin, go to bed. There you are, your fingertips all black and blue. You don't feel it, all of a sudden it quits hurting. First they're tingling all over. Then after a while, you're getting used to it, you don't realize—you have gloves on—and you start realizing when you go to grab something, you can't pick it up. You can't bend your fingers. Then you go inside, and usually by then, if it's that bad, your fingers will have turned white already, it's frostbitten. Then it starts turning, looks like a bruise. Puffs up and all that. If you really get it bad, amputation, that's the only thing they can do. One guy lost all his toes.

I spend at least five hundred dollars a year on work clothes. That's minimum. For someone who's going to the Slope right now, for a full year, the gear alone costs at least three thousand or more. Like, you're working every day. You've got to have five pairs of refrig-wear at a hundred fifty cash. Big Buddy boots in the wintertime, big white combat boots. Face masks. Usually you can't keep it on though, you can't see. You kind of just grin and bear it. You constantly pull the mask up so you can work.

Twelve-hour days, with a half an hour break. You get coffee breaks, fifteen minutes. If you get time. With no union they can flush you right out. You say, "I'm going to take a little longer break," and away you go. I don't know anybody that works up there that enjoys it. It's the money. Money. But without money . . . that's survival. Without money, the way the system is, you can't do anything without money. If it was a hundred years ago . . . If I had to choose between working here and in the Soviet Union, the way things are now, I'd take this work, I'd take the risk. To me, the other would be about like going in the army. To hell with it.

If I can't enjoy life, working is not rewarding for me. Not at all. Work, it's something they set up, everybody's got to do it. But as far as being rewarding, I couldn't dedicate myself just for the money, no. I take pride in my work, don't get me wrong. But they got to pay me too.

Prudhoe's like a city. It's got a swimming pool, gym, everything. The companies fly you up there and back. It gets pretty wild up at Prudhoe. Not many women. Most of the women are like bull cooks, they make up the beds and stuff. They've got a few secretaries up there, all the oil companies have offices up there. They've had, like women roughnecks, but not that many. Drinking? No way. No bars. But there's bootleggers. It costs you twenty dollars for a case of beer, fifteen dollars for a fifth of R&R—that's rotgut whiskey. You can buy it in Anchorage for six bucks a bottle. I've done twelve weeks max in a row up there. By then, you're a damn lunatic when you come down.

Rex's friend, Bill, has lived in Alaska seven years. He is a postal worker in Anchorage. Bill feels as strongly as Rex about Alaska's problems with the federal government and oil corporations. He told me, "There's a couple good reasons why they don't allow alcohol on the Slope. One is, these guys working twelve, eighteen hour days, if you drink in an off-duty time, there's gonna be trouble. Then too, in winter, with all the darkness, being closed in, if everybody was tanked up, it would turn into a big brawl. It's hard enough to fight cabin fever without alcohol adding to the problem.

"And on seceding from the Union. The federal government owns 90 percent of the land in Alaska.* About 5 percent is owned by the State. Three percent is owned by municipalities and boroughs. Less than one percent is in private ownership. That's the lockup people up here are screaming about. And the federal government can tell the people down in the Lower '48, feed them the story that they're preserving it for them. They're preserving it not for the people. You can't touch it, you can't land a plane on it, which is the only way you can go unless you walk. Like the average Alaskan, I only have about six months a year when the weather's where I can go hiking. The places that are accessible by road are the ones that are off limits. So the average Alaskan has been shut out of his recreation. And Watt,† he's pro business. The people are locked out, but big businesses aren't.

"Another thing, Alaska retains the mineral rights on any land a person might buy. And leases them out to the oil companies. Say you build your homestead on that land. Any time they want to, they can come in your front yard and drill. You will be compensated for damages to the homestead you just broke your ass to build. But their money doesn't make up for the fact that you lost your homestead. The oil companies have won it away from the people and now you've got an oil rig sitting in your yard.

"And the politicians here, the ones that own big pieces of land, they're selling land to the Japanese. And businesses. The old-timers out in the bush, they're screaming and they have a right to, because they're losing their way of life. But the politicians, and the rich old-timers who own the banks, the stores, live in the fancy neighborhoods in Anchorage, they're selling out. It's all just very political—who's got the

---

*This figure includes the 12 percent of Alaska land returned to native tribes.
†Ronald Reagan's secretary of the interior, James Watt.

money profits. Most of these people, they have their homes out of state somewhere, they have other investments. They pump you full of lies, their back pockets are full of money. Prices are rising, for the average Alaskan—the average house costs a liver and a lung, a hundred fifteen thousand dollars. The corporations and politicians drove the prices high. And now they're trying to bust the Indians who finally got some rights. Anchorage right now is nothing but a miniature Chicago, New York. The crime rate's incredible."

Rex

On a rig, there are fifty people on location, the crews and everything. If you're working on the log and you notice a shift in pressure, you better shut it in. Alert the drilling floor and close in the wall. If it looks bad, hit it. Once you're shut in, you're stuck for eighteen hours, doing nothing. Lost time and everything else. It costs the company about fifty thousand, just for the initial shut-in. You'd better be right if you make a decision to hit it, have some kind of indication to back it up. If not, you'll be packing your bags. But if something goes wrong, and you don't react, there's no place you can run, you get off the pad and you sink in this deep tundra, you ain't goin' nowhere. So you hit it, shut it in. It's costing three and a half million to drill a well up here. So what's another fifty, sixty thousand dollars?

They don't understand the permafrost yet. They can't even get a highway up through it yet.

I got laid off a few months back. I decided I wasn't going back up to Prudhoe again. Figured I'd work in a grocery store, settle back down into the groove. Making eight dollars an hour.* Bullshit. Can't live on it. I've made up my

*Wages in Alaska are higher than in the Lower 48. So is everything else.

mind that I'm not going to work for some mentality, just going to work for the money. And up here, the money's on the Slope. It's human nature to want to survive.

Mining, oil fields, any jobs like that, you are constantly dealing with death. There's always the chance that the next minute it could be you. You form a bond, people working together, you form a bond.

I'm not an atheist. I believe there's Somebody up there. But as far as organized religions go, I can't see it.

Look at the Soviets. They have painted a pretty bad picture of us. Their government has. You get away from the government and you get down to the people, there's not much difference. Can't be. Same here. It's propaganda we get about Soviet people. Got to kick the government out. Our government is about as close as it comes for true representation, but it's still the Big Chiefs and the little people, even if everyone goes to vote and whatever. Got to kick the government out.

The big corporations, the oil companies and the politicians, they don't think about the future.

Tarzan Fan

Around the bend, here comes the GEM of Egypt
Her measurements are perfect for a stripper
   quite so tall
The biggest act to ever hit the mountains
She takes it off the top and she leaves
   the rest to fall.

And when she moves, she strips and grooves
Little Egypt can move mountains
   with a solitary yawn.
And when she strips, she tears and rips
Away the seams of old Ohio hills left barren
   when she's gone.

                 —song of an Egypt, Ohio, stripper

Nothing is more troubling than power devouring beauty. This thought occurred to me one cold winter morning in Siberia as I stood in the cabin of Afanasii Kulagin's strip mining machine watching technology gouge a hole in hard rock that was once a mountain. Afanasii's breath turned to ice crystals that sparkled for a second, then melted when it hit the blast of the cabin's heater. His co-workers, two dark Georgians, stood behind him, admiring Afanasii's control over the big machine. She groaned, yawned, swung her neck twenty degrees, and opening her jaws molar wide, bit about two tons of rock off the cliff. Clouds of iced granite dust steamed from her mouth, puffing out like dragon's breath. The cliff rustled, shook, rumbled. Afanasii jammed her into reverse and moved her along to the next bite. She plunged for granite like a starved dinosaur. I looked around the cabin.

It was big as a living room, with frosted windswept windows that slid open to reveal southeastern Siberia's ice sculpted mountain taiga. The furniture was sparse, just one chair for the operator and standing room only. The gray steel walls were decorated with a list of operating regulations in Russian and a handcarved wooden figure of an angel praying. There were five persons in the cabin, and we all wore fur hats, fur or felt lined boots, heavy coats, woolen scarves and gloves. Because it was cold. The cabin's heater blasted hot, but Afanasii Kulagin liked working with a window flung open, and it made sense because the windowpanes were iced over with delicate crystalline etchings. Through the open window, Afanasii could see where we were going.

We were going to the next granite cliff, where the stripper would perform her act again and again until all the granite had been inhaled and spit out in piles for trucks to haul away. Where the granite used to make a high cliff, Siberia's richest coal seam, Moshchnii, would appear, bared to the sky—black beauty exposed to men of progress. An American named James Watt would adore the sight, and probably be fond of Afanasii Kulagin too.

Afanasii Kulagin is a realistic man. Progress is good for people and people need coal to fuel industry, which drives progress forward. Besides, Afanasii assured me, the land would be carefully and lovingly reclaimed, covered over again with rock and topsoil, almost-a-virgin piece of land. I allowed that it would never be the same, land defiled by human technology's strip mine inventions. This machine was altering Nature permanently and irrevocably. "Ah," smiled Afanasii, "but what is permanent in Nature? Nature is always changing, and humans are a part of Nature too. It is our responsibility as intelligent beings to improve the whole of Nature."

He had a point. But I still wanted to argue. "Okay," I said, "I'll accept the part about humans being Nature's children. I'll even accept that all of Nature is constantly changing." I gestured outside, where a Siberian hillside lay guts open, bleeding black rock. "But how is this mess an improvement on Nature? Tell me that."

We went around the question a little while until the interpreter got cold and tired, then I left Afanasii Kulagin in his office with his two teammates and the praying angel. He said if I'd drop by his flat in Nerungrii that evening, he'd introduce me to his wife, Lyudmilla, and maybe reminisce a little about his first years in Siberia. Climbing down the ladder on the monster's foreshank, I called up to him. "Thanks for the demonstration," I said.

He said something in Russian that sounded like, "You ain't seen nothin', kid."

Nerungrii, where Afanasii Kulagin lives, is a typical Siberian boomtown. Raised in haste in the early seventies, when nearby coal seams were opened for pit mining, Nerungrii has the rough and tumble, primitive flavor of old Alaska Gold Rush settlements. In late winter, scrubby pines and rough wood buildings cast long shadows when sunlight hits the frozen ground. Convoys of Japanese and American mining equipment roll along the highway between Nerungrii, where the strip mine enterprises offices are, and the rolling mountains a few miles distant, where the ground is being opened. On the edge of Nerungrii, a concrete apartment complex is almost ready for occupancy. With its raising, the citizens of Nerungrii are making a statement. Nerungrii may be just a boomtown, but its residents believe that, like Siberia's largest coal seam, the community that houses its miners will have a long life.

Afanasii Kulagin lives in a small, wood-frame apartment building, in a three-room flat with his wife, Lyudmilla, and their two children. Afanasii and Lyudmilla's living room doubles as the children's bedroom. Its walls are blanketed in thick red and gold Oriental carpets that brighten the room and retain heat. Lyudmilla had made a batch of Siberian meat dumplings and a garnish of frozen *brusnkia* berries the evening I visited them. After we ate, Afanasii Kulagin leaned back in his chair, folded his hands contentedly over a full stomach, and said:

Afanasii Kulagin

Maybe you remember the film *Tarzan*? As a kid, I saw this film many times. It's an exciting film, of course, and naturally it pushed me in adventurous directions. So, you remember how they jump from tree to tree? We kids would try to imitate this. We'd take ropes out of the house when our parents weren't watching and we'd take them into the taiga and hang them on the trees and try to swing like Tarzan. We usually played the game deep in the taiga so our parents wouldn't discover us. Then when we'd go with our parents into the taiga to pick berries and mushrooms, they would suddenly discover, "Why, here is my rope! Why is it hanging here in the trees?" They couldn't imagine how it got there.

When we were kids down in the south, our family lived near a railroad station, and of course we kids were interested in the trains. One day, we kids decided to go locomotive riding on a steam engine. So we climbed onto the roof of a train car—needless to say, without a ticket—and hid up there. But the deputy engineer noticed us. He put on his most soiled working gloves and rubbed our little mugs with them. So we took off to the riverbank and tried to wash our faces clean. But it was oil, lubricant, it wouldn't come off with water. So we tried rubbing it off with sand. That didn't work. We finally had to go home with our faces like that, all covered with grimy engine oil. So what happened when we got home? The belt of course . . .

It was a long time making the decision to move to Siberia. I was working in the west as a miner. In the newspaper *Soviet Miner,* we read about this construction of a coal mine in Siberia. So myself and some other miners, friends of mine, we decided to just go up there and take a look around. We came here to Nerungrii and we had decided that if we liked the place we'd just stay here. At first the women, our wives, they agreed with us. But then something changed their minds. On the morning before the holiday—we were going to check it out during our holiday time—we went to the railroad station and ordered tickets for the trip. When our wives heard about this, they said, "No, no. There's taiga and frosts there. We don't want to go." But we men, our decision didn't change. And so we came out here, had a look around and liked what we saw. Then we went back home and settled up at our jobs, got our severance pay and began packing up to move to Siberia. As we were leaving, our wives came to the station and saw us off. But the separation wasn't for long. Not more than a month went by when the telegrams arrived: WE'RE FLYING IN. MEET US AT THE AIRPORT.

Of course, there were troubles at first, but together, her and me, it's easier to overcome all these things. When we came here, it was just a working settlement, people were living in tents. There was an old pit where they mined coal. Then, after the geologists explored the territory, they began construction of a territorial center for exploring deposits. As soon as I got here, I began working for the exploring center. In those days, there were only about three hundred people working here. We arrived in September of 1975. There were teams of geologists and builders. This was before the big seam of coal was mined. Where we live now, there were a few wooden houses. And nearby there is a place where the first settlers would go to pick berries and their favorite mushrooms. There was lots of bog around here, so we had to cover them with soil. At first we lived in tents. But we had electricity because a big hydropower dam had been built in Chulman, not far from here. As I said, it was just a working settlement. We covered the tent floors with a layer of soil and then we laid wooden floorboards and made our tents over this. We lived in tents for three months and it was cold outside, but inside the tents it was hot. We had wood stoves, coal burning stoves.

At first we worked as carpenters. We couldn't work as miners yet, we were still building the town. Then, when the excavators arrived, we began mining the big seam of coal. Moshchnii, the big seam, was discovered in 1955.* In '57 they began to uncover it bit by bit, and when the topsoil was removed, they could follow it. And finally we began mining it.

There were no courses for studying our work. But some people who were experienced came and taught us how to do this sort of excavating. Now we have a training center for new miners in the open seam operation. The people who trained us back then, they were Soviets. But the first machinery from abroad came here in 1977. They were called "Marion" and they were from the Sumitomo Company in Japan. At the end of '77, we got some American Unitraks for transporting.

* *Moshchnii* means powerful. It is the name of Siberia's largest known coal seam.

310

In open pit mining, we remove the top layer of soil and reach the coal. It's very simple. This differs from deep mining because we mine in the fresh air, not underground. And we have to blast away the layer of topsoil. When we're going to blast an area, we clear it of all unauthorized personnel. Then no one is allowed into the area after the chain of explosions until the explosives specialists have made sure all the explosives detonated, that none failed to detonate, that the area is safe. After that, we move in with the excavators. Of course, all the machinery has been removed until after the explosion. So then we bring in the excavators, we move along the seam, removing sections of soil, then sections of coal, then sections of soil and so on. Me and my team, we remove the soil. Mostly it's stone, and the first layer of soil is eternal frost.

Eternal frost covers the territories beginning a little south of here and goes way up north. All the territories here in Siberia are covered with eternal frost soil, both the tundra and the taiga. Taiga is covered with coniferous forests, and the trees are very small and sparse. Tundra has no trees, or very few trees, but in the summer it has low vegetation. Tundra looks like snowy steppes sometimes with sparsely scattered dwarf trees. The whole area is on eternal frost soil. The main difficulty with eternal frost is, when we are preparing the next area for explosions, we have a number of feet down which we need to drill. After drilling, if the sun begins to shine and the soil begins melting, then there'll be a column of water inside the drilled hole which will freeze up. Then we have to drill them over again. But it's only a problem in the summer, in winter it's the best time to drill.*

Under the very severe climate we have here, we need to

* The chief engineer of the Moshchnii strip mine operation told me that Soviet experts had not yet devised methods to reclaim Siberia's eternal frost blanket, which is being torn open by this procedure.

311

pay a lot of attention to our equipment. You can't imagine how many things we have to do to keep our equipment operating properly. Besides, we're dealing with a very solid kind of stone here. According to the scientists, this rock has a 13 or 14 percent rating of solidness. What it is, it's very solidly compacted sand.

For us miners, we can go to work in any temperatures. But it's not allowed for the machinery to work at more than 40 degrees above zero and not less than 40 below zero.* These particular excavators must keep to that limit, but we have another excavator, a stepping excavator, which can't go below 30 below zero. We work under any conditions. But the temperatures will become so low that sometimes it's impossible for the bus drivers who take us to work to start their bus engines. And so we have our days off.

We have our injuries on the job. Usually it's when a worker doesn't pay attention to the safety rules. Maybe he jumps from a place too high or maybe he hasn't taken his equipment in for maintenance as we're required to do. We're really working to improve safety for workers. Our union's interested in safety as much as the enterprise is interested in it. For example, the noise you hear inside my excavator, that's the heater which keeps the excavator defrosted in these conditions. And there's noise from the ventilation system which blows fresh air into the cab. But according to the noise decibel system, it's not a dangerous noise level. Anyway, we're supplied with earplugs, but we don't like to use them.

I can't recall any deaths on the job since I've worked here.

My team consists of eight guys. We all work on the same excavator. Now I have new comrades† on my team

---

* −40 Celsius = −40 F.
+40 Celsius = +104 F.
† In Russian, the word for comrade is *tovarisch*. It is used as frequently as Americans say, "friend," "fella," or "buddy."

because the veterans went after a new-type machine. They wanted to learn to operate the new type of equipment, and I wanted to stay here with this excavator. The men I work with are all different ages, but most of my new team is young guys. They're training, and yet we've overfulfilled our quota for the first quarter of the first year of this Five Year Plan. Now that I've got my new team, we'll work permanently together. Right now we have a lack of trained excavators, so I take trainees and teach them, and I really enjoy it. Every day we're getting in new machinery, and we need trained people to run them.

Basically, I like the guys I work with. They know their work well. They're very gentle. And we never quarrel.

Here at our mine, I'm sure there isn't one person who doesn't belong to our trade union. All of us who work at this excavation site belong to the same union. And our union is a working organization, it is active. It defends us against allegations of rules violations. It takes care of getting vouchers for summer vacations and for sending our children to summer camps. Naturally, the union takes care of our health benefits. Our union is very popular here. Now we have a new resort under construction, And a preventive health care clinic. You may ask why we didn't have a health spa before now. Well, until recently there weren't that many people working here. And now since we plan to double the production from this pit, next year a lot of people will be arriving to work. We'll need a health spa then.

Lyuda and I, it's not our habit to be unhappy. We spend a lot of time with our friends. Mostly, we like to entertain in our home, but we go out a lot too. And Lyuda cooks those famous Siberian meat dumplings for our guests. . . .

Well, if I could send a message to miners in the U.S., I'd say, first of all I wish you health. It's important for everyone, but for a miner especially. Secondly, I hope that all their requests, all their wishes will be fulfilled. Regards. And my best wishes. But it would be better if your miners' union members could connect with our miners' union members. It would help strengthen relations between us.

Nerungrii is just a small Siberian town, and yet walking through its snow-packed streets, I noticed several big billboards which carried a simple message: MIR and MIR Y DRUZHBA. Peace. Peace and Friendship. I asked 'Afanasii Kulagin if the billboards were advertising for world peace. *"Konechno,"* he said. "Of course. What could be better to advertise than world peace?"

The next morning, Lyudmilla invited me over to her house for breakfast. She had made a special Siberian breakfast treat. Homemade ice cream.

Crafts and Shamans

When eternal frost wraps Yakutia in a glistening white winter coat, wise Yakutians slip *unti* on their feet and consult the modern shamans. Yakutians have always depended on reindeer fur boots and shamans' secret organic brews to survive the dark, cold winter months, and Siberia's Russian and Ukrainian immigrants have adopted Yakutians' survival secrets. Today's urban industrial Yakutsk is a center where native crafts and shamans are very much in demand.

Anya Sleptsova is a seamstress in the Yakutsk souvenir factory Sardana, which produces native crafts like unti—boots made from reindeer hide and fur. Sardana also uses the pelts of Siberian polar foxes, sables, squirrels and Yakut horses to make luxurious fur coats and hats. The factory produces birchbark bowls, a Yakut musical instrument—a Siberian version of the mouth harp—and other traditional Yakut and Even crafts. It is a state financed operation, unlike Alaska's native crafts industries, which are either operated by native regional corporations or are total shams run out of the Orient. The native crafts of

Alaska and Siberia are strikingly similar—unti and *kammiks* are basically the same boot—but the production of traditional crafts differs in one important aspect. Alaska's department stores and tourist traps are loaded with "Alaska souvenirs" fabricated in Hong Kong or Taiwan, and one must forage through the fake articles to locate the genuine Alaskan product, the beautiful artifacts made, for example, by Inupiat Eskimos. In Siberia, anything advertised as a Siberian souvenir is the real thing. The Soviet government encourages production of traditional crafts among all its nationalities, and by investing in craft industries, provides jobs that encourage workers to keep in touch with their national origins.

Anya Sleptsova is a young Yakut woman—too young to remember the old shamans. But she has a thorough knowledge of her people's origins, cultures and traditions. Reared in a northern Siberian village, as a child, she could look out over the Arctic waters and almost see the North Pole. Now a young mother, Anya has settled down with her husband and children in Yakutsk. Urban living suits her, she told me, her face as round and glowing as the Siberian full moon. Working as a seamstress in a Yakutsk crafts factory, Anya Sleptsova said, not only helps support her family's urban lifestyle. Anya Sleptsova is creating new versions of ancient Yakut artistry, adding a nostalgic and necessary warm touch to new Siberian Soviet lifestyles.

Anya Sleptsova

Both my mother and father are Yakut. My father returned from the war very seriously wounded, without a left arm. He was the village librarian. When I was born in 1951, just a few months later, he died. I was one or two months old. For a while, my mother stayed with his family, because she was all alone with just me, but then their place got crowded and so my mother had to move. This was in Namtse, not far from here, eight kilometers maybe.

I have two sisters from my stepfather. My stepfather was a communist. He was chairman and founder of the Yakut State Farm not far from here. Then we moved to Bulunskii, very far from here in the Tiksii region, where my stepfather helped to found another state farm, and then he was founder of another one before he retired. He was twenty years older than my mother. After he retired, he worked on a polar fox farm. And in 1969 he died. He had high blood pressure.

My mother worked in the state bank, and she had been an accountant on the farm before that. In the bank she worked as a teller, but four years ago she retired. She is fifty-four now. Her pension is one hundred twenty rubles monthly.

In Bulunskii, after I finished school, I worked as a *vospitatel'nitsa,* working with small children, like a counselor. The children were . . . how old are they in the youngest grades? . . . ten, eight, nine. I was seventeen or eighteen. It was the Far North settlement, and it was a boarding school where I worked. In summer, the children went to camp not far from here in Yakutsk. Then, before I was married, I worked for a while in what they call a fur shop. We took beaver and squirrel skins and sewed fur boots, hats and other sorts of winter clothing. And in Yakutsk I met my husband. He was studying at the university and working in the technological division of the department for mountain research in geology. We recently celebrated our seventh wedding anniversary. We have a six year old boy and a four year old girl.

My husband is from a small village called Vugu. *Vugunekhta* is the word for "hills" in the Yakut language, and this village is situated in the hills. After he graduated from the institute, we moved to the south of Yakutia, but we weren't there for a long time. Our son was born there, and the climate wasn't very healthy down there for him.* He was sickly. So we came back up here.

Every year we celebrate *Sekhr* [the summer solstice]. All the Yakut people put on national costumes. It's sometime in June. My grandmother always knew how to sew well. She could sew our national costumes which we wear on Sekhr. She was also a master in fashioning a special kind of birchbark bowls called *tuyesok*. They can be made so perfect that they can keep water and it takes on the birch flavor. There were lots of grandchildren, but I was the oldest and therefore the favorite. Once a year she'd come here to visit. In summer, we would go to visit her. She was a very good cook. Even now it seems that nobody can cook better than she did. I especially liked the special kind of porridge, *salamats*. And pancakes. Lots of meat dishes then. And for a dairy dish we would like *kircha*, whipped cream, very, very fresh with strawberries. And then you freeze it sometimes. It's a wonderful dish for breakfast. And *sora*, a kind of sour milk product.

Oh, how do you explain? It's natural my grandmother didn't want to give up the old traditions. But she was happy to live under modern conditions.

Very many, it would seem, Yakut fought in the Great Patriotic War. Two of my uncles went off to the war and didn't come back. Generally, every family, I believe, had someone who went, because my husband's father, he went to the war at seventeen, he added a year to his age so he could join. He came back an invalid. My father, then my uncles, then lots of them, even in our small village where I was born near Namtse. Many, many fought; it's called *krasnaya,* in areas where there weren't so many men, every household sent a man to the war.

When the Russian tsar ruled Yakutia, our people lived under Russian princelings, under merchants. Generally

* Southern Yakutia is "warmer" than northern Yakutia.

318

speaking, under oppression. And my stepfather took part after the Revolution, there were many . . . my stepfather took part in the civil war. He was a partisan, and in those years he was just a boy of fifteen or sixteen. Well then, the collective farm, and then the war, and now . . .

You see the picture of embroidering on fur. They didn't use Yakut horsehide,* they wore calfskin, they used reindeer. Now a factory has been opened which puts out fur coats, boots made of horsehide, the Yakut horse. There are problems with the dressing of the horsehides. They don't curry as well as reindeer skins. In my opinion, if it were easier to curry, if it was softer, it would be used even more frequently because it is more perfect than reindeer skin and more beautiful, in my opinion.

The Yakut people worshiped wooden idols, like a talisman which they hung on the walls. Baiyanai is a taiga spirit, the protector of hunters. He will do everything you want, save you from any evil. You needn't speak words. Besides Baiyanai, there were wooden gods, lesser gods. It's like a fairy tale for us, Baiyanai is a legend. The protector of hunters, for luck in the hunt. The old gods were made like Chinese dolls with bowed heads, but the heads didn't rock. Little figures. It was as if these lesser gods prayed to Baiyanai. Not prayed, bowed down. If they had brought food, the hunters would break off some and give it to the god. This means they were asking luck of the Baiyanai. It became a tradition. This is a gift for the god. It's become a tradition of the taiga, and when we go to pick berries we give to this god. We keep the old traditions very closely. There's another tradition we observe.

There is a house for hunters in the forest. Just a wooden house, a house like anywhere. You can just go there . . . here's a little stove, next to the stove, dry firewood, and

---

*The Yakut horse is small and Shetland-like, with a very long fur coat. Its meat is Yakutia's "national food."

canned food. Go ahead, use them, heat the stove. But when you are ready to leave you must replenish the supply for the next person who may run into a misfortune and come here. For us it is a very serious tradition. And there are others too. Giving pieces of food to this god shows it. And then it's lonely for hunters usually, just one or two. You have a chat with Baiyanai, the spirit of the taiga, and it's more cheerful.

Here in spring and fall, the hunters are allowed to hunt ducks for a few days. All the men seem to go out of their minds. They can also hunt rabbits. If they can get a license in winter, they hunt moose. And the professional hunters hunt for muskrat. In the old days, hunting was not the only means of existence; we bred cows. And now we are breeding cattle, for example, my husband's parents have cattle . . . babies, grown-ups, we traditionally use cow's milk, but further north there's reindeer milk. We prepare *kumis*, a favorite Yakut drink.

In the old days, there was *kamlanya*, the shamans, they were healers and sometimes they'd call forth . . . we had these devils and demons. Exorcism, it's called. They would throw different kinds of grasses and food in the fire, and as is usual, the corpse is there. The grave markers are little houses made of wood, with a sloping roof, and they were beautiful with their wood carvings. And till nowadays we have lots of them in Namtse, like little castles made of wood with different carving and pictures of lovers and animals. When someone died, their spirit went to good hunting and lots of animals.

I work in a fur hat department of our local native crafts factory. I get up at half past six. My mother gets up a little earlier, because she is retired now, and she makes breakfast for us. I wash up, I do a little exercise, rinse off and go eat. And then I wait for the free bus at half past seven. And at twenty till I'm at work. At work, I change into my work clothes. And if I have no work waiting for me at my bench, then I go to the preparation shop and receive my work. We wear smocks at work. They give us the pieces of polar fox for the hats. Usually we sew on a machine, but sometimes by hand. We sew both fox and polar fox.

We have no timers, no clocks on our machines. We have a planned month. And we can regulate and plan for ourselves day by day. It also depends on how we are given the pieces. It happens that they sometimes give us more at the end of the month. If there's nothing at all to do, we sew fur coats or make souvenirs. I know how to sew fur coats and hats and boots.

At ten o'clock we have a ten-minute break. We do exercises. Then we have lunch from twelve till one. We can go anywhere. We can walk around. We have a dentist we can go to. And at three o'clock, we have another break. When I finish my day, the bus leaves at five fifteen, so I finish at five fifteen. If I don't stop to look in the shops, I'll go home. I'm usually there by five forty-five.

At work we regularly have lectures on safety. We sign a special form that we know all the rules and will try to follow them. "Don't wear heels, wear flats. Be careful not to let your hair fall in the machinery. Keep track of the on/off switch on the machine. Make sure there's good light for working."

Working in native crafts connects me with the traditions of the Yakut people, my people. There have been changes in our lives, literacy first. There is no illiteracy now. And the fact that we receive free medical care. Our children have received the opportunity to study towards whatever they want. We don't need to save for a rainy day.

I have heard lots of stories about our national hero, Manchary. He took treasures from the rich and gave them to poor people. We also have lots of legends about Nugun-boutu, a fairy tale hero who fought against enemy invaders. Manchary was a real person, though. Vasily Manchary, he was a reality, not from a fairy tale. In

Yakutsk there is a tower where he was imprisoned by the wealthy. He lived at the end of the 19th century. I don't know how he died, but he was old when he died. It's even been shown that there was an incident when he was very old and gray as a polar fox that the rich people asked Manchary to show them how he took from the rich and gave to the poor. One rich man asked Manchary how he did it. So Manchary called together all the wealthy people who lived nearby. It looked as if they were going to a concert, everybody was in a state of expectation, everybody waited for Manchary with bated breath. Then Manchary appeared on a white steed and seized that wealthy man who'd asked how he did it. He had a *batiya*, a kind of spear with two blades, in his hand. He pricked the rich man with this spear. Then he rode off on the white steed. The rich man was so humiliated in front of his wealthy friends, he was so ashamed that he broke all the locks on his treasure chest, opened up his rooms filled with treasures, and fled.

Saturday, we are going to our parents' place to help them out. They don't have heating, central heating, they heat by oven. My father is an invalid so he can't chop wood or carry it. He was wounded during the war. They are living in Bugnyekhtakh, one hundred kilometers from here to the south. It takes us two hours—we have a Zaporozhets, our private car.* It cost us 3,800 and something rubles. Now they cost four thousand something rubles. We bought it with savings. It didn't take us long to save the money because our parents helped us as well. There is no problem buying gasoline; we usually buy tickets in the store and then we pay with them at the gas station. It's the common way of buying gas. It's very common to own a car here in Yakutsk; lots of people have

---

*The Zaporozhets is the smallest and least expensive Soviet automobile, manufactured in Ukraine. Anya's cost the equivalent of $5,700.

private cars. Our enterprises have this special fund annually for selling cars to the best workers. That's why there is no problem buying a car if you're a good worker. The same with bicycles and motorcycles.

My children go to a daycare center while I'm at work. I stayed home for a year after each child was born. Now they've started paying for the women who stay home with their young babies—they are luckier than me because they receive money during their whole first year at home. The sum equals their usual monthly wage. This is all just since the last Party Congress. And the state guarantees a woman her job for seven years when she has a child. We have a law that a woman who's expecting a baby works until the sixth month and then stops working until after the baby's born.

When I was pregnant, I followed my doctor's plan and visited the doctor once a month. In the sixth month I had some problems, not very serious. And the doctor sent me to a confinement hospital for a month until I was well. Then for two years after my child was born, pediatricians and nurses would come visit me. Also, I visited my patronage, family nurses, who are a special kind of nurse for children, who visit you during the first year and help you, teach you how to take care of your baby. They do it automatically, not only for the first child, but with every child you have. Besides visiting me, she gave inoculations to the children at home.

As for me, I prefer ordinary childbirth. I had a very ordinary labor and birth in a small village with my second child, in the only hospital in town. With my first child, we were living in Tiksii and I had to go to a maternity house. They took me by plane. Usually the stay at a maternity house is nine days. Having children at home sounds frightening to me.

What do I wish for the future? Certainly health, health for my family. I dream that our grandma should live a long time. And I want my children to be obedient and clever. And that we should always love each other.

Anna Arinosova is a modern shaman, working as a practical nurse with Yakutsk's public health clinic. Her patients rarely come to the clinic for treatment, though— Anna goes to them at factory workplaces, into neighborhood centers and homes, or wherever she can carry modern medical techniques that help people maintain health. Calm and reassuring with her patients, the idea of meeting an American caused her a spell of apprehension. When we were first introduced, she bowed her head so low over medical charts that her wide white nurse's cap hid her face like eternal frost conceals Siberian tundra. When she finally raised her head, a beautiful Asian face was revealed, blushing deep crimson. "I think there is some mistake," she told me. "Maybe my life wouldn't be very interesting to you."

I told Anna Arinosova that her life would probably interest a lot of people, and suggested we might meet later at the Hotel Lena in downtown Yakutsk, where we could talk in surroundings less crowded than the Yakutsk public health clinic. Anna Arinosova said she might show up at eight o'clock that evening.

The young Russian doctor who works with Anna Arinosova told me that preventive health care is a priority at the clinic, and that often she and Anna go through workers' neighborhoods searching out people whose medical records indicate they require treatment. "If they won't come to us," the doctor said, "we'll find them. It is our responsibility to keep our patients in good health. Sometimes our patients are very stubborn, they don't want to be disciplined about maintaining their good health or treating an ailment. We try to talk to them, try to convince them it is important for each person to maintain good physical condition."

I asked the doctor if the old shamans' traditional methods of hypnosis and herbal cures were practiced as part of today's preventive health care treatment. "Certainly," she said. "We use many of the traditional treatments, combining them with scientifically advanced ones. For example, we teach self-hypnosis, which the old shamans taught, only our methods are more effective because today we understand more about the science of hypnosis and about other traditional healing methods. We also use acupuncture, herbal preparations, and cupping methods to draw out infection. We combine these traditional methods with new technology."

Yakutsk is not a tourist town, and precisely because it isn't, the industrial town built entirely on eternal frost seemed a more genuine model of urban Siberian life. Some of Yakutsk's older buildings, ancient log cabin structures built by Russian settlers before they understood eternal frost, have sunk into the soil that melted with the heat of their weight. In contrast, the newer buildings, designed and constructed with advice from Yakutsk's Eternal Frost Institute, are sleek concrete structures that stand confidently tall. Most of the public buildings and private dwellings are decorated with plants—botanical gardens that compensate for the scarcity of trees outdoors.

The Hotel Lena is one of Yakutsk's "in between" buildings, neither ancient nor new, a ramshackle residence hotel for workers who have temporarily located in Siberia, such as construction crews and miners. The Lena's halls are narrow and the lobby is dark; bedrooms are small, and those with private baths occasionally delight a guest when the cold water tap and toilet plumbing actually work. The Lena is no luxury hotel, but it is probably the most hospitable one in the Soviet Union, and somehow the warmth of its employees makes living in the Lena a cozy experience. Exciting too, if you happen to wander into the lounge any evening of the week.

At night, workers pack the tables of the Lena's lounge

and sit drinking vodka and beer, listening to the music of a local rock band that plays Soviet "jazz." The lounge serves substantial meals of Yakut horse meat shishkebab—though I confess to never having tasted this Siberian delicacy—fresh, hothouse grown vegetables, and sturdy bread. By seven o'clock, the place is packed. Men wear suits and ties, and women are dressed to the teeth in vampish frocks, powdered faces, both Yakut and Russian, high-heeled pumps and lots of long, coal black or platinum blond hair. By eight o'clock, the band is warmed up and the room throbs from an overloaded bass amplifier. An unescorted woman will be approached quite openly by rugged construction workers and miners, spiffed up for a night on the town, who politely request a dance or suggest joining them for a drink at one of the tables filled with bottles and surrounded by laughing people. Under a heavy blue smokescreen haze, would-be lovers longingly survey the dance floor, and lovers with their partners in tow move off into corners to hold hands and whisper in the dark. (Private love nests are extremely difficult to find in the Soviet Union, unless a man and woman are married, in which case they may have a flat of their own. In the U.S.S.R., it is illegal to engage a hotel room in the town where you live. The unmarried lovers of the Lena's lounge just have to use a lot of imagination.) The scene is reminiscent of the workers' barrooms in Anchorage—the rugged energy of adventurous free spirits prevails. Anything might happen in this Siberian honky-tonk. A vigilant chaperone will snatch her charge out of the Lena's lounge just when all the fun is beginning, admonishing that "there is no time for relaxing."

Anna Arinosova arrived at my hotel room at eight o'clock on the button. She was more relaxed than she had been in her workplace. She had only one hour to visit, she told me, but she ended up staying two. After she left, I wondered if she had gone downstairs to join the revelry. I went to have a look. Anna was not among the party crowd. From what I knew of her, she was probably over at the Komsomol League's coffee house, where a crowd more suited to her tastes was gathered.

Anna Arinosova

I was born in the Ordzshonikidze region. The village was called Sinsk. I was born in 1956, on April eleventh. We were ten children in our family, eight girls and two guys. I am the seventh child. My parents . . . my mother is working in the vegetable garden on the Yakut state farm, my father is a disabled veteran of the war. He was director of a collective farm for twelve years, and then he worked on the state farm, and now he works in a hospital, as assistant manager for procurement. Now they are both retired. My mother was decorated. *

My brother is a family man, my older brother. He lives here in Yakutsk. He has his own flat and they have one child. My oldest sister is working as a vospitatel'nitsa, a teacher of very young children. The third is also a sister. She is working as a master in the garment industry. Then my next sister works at a brewery. The fifth sister works in the procurator's office. She's a procurator. The sixth is working for the planning organization for industrial construction. She's an industrial engineer. I'm the seventh. I graduated from the Yakutsk Secondary Medical School. The eighth, my brother, graduated from the Omsk Aviation Academy, and he's working in Bagatai. The ninth girl is studying in the tenth grade [a senior in high school], and the tenth, my little sister, is in school in the seventh grade.

Yes, certainly, I like the idea of a big family. For myself, I don't even know, 'cause nowadays it's not so common to have such hard labor so many times.

My family speaks both Yakut and Russian. At home

* As a Heroine Mother of the Soviet Union. Mothers who give birth to and rear ten or more children are honored with this award.

when we converse with our mother and father we speak Yakut. Our father speaks almost no Russian at all. He understands everything, he can speak some Russian too, but he thinks that Yakut has been our native language, so we speak it. But he understands everything. It depends. We can speak Russian as well as Yakut. That's why we sometimes don't even watch which language we are using at home.

We have our Yakut traditions. In summer, for example, every year we celebrate Sekhr, the solstice, and the whole family gets together on this holiday. We all go to the village where our parents live. All the relatives, all the brothers and sisters, it's very joyous. This is a very big celebration in the village, and it's very interesting. There are national dishes. There's *kumis*, that's made from mare's milk, then there's lots of meat dishes, and we make *shashlik* [reindeer shishkebab]. There are also sports competitions, with specific national games. We wear national costumes on this day. Usually we have a competition for best costume.

It begins. Everyone gathers in a circle and dances a round dance. They're dressed in special costumes. This round dance opens the celebration. There is a kind of traditional pole in the center of the circle. It's called a *sergeh*. It's a kind of pole and it's covered with ornaments, and at the top there is usually a kind of Yakut souvenir. What are the *Kanavyasi*? These Kanavyasi, many years ago, were put into the ground near the house. It's a symbol of hospitality. That is, "Come visit me, be my guest. Come on your horse. Hitch your horse and come to me as a guest." It's also a symbol of the good life. That is, "I have the means to receive guests, so stop and come inside." Another interesting thing, when the railroad came here to Yakutia, that is, crossed over from the Amur region to Yakutia, we put three enormous iron sergeh on the border made out of iron. That is to say, "Come hitch your iron steed and please be our guests in Yakutia."

The round dance can be around one pole, but every year we put in a pole, so there are many of them.

Usually my father told us the old stories in my childhood. I don't know how to tell it in Russian. In Yakut the story is called *Bedoro-konyatsin* . . . that means five-cow grandmother. In Yakut *bes,* that's "five," *inostak* means "cow"—*bedoro-konyatsin.* In translation it comes out approximately like this: grandmother with five cows, "Five-Cow Grandmother." I don't remember the fairy tale exactly.

There was a grandmother long ago, and she had no children. She had five cows, and she was with them every day and night. She usually put scissors under her pillow. (Why, I don't know.) When she went out to milk the cows, right away the scissors started to click and she thought, "There's nobody home," and rushed into the house. But she didn't notice anything. So then she went out again and started to milk the cows again. In this way she went back and forth several times, because she heard the scissors. And when she went in for the fifth time, there on her bed she saw a child. She was delighted of course to find the child, because she had no children at all.

It ends . . . well, the child will stay with her as if it were her own, as happens in fairy tales, she'll be very satisfied, will live happily ever after.

Over the past almost three and one half years, I've worked as a district medical nurse. That is, I've been working with one doctor. We have our own office in the clinic where we work with our patients from our defined district, the district assigned to us. As for me, I worked in the 16th District. I work with Dr. Lyudmila Georgievna Kholodezhnikova. The population of our district is more than two thousand. In our district we have a number of organizations which send their people to our clinic. We are a practical clinic. We provide the practical services. For example to prevent flu we give flu shots. Also tuberculosis.

Flu, TB, and some kind of fever. It's free. In addition, we also receive patients from our district with chronic illnesses and put them in our register. For example, the diseases chronic pneumonia of the lungs, chronic cystitis, chronic bronchitis, myocardial infarction, systemic heart disease, for all the kinds of diseases we have a register so we can keep track of their histories and call them in for regular appointments.

Over a three or four hour period the doctor and I receive patients with various illnesses and ailments from our district. And afterwards, we go out to the district to make house calls, and she examines them, and I sit with the patients and sometimes give injections. We administer various treatments: we do *banki* [cupping] and mustard plasters. Cupping is used for patients with aggravated chronic pneumonia, such diseases as chronic bronchitis, tracheitis. We put them on the thorax and back. The main service of our public health system is preventive treatment for the people, which is why I work in inoculation clinics. We give inoculations against infectious diseases like influenza and other diseases. Gastrointestinal disorders especially before the summer. We set up clinics at warehouses and in the local shoestore. We go around to the warehouses, wherever people work. There is only one big enterprise in my district. But sometimes there are many factories and enterprises, as in the 11th District, right next to ours. They have a larger population to serve. The 11th District has a pathology clinic at Yakutstroi. Also, often we help whoever has more population in their district. We must help each other.

I work five days a week. Seven and a half hours. My monthly salary is eighty rubles and besides everything I need for working in a very difficult climate, so-called "climatic zone," it is in the vicinity of 25 percent of my salary. On the whole it is enough money, but when I need more money I can take another district to earn extra money. In my free time I take care of things like house-work. Besides that, I go to the movies. In addition I work out in track and field, running. I run eight hundred meters and one thousand meters. I'm a class B runner. And I like to disco very much. Most of my free time I like to spend at the youth coffeehouse which opened recently not far from my home. It's called the Youth Café. You know, this café was opened by the Komsomol organization. You have to buy tickets. They have records and tape recordings. I like the music there very much. And they have discussions about the bands who perform on recordings. We have all kinds of music, and I go there when I have free time. Maybe two or three times a month.

Sincerely speaking, all my male friends are where I was living before. They've all gotten married now, and when we go there I visit with their families. I don't really have any male friends here. I don't even know too many. Well, I'm not that kind of person. Besides, my life is such . . . I'm so busy. I don't know. I don't look at others. There are girls who are more active, who are trying to be more aggressive.

As for a husband, I would want him to be a simple and good person, and certainly, I'd like him to be a smart [stylish] person. His occupation is all the same to me.

Usually a person who arrives here in Yakutsk makes arrangements beforehand. They're provided apartments, a job, other facilities. It supplies everything they need. I was about seventeen years old when I came here with my sister. Well we . . . you see, my parents are living in the district and my sisters and brothers are here. Most of them have their own families. I am living in the house which belonged to my parents before. They wanted to move here and they bought the house, but then they changed their minds, so now I am living in my own house with my girlfriend, here in Yakutsk. It's possible to buy a house in the suburbs. It's made of wood.*

I lived in a workers' dormitory, then I lived with relatives who had bought a co-op apartment, and now I'm living in the house. It's better to live in my own place, instead of with other people.

I haven't met any man yet with whom I'd like to go anywhere. We just arrived here recently, after all. As for having a husband, yes, I'd like that. As for having lots of children, as I've already said, the largest families have three people, maybe four. In general, we have the situation where you can stay home with the child for the first year and I would rather sit home with my child for a year.

I don't think about war, and I don't want to think about war. I would like the U.S. and the U.S.S.R. to have friendly relations. If we had good relations, there would be more contact between our doctors and scientists and that would be better. Certainly, I would take the opportunity to visit the U.S. I think it would be very interesting. I'd like to visit any area, because I can't believe that people can be in such difficult conditions. It's hard to believe that all their medical treatment has to be paid for.

In my country we study nursing two and a half or three and a half years, depending on the specialty. We also have practical courses in our nursing schools. If there was one thing that I could add, I would graduate from the university. That way I'd know more and that way serve my patients better. I would learn how to diagnose illness by myself and serve them better. I am going to go further with my studies. One day I hope to become a doctor.

* People may buy or build their own country home in the Soviet Union, but not within city limits. They may *not* own the land on which the house is built. Anyone wishing to build a house gets permission to use a plot in perpetuity from either civil authorities or from the workplace. Large enterprises usually have the use (not the ownership) of a certain amount of land for this purpose. If the government should ever wish to use the land on which you've built your house, they will either pay you its cost or provide you with a similar one in another area.

Service Elevates

When Lou Williams was a child, she picked cotton and grew corn on her grandfather's farm. Raised in a Creole family in rural Louisiana, Lou's childhood memories are woven from blossoming chinabowl trees, children's "rain play," Creole dance bands and Fats Domino music spurring agile feet to shuffle over parlor floors, gumbo made with rue, and family bonds so close she always felt secure.

Lou Williams' life changed after she married and went to Germany, where her husband was stationed in the army. And it changed once again after her divorce. Through a long chain of events, Lou landed in Fairbanks, Alaska, with two children to support and no job. After the Alaska pipeline boom died down, work was hard to find in Fairbanks, especially for women with no occupational skills. Like most women who find themselves in Lou's position, she took a service worker's job. Today she works at Fairbanks Memorial Hospital, in the housekeeping department. In her early forties, although she appears much younger, Lou is performing one of society's most unpopular chores—cleaning up after others. Her wages and benefits are not the highest in U.S. service occupations, but she lives in a large, comfortable apartment and manages to support her teenage son and daughter. To this beautiful Creole woman, I dedicate the following story of an ancient *babushka* housekeeper in Moscow's finest department store, GUM.

Babushkas, as grandmothers and other old Soviet women are called with affection, are often hired to sweep the streets and subways of Moscow, Leningrad, Tashkent and other cities. Their broom brigades give urban U.S.S.R. its spit-and-polish coat. Occasionally a babushka janitor can be heard grumbling over her broom or mop pail. She got a bad shake out of life and she knows it. Many lost their husbands or entire families in World War II; many live alone or crowded together into dingy flats. Their wages are among the lowest in the Soviet Union and their working conditions among the least enviable. Yet babushkas are probably the most patriotic Soviet citizens. Witnesses of revolutions, civil war and Nazi terror, they are grateful that the Motherland is peaceful today. The broom brigade is hardly prepared to rise up against its deplorable working conditions.

If Soviet society wanted to be genuinely pristine about glorifying workers, then somebody in the next Party Congress ought to raise the issue of babushka janitors and street sweepers. A society that has increasing problems with vagrant youth gangs and hooliganism could surely find replacements for the old women maintenance crews. And if the women still wanted to feel useful to society, or if their pensions were inadequate, they could be assigned to child-care centers or youth hospitals, where age and wisdom are appreciated by hearts and minds yet untainted by the universal syndrome of middle-generation cynicism. If any segment of Soviet society needs material uplifting, it is the service workers—housekeepers, waitresses, and, most of all, the babushka scrubbers brigades. And bent old men. The few who survived the war.

I did meet one babushka who loved her work. It was an accidental meeting on May Day. I was on the reviewing stand in Red Square, directly across from Lenin's tomb, watching millions of workers parade by, celebrating the workers' holiday invented in the United States but most heartily observed in the Soviet Union.

The sky was clear blue this Moscow spring morning, and a pale sun cast thin beams over Brezhnev and Kosygin, who were reviewing labor's celebration from their stand high on Lenin's tomb. The air was cold and I shivered under a light jacket.

Thunderous voices boomed the *Internationale* as men and women wrapped in woolen coats and each other's arms marched ten, twelve, fourteen abreast past Lenin's resting place. Fathers lifted babies with round laughing faces, holding them high, where infant eyes could wonder at the sea of pink, blue and green balloons, the floats and banners, the confetti snow. For one day, at least, workers were putting aside their personal problems, their workplace gripes, their beefs with the system, petty or profound, and were celebrating the achievements of their own toil. A man standing next to me lit a *papiros*, a cheap sweet smoke, and, clamping the two-inch cardboard filter between his teeth, ripped the muffler from his neck and flagged a passing brigade of steel workers. "*Slava!*" he shouted past the papiros, "*Slava!*" Glory. Glory to the working class. His two adolescent daughters giggled over a handsome Red Army honor guard doing a goose step. Another man's young son cried, "Papa, I can do that step, I can!"

Watching the parade through Red Square, I noticed a total absence of armed militia. Even the honor guard were not carrying weapons. Thinking back to demonstrations of American workers, either supporting or opposing government policies, where local police squadrons and sometimes National Guard troops were inevitably lurking in the

335

shadows of the demonstrators, this apparent absence of armed militia seemed stunning. My escort explained there was absolutely no need for them, even for crowd control, on May Day.

Later, after the parade ended, we stepped into Moscow's beautiful Metro station, where, packed into the entrance tunnel, steps away from Red Square, were about one hundred strapping young Red Army soldiers, toting rifles. I asked my escort what these men were doing in the subway, facing Red Square, if they were not security forces. She said, "They came to watch the parade. The parade is over. They are going back to their barracks." I asked why they were carrying rifles if there was no need for a security force on May Day. Rather angrily, she replied, "They are soldiers, so they carry rifles. They will only use them when they go back to their barracks. They just picked them up on their way home. Besides, it is not our business to ask why soldiers are here. They are in the subway, like everyone else." It is illegal for a citizen to own a handgun in the Soviet Union, let alone tote a rifle in a subway tunnel, so the Red Army soldiers were not really "like everyone else." The presence of armed security forces at a workers' demonstration was certainly nothing new to my experience, and if my escort had only understood how similar the United States and Soviet Union are in these matters of official policy, she might have been less defensive. I felt sad that the hostility between two governments had raised such a wall between two women who were having a hard enough time breaching a language barrier.

The parade swept on, hundreds of thousands of feet tramping over history worn cobblestones. Huge banners were lofted, red slashes bearing a golden message, MIR. MIR Y DRUZHBA! Peace. Peace and Friendship. They were addressing the world, and near the reviewing stand, a bank of television cameras recorded their message. *Mir!* roared through Red Square and bounced off Lenin's tomb, and off the façade of GUM Department Store.

My feet were frozen in my boots. I pointed to my escort's red nose and suggested we go indoors to defrost. We found refuge in the women's room in the basement of GUM. At the back there was a door on which a sign said, EMPLOYEES ONLY. DO NOT ENTER. Curiosity guided my hand. The door creaked, then swung open.

"Come in! Come in!" cried an ancient woman. "Come inside, *devushka,* and have a cup of tea. You are frozen to your toes."

We entered a little housekeepers' service room, about ten by twelve feet, lit with one dim bulb hanging by a string. The babushka turned her back and filled a pot at the sink. I looked around. On a chair in one corner sat a middle-aged woman, kerchief framing Russian round cheeks and wide sad brown eyes. She was speaking to a dark young man who wore a black leather jacket, thin black tie, and white shirt, and who looked somehow official. The woman nodded casually and continued talking to the man. Babushka turned around. She stood about four feet eleven, wore a light-blue service smock with a medal pinned to the breast and a dark bandanna around her head. She was at least eighty, I knew, her face as wrinkled as a traveler's roadmap, thin, but round still, and her eyes were Siberian glacier blue. She had good teeth, small pearls that glistened when she smiled. She pointed to a hot plate standing high up on a shelf, for her a tiptoe reach. She wanted me to plug it into the outlet, so I did and she stretched and placed tea water on to boil. She was shy, I could tell that; she kept her eyes down a lot, like a servant would. She pushed a straight chair at us. Her hands were gnarled oak, polished. My colleague and I declined the chair, so with a little shrug Babushka sat down. I sat on a ledge against the wall and studied Babushka's roadmap. Deep below the gentle smile lay an ocean of memories. Some were *strashnii,* worse than horrible, terrors of war.

I realized none of them knew I was a foreigner. To them, I was just another local *devushka* from GUM's women's room. And they were serving me tea to defrost my toes. This could have been a small-town scene in eastern Kentucky.

When the water had boiled, Babushka shook tea from a tin and placed the pot on a wooden table scarred with children's etchings. After a while, she poured hot brown liquid into one china cup and one enameled tin cup. The tin cup was hers; I could tell. She gave it to me, watched me wrap my hands around it, and the room flooded with light when she smiled.

"Are you enjoying the parade?" she asked me.

"*Da, da.*"

A small frown creased her brow, but she didn't speak again for a while. She sat down on the chair and traded us for some reverie. The middle-aged woman spoke up.

"So you see, this is our office. We are housekeepers here at GUM. We don't work today, GUM is closed, you know. But we're here anyway, just in case someone needs us. Someone might get cold, need a place to go. Like you girls." She explained that the young man was head of Red Square's maintenance crew, preparing to run a cleanup brigade through the square when the parade was over. He nodded to us and bustled out a door that led somewhere into the bowels of GUM. The middle-aged woman said, "What school do you girls attend?"

My colleague explained that we were "older than that" and in fact she had graduated with an advanced degree from Moscow University. The woman turned to me. "And you, *devushka,* where did you go to school?"

"America," I answered. "*Ya iz ameriki.*"

Babushka's head shot up. The middle-aged woman sat up in surprise. "*Ameriki?! Tak! Devushka,* please tell us, where is the rest of your group?"

Soviets are not accustomed to Americans traveling alone in their country. I explained my situation. Babushka listened carefully, the Siberian glacier eyes sparkling.

"Oh, I see," said the other woman. "In that case, you ought to talk to the old woman here. She is a very conscientious worker. Look—she is eighty-four years old." Babushka blushed and flicked at invisible dust on her smock. "She is an old woman, *da?* But look how she still works, and she doesn't have to, you know. She has a pension. The old woman likes to work. Work elevates. Besides, she is keeping busy. Now me, I am still working age. I have a family to support, children. But the old woman . . . well, she . . ."

Quick as a cat, Babushka jumped up and straightened her kerchief. "I'll be back," she said. "I'm going to watch the parade." She fled the room, and I was suddenly aware of the thunder of marching feet overhead. How many millions had marched through Red Square already? How many more to come?

The middle-aged woman confided, "The old woman is all alone, poor thing. She has nobody. Nobody left. She never married, you know. Never had a chance. Wars. Her whole family was lost. Now she is alone. But, you know, she is a decorated worker. Did you notice her medal? She won't mention it. Anyway, the old woman hardly talks much."

I had seen so many decorated workers that Babushka's medal was like a popular breast ornament.

After a while she returned, her cheeks glowing with cold and excitement. "Oh, it is beautiful out there!" she exclaimed. "So many people here this year."

I asked Babushka if I could photograph her. "Me?" she looked puzzled. "Me? Why me? I am just an old woman, just a simple worker."

The light from the single hanging bulb was dim, but her eyes shone from inside. She stood, fingers clasped, with a schoolgirl's bashful smile. Then she removed her kerchief, maneuvered her chair up close to me and said, "Now then, *devushka,* what can you tell me about American workers?"

339

To Babushka, I dedicate a younger American woman's story, told to me by the woman who lived it, the Creole woman, Lou Williams.

Lou Williams

Mother and father were both farmers, and on my father's side, his grandfather owned a lot of land . . . they were rich, really. They had a very large house. As a matter of fact, they also had servants in their home. That was in a town called Lawtell, Louisiana. Lawtell, where my father was born and raised, was St. Landrey Parish.

We spoke what you call Creole. And English. It's a real funny thing, because . . . I guess because we were born into it we didn't really have any problems learning it. Creole music . . . you know what a washboard is? An accordion and a washboard, and they use knives and forks, and just make the music. Some Creole is the same as French. *Bonjour.* Like the months, I think, and the days. There's a lot of words that's very close.

When I was a kid, we had a lot of relatives, and it seems like all our neighbors were really our relatives. We used to go visiting at night and play a lot of cards. And make believe that we were making dances. We'd get the wash-tub and pots and pans and spoons and stuff and just make a whole lot of noise. Then we'd put up like a screen, with a light in the back so we could see shadows, and we used to really have a ball. That was our entertainment. We didn't really go any places except when we got a little older, then we used to go to school dances. We were brought up very strict Catholics, and we used to go to church dances and church fairs, bazaars and stuff like that.

We all farmed. On my grandfather's property. We raised everything possible, everything you could think of. We had cotton, corn, sweet potatoes, Irish potatoes, greens, peanuts, sugarcane; we had an orchard. We had apples, grapes, peaches, plums, figs, pears, and my grandmother had a beautiful flower garden that I used to help her take care of because she was paralyzed on one hand. She couldn't use her left hand, so I used to help her in the flower garden. We raised cows, hogs, chicken, geese, guineas, ducks, turkeys. You name it, we had it. I would say probably about three hundred, two hundred and fifty to three hundred acres of land.

We were seven kids, but only four of us was old enough to work the farm, and my father and mother. My mother worked up until it was time for her to have her baby, because she was just pregnant so often. She really worked out there. She used to, come harvest time, used to put up a lot of food in jars.

Also we used to butcher. There was one season where we just butchered and got ready for the winter. And they would butcher like three and four hogs at a time, about three hundred pounds apiece. My grandfather had a slaughter pen, where every other Friday, the men in the community would come by, and they'd slaughter over at his slaughter pen. The way it was, my grandfather would slaughter once a month, then all the men of the community would come and buy beef from him, then maybe in another month it would be another one from the same community, and then they would just buy from each other.

We'd get wages. For instance, do you know anything about farming? If we go out and pick cotton, and if say you pick a bale of cotton, which consists of I think one thousand five hundred pounds of cotton. So that was considered the bale of cotton. You take it down to the cotton gin, and you sell it, and then you'd get paid for it. I used to pick five hundred pounds a day. The cotton is planted around April, Holy Week. Then the latter part of June, preferably the first part of July, is when the cotton is ready to be harvested. So you pick it. By hand. We had a sack. Just a long sack that had a halter on it, and you just put it around your shoulder, and then you picked the cotton from the stalk, and stick it in the sack. When the sack got full, then we'd weight it and dump it into the wagon. One of us just had to keep count how much we picked that day. In about two days we had a bale of cotton, which consisted of about one thousand five hundred pounds. If you was out working for somebody else, you get paid by how many pounds you picked. But with us, we would just sell the thing and my grandfather would get the money, and everybody would benefit from it.

We had a tractor, and we had a plow behind it, and what you did was . . . the potatoes was planted in rows, so what you do is you take the plow and lower it, go underneath the potatoes and lift it up, and we'd just go and pick them and trade them. We mostly kept the produce for ourselves. For instance if there were other farmers who didn't make out so well, their crop didn't do so well, then we'd sell it to them. Like corn. Not cotton, though. Corn and potatoes and vegetables and stuff, and we had lots and lots of watermelons, too. I can't even stand them today. I don't even eat them, and tomatoes either.

Cotton was the cash crop. And the corn, we kept most of it to feed the livestock. I can remember a few times, when we had a cow that just wouldn't give any more milk and my father felt like we just didn't need it, to butcher it, but that didn't happen too often. Then they sold it.

The big house, my grandmother's house, had a very large front porch, and there was four bedrooms. We had a large dining area, and a very large kitchen. Just a wood frame house with a tin roof. A very large front and back yard, and of course my grandmother's flower garden, that was really beautiful. We had lots of . . . do you know what a chinabowl tree is?* A chinabowl tree, it grows very large

* Also known as chinaberry tree.

and it grows very tall, and it's spread out. The chinabowl is a little green ball, it grows in a bunch, but all over, and before the chinabowl comes, it's real pretty purple flowers, before the chinabowls come out. I never knew what purpose it served, but we used to make swings in it.

We also had pecans, lots of pecan trees. Those were great big trees, very tall. We had over twenty pecan trees. Some families wasn't fortunate enough to have some, so we would sell a lot, and keep a lot, too.

The house, to me it was a very warm place, because we could leave our little house and go to our grandmother's house, and it was like a feast really. There was lots to eat, and we were around the grandparents, so it was really good. We had a good time there.

I went to a Catholic school. Ten years. And our church, it was all black. The priest and the nuns, they were white. But the whole community was just black people, because the white people had their church, in a different location. There was definitely segregation. I didn't know any different. That's all I knew, black was black and white is white. It was just after I grew up that it, to me, was a change. When I was growing up, that was the way it was. That was in the 1950s; 1953 to 1954. Nineteen fifty-five, I think I was fifteen. When I was growing up, it was our own little world. I didn't even know anything about the Klan until I grew up older. We just never really had to worry about it, or never did worry about it. I never heard my parents talk about it either. We had white neighbors, if you can call them neighbors when you are out in the country, like three or four miles away. Like if we go to the store, we had stores out in the country, and we'd see them, but it was never no hassle or nothing. As a matter of fact, the only white people we were around was like the nuns and the priest. We just accepted it. It maybe made a difference to our parents, but they didn't say anything about it. We had one priest, Father Barnett, he spoke Creole. There was a lot of old people that spoke Creole when they'd go to confession, so Father Barnett was there for them.

We used to have a lot of house dances; we didn't call them parties, we called them house dances, and that was all in Creole. It was really fun. The reason why, when I was growing up, I didn't get to go out too many places. Just like, say, to a house dance, and then the younger kids would get together every Sunday and have . . . this may sound silly. We used to call it "rain play." One Sunday we'd have rain play over at our house, and a whole bunch of kids would come, and another Sunday at somebody else's house, and we always knew where, so we'd go. What you did was just go out and play games and dance, dance to records, instead of bands and stuff. It wasn't the Creole music. It was like maybe Fats Domino or people like that. That was really good, because it was something different. We used to play a game called Post Office and stuff like that. That was rain play. But what I called a house dance, it was mixed, with older people and younger people, and the older people would have their section of the floor to dance, and the young people here. They had pops for the kids and beer and whiskey for the older people. Live Creole bands.

Mardi Gras . . . a lot of people would just go to New Orleans for the Mardi Gras, but I never have been, and I can't remember too many people in my family have been, either, because it's very dangerous. People just commit a lot of crimes, because everybody is all masked up, and they know it would be hard for them to get caught. Back in the country, we had our own little celebration. On Mardi Gras day, a group of men would get together and dress in real funny clothes, mostly dresses, long dresses, and masks. They would come over, and they'd ride in a flatbed truck, and we could see them coming for miles. We'd prepare for them. One guy, he was called the Captain, and he'd have his three helpers. They'd come by, and we'd present them

344

with gifts. They would always consist of food, but on the other hand, the other guys, the "bad guys," would sneak around the back, and they'd steal chickens, eggs, they'd go out there and steal fruits from the trees and just anything they could get their hands on. Sometimes they would even get in the house, we would have to watch them really close, because they'd be sneaking in. They didn't mean no harm, it was just a fun thing, and they wouldn't take nothing of value, just the food. Then after they'd go from place to place and collect a lot of food and stuff, then they would pick one house or one place, where they would all go and cook up all this food and everybody in the community would just go. They would like just party until morning. Everybody would be soused.

We moved away from the farm after my mother died. I was twenty. Our father just went berserk after my mother died. So we moved closer to my aunts and uncles in Lake Charles . . . they had moved out there by then. . . . So my aunts and uncles could help me with the kids. At first I really didn't want to. But then I was going through such depression there, and it was just so lonely. After I made the move, it was great, the change was really good for all of us. Raising my brothers and sisters, it didn't even, should I say, faze me. I don't know. Because that's the way I was brought up. It just didn't faze me, it didn't bother me at all. But I have an aunt that shooed me off to get married, she told me, "Go on and get out, it's time for you to start living," and I did that. Then she took over raising the kids.

I really hadn't had a teenage life. And I still don't have it because I'm still stuck with these kids. And I'm forty-two years old. I tell my kids, "Don't bring my grandkids here, just keep them." I don't want them. I started feeling that way about three years ago, because I just sat back and I thought about it. I've been around kids all my life, and I don't mean it in a bad way, but it is the truth, I've been around them all my life.

I got married pretty young, I guess. My husband was sent to Germany, in the army, and I went on my first airplane flight, to be with him over in Furt, this little town close to Nuremberg. It was my first plane ride, and I felt like a country girl finally getting wings, you know?

When we got to Luxembourg, I had to catch a train to another town. On the train, I got up to go to the bathroom. There were a lot of German soldiers, and they were standing out in the hall of the train. When I went by, one of them grabbed my hand, but very gently, and it really frightened me. About three or four of them came up to me and touched my face, touched my hair. They were just feeling all over me, and here I was. After a while, when I saw they weren't going to harm me, then I relaxed. So this German guy who speaks English, he saw the soldiers doing this to me. He started talking to them. Then he started laughing. What was going on here? He told me, "The reason why they're looking at you and feeling you like this is because they have never seen a black person before. They are saying good things about you, don't be afraid."

I said, "Well!"

After my husband and I split up, I moved to Fairbanks. I had to find a job. I'd pretty much always been a housewife while I was married. Finally, I found this job at the hospital.

What I do in the hospital is, I am a maid. I work on the first floor, and what I do there is clean bathrooms, pick up trash, clean in the emergency room, and we have a doctors' lounge, we clean in there. I take care of the whole first floor, it consists of a lot of departments like the X-ray department. Go through there and do a little dusting and pick up trash, and there's five bathrooms in there. Clean bathrooms.

We have the lobby. I clean off the chairs in there, ashtrays, and there's a whole floor, the first floor has about five water fountains. I clean those. We have a meditation room, I clean in there. All of the business offices is down there. I don't really do anything in there except pick up trash. Some of them have bathrooms connected to it, so I clean in there. Occasionally I clean the morgue. I really don't see anything in there. After they have a post, then they usually clean up pretty much behind themselves. We're two people go in there. There's the bathroom, I take care of the bathroom, and the janitor takes care of the floor. Everything else is pretty well cleaned by the time we get in there, if it wasn't, I wouldn't go in. No way. There's always some body in the freezer, though. It really doesn't bother me.

Housekeepers, we have the second largest department. The first largest is the nurses, and we have the second largest. I'm going to only give you roughly. We have three different shifts. I'll say probably about thirty-five on the day shift, and we have five people on the evening shift, that's from four o'clock to eleven o'clock or twelve o'clock, then there's another shift, which is graveyard shift, it's only men. They are like the wax crew, and that's about fifteen to twenty people. That's only roughly. Our hospital has an extension, which is what they call a Native Clinic, and there's one lady takes care of that during the day. Then they have the wax crew going in on the graveyard shift and doing the floors and stuff.

It's a privately owned hospital, it's the Lutheran church's hospital. Fairbanks Memorial. It's a capacity of one hundred and fifty bed patients. A lot of patients are flown down below to Virginia Mason Hospital in Seattle. Something more serious, like maybe heart surgery or something like this, they fly them out.

In the housekeeping department, we start out at five dollars and eighty-three cents, but since . . . as a matter of fact, on our next check, we should have this cost of living raise. So I think starting wages is, for housekeeping, is gone up to six dollars and twenty-four cents, I think. Raises, if you're not doing your job, you don't get it. Or if you're missing too many days, you don't get it. They are very ornery about that. Which I think is only right. You have ninety days probationary period. Then after ninety days then you get a raise, and don't ask me what percent, because I forgot. I've got it all in my little pamphlet thing. Then after that, then you get like, around this time of year, which is July-August, you get a cost of living raise. Every year. We just got one, it's supposed to show up in our next check. After you're there a year, like if your attendance is good, it's because of your attendance and your work performance, and of course your attitude, then you get a yearly raise. The supervisor makes the decisions about your attitude and performance.

We start at eight o'clock in the morning, then at nine thirty we have a fifteen-minute break. Then we have a lunch break starting at twelve o'clock. Then in the afternoon you have another fifteen-minute break from two o'clock to two fifteen. Then you work on until four thirty. The only benefit, we get a discount on medication. I think it's 10 percent off medication. But the insurance, through the hospital you can get the Blue Cross-Blue Shield insurance. I have myself and my son, because my daughter has her own insurance with her job, and I pay forty-two dollars a month. The extra ten dollars is for dental and eye care. That doesn't come until after you are there for a whole year.

After you work there for a year, you get three weeks paid vacation. Then the hospital grants you three days for death. They have another term for it, I don't know what it's called. They grant you three days you get paid for. You get sick leave, too. You acquire one and a quarter days a month. That is one thing you have to watch, because if you call in sick too often, then that can really put a damper on your raise. You can only take sick leave when you are really sick. Like some days, you don't feel like going to work, you call in sick. That's okay. But if you do that too often, then somebody's going to . . . "hey, something is wrong here." If you want to leave, you put in your two weeks notice, and if you have twenty-six sick days, then you just lose them. Vacations have to be worked out. You request it, and if somebody else has requested that time, then you're out. You just have to take another time.

The wages are enough if you don't overload yourself. Because this apartment here is through HUD,* which is . . . this is what you call low-income apartments. These are new apartments. I was the first one to move into this apartment, three years ago. I moved in here in June 1978; it's just three years since I've been in this apartment, and they are all new. It's according to your income. I pay one hundred and ninety-seven dollars a month here.

In the summer here, people just go wild. They really do. Everybody is just so happy to get out of these heavy parkas, and they can go out and get in their car without having to go and warm it up for two and three hours. There's a lot of drinking here, and people drive. They drive, especially the younger generation. They drive crazy during the summer here. It's just really nice in the summer, and I suppose the reason why people feel that way is because they've been cooped up inside so long. Or during the winter, everything is at a slower pace, naturally. There's still a lot of people out, though. People don't just stay in. Just because it's cold. People just go on about their business, like in normal weather. It gets very cold. It can get as cold as seventy below. Usually it starts getting below zero in the latter part of December. Somewhere in there. The thaw comes way in April.

What cabin fever is, it's a person who just doesn't care to

* The Housing and Urban Development program for low-income wage-earners.

get out in the wintertime. And they just stay inside. I guess it does something to them. But I would never get cabin fever, because even if I didn't have a car, I'd take a bus somewhere, somehow. Some people are like that, they just don't like to get out in the cold, they get stationary for that day, then one day goes by, and then the next day, they just don't get out and do nothing. But I have heard a lot of cases where people get that way, and it could cause a lot of problems. Yes, mental problems. Alaska, we're either the first or the second for alcoholism. It's somewhere up in there. I really don't know how to describe that. I really don't know why. It could be because Alaska is so different from anywhere else.

BAM

On April 27, 1974, the Soviet Union's Young Communist League, Komsomol, sent its first contingent of volunteers to Siberia, where they would break new ground, both literally and historically, in service to their Motherland. Komsomol youth were going to build a railroad through Siberia. Today, their task is nearly completed. The Baikal-Amur Railway, BAM, starts at Lake Baikal, Siberia, and reaches to the Pacific. It is the second Soviet railroad line that extends from Eastern Europe across Central Asia to the Pacific, and it represents the magnitude of the Soviet Union's national priority—industrial expansion.

The Soviet Union is moving rapidly into Siberia, where once secret motherlodes of wealth have been uncovered: coal, iron, copper, gold, oil, diamonds, and more. Siberia's resources guarantee the nation's energy independence and economic stability, probably for many centuries to come, and BAM ensures that the resources, once mined and processed, will reach every Soviet republic. And as BAM nears completion, new Siberian settlements have been added to Soviet cartographers' maps.

Beginning as primitive tent villages thrown together by the first waves of Komsomol volunteers, BAM's legacy settlements have evolved into modern industrial towns, huge urban centers scientifically constructed to stand firm on eternal frost. Some of the newer buildings have been raised on pillars, elevated off the ground to leave untouched the eternal frost beneath them. These modern Siberian structures are brilliantly designed and executed, magnificent proof that the U.S.S.R. has no lack of technological expertise or construction materials. They stand in stark contrast to many Soviet Eastern European structures, where shoddy materials often cause new high-rise buildings to look ancient before they are occupied. BAM's new towns must be the pride and joy of young Soviets. And because wages and job advancement opportunities are so much better in Siberia, they flock to them. Siberian cities are booming.

Many parents are disturbed by the youth migration to Siberia. Fathers and mothers who spent their working lives planning how their children would live better than they did, expecting them to attend Eastern European universities and settle down as professionals in Moscow, Leningrad or Kiev, are shocked to their socks when their offspring come home one day and announce, "Mother, Father, I am leaving in the morning for Siberia." Hundreds of thousands of Soviet youth have spoken these ominous words, and turning their backs on the older generation's dreams, have taken up the proverbial knapsack and headed out to the Last Frontier. Parents wonder what will become of these rebellious young people living in the hinterlands. Meanwhile, the government rejoices. Komsomol youth, the state tells children, are the hope of the future Motherland. Komsomol or not, most young people are intrigued with Last Frontiers. If you are seeking adventure, a better wage, rapid promotion and more independence from bureaucracy, Siberia is Soviet heaven.

Working on the BAM, a railroad engineer sees hosts of

young people come and go, trying out Siberia for a year the way so many Americans try out Alaska, failing to overcome cabin fever, their bodies refusing to adjust to harsh climatic conditions, and drifting back to milder, more comfortable environs. The engineer sees progress too, as he runs coal trains along BAM's mainline, from Nerungrii to Birkakit. Many people, including himself and his wife, have settled down in Siberia, reared families and become Siberian citizens.

Valery Samuylov is a coal train engineer who has worked in Siberia since the first Komsomol call for volunteers in 1974. Moving from Ukraine to Siberia was not just going to the New Frontier for him—he was returning to the place of his birth.

When I arrived at Nerungrii railroad station to interview Valery Samuylov, he was out on the rails, behind the controls of a diesel engine pulling a load of coal from Nerungrii to Birkakit. Waiting in the station for him to return, the stationmaster told me a little about the railroad workers' job.

"Well," he said in a thick Volga region accent, "we're working for the second year now, under the Ministry of Communication. The main task is transporting Nerungrii coal from here to other places. For this we are preparing carriages. We clean them and repair them. We take supplies to the pit and come back. Well, so we service the builders of the railway line . . . Generally speaking, we service the new district.

"We have one passenger train a day, which comes here only from Birkakit [the next station on the line]. But for the future we have planned a string of passenger stations between Birkakit and Nerungrii, and then we'll be very large scale. So what else? Right here we have maintenance operations so that there'll be locomotives, so that the locomotives will work . . . we maintain the line. We are working to an exact schedule during the year.

"We have passenger trains and freight trains. We have

diesel engines and some steam engines. We don't have electrical ones here yet. How long they last is a question for engineers."

Valery Samuylov walked into the station just in time to answer this question. He was a handsome Russian, fair face chafed red from working outdoors. He wore a sleek fur hat, heavy boots and a lightweight jacket. He sat down at the table across from me, and without waiting for a formal introduction, began talking about freight trains.

Valery Samuylov

Well, as a rule, our freight engines don't stop work, say, as a result of climate conditions. In general, from the moment a diesel leaves the factory until the time it must be written off it works, I'd say about twenty to twenty-five years. Depending on the type of work. Freight hauling means a bigger load, so the engine would work a slightly shorter period of time.

We also have beautiful passenger trains, sleek, beautiful cars that sleep two people to a compartment. We have sleepers coming in here. We think and hope that by the summertime our best passenger trains will be coming here into this station. This place is the Last Frontier. The extent of our railways is much better than in the U.S.A., much more extensive. That's why we don't have too many superhighways here yet. This is because the great concentration of freight is on our railways, you understand. Oh, let's see how I can put it simply? We have many trains running. The length of our railways is less than theirs, but we carry on a slightly greater volume of work. If in the U.S.A. . . . I don't remember, if I'm not mistaken less than one third of the total freight goes by rail. I think you have more road vehicles. Somewhere around one third. You have primarily automobile traffic.

We also have electrified rail lines. Generally, it's the older stretches which are electrified, mostly in the west.

And the new lines, like our BAM, for example, will be fully electrified. For now we use diesel. You see, to electrify we would need more time, more technology and greater means, more money allocated. Diesels are autonomous mobile units, they don't depend on contact, say, with electric power lines.

I was born in '47 in Ulan Ude. In Siberia. It is the capital of the Buryat Autonomous Region, on Lake Baikal. I was born in August. My family, well, I was born into the family of a military man. My father was an officer. Because of my father's work, we moved to the west and lived in Ukraine. I went to the first grade there, so I must have been seven years old then. When I grew up, somehow I wanted to go back to the place where I was born, just to work a little, and so I came here. In fact, my parents told me a lot about the Baikal area, the far east, about this place where we live. But, of course, I didn't remember myself. I was still little then.

I came here actually in 1974. So, how did I come back? I also worked in a locomotive depot, the same as I do here, in Kharkov.* There was still a great need for people in my occupation, and I wrote a letter of inquiry to the depot of the Baikal-Amur Railway and received an affirmative response. I gathered up my family and came here.

How do I say it? My son (he was our first, the only child at the time) was little. We didn't ask his opinion of course, since he was all of three years old, even younger, two and a half. My wife, generally speaking, supported me, though she's Ukrainian. I told her, "I want to see this place where I was born." She agreed with me. We came like everybody did, we took the train. At first I lived in Skovorodino, that's four hundred kilometers from here on the Trans-Baikal railway. And then, you know, as they were just building BAM, so that's 1978, I decided to move to BAM.

So what's my work like? I am a locomotive engineer. So,

* *Kharkiv* in Ukrainian.

you know, I have to do maneuvering and then hauling. That is, until the trains are maneuvered, I'm at the station, and then I transport freight from one station to another. That's my job. My workplace is in the locomotive. When I am working on maneuvers, then I work from eight o'clock in the morning till eight o'clock in the evening, and from eight in the evening until eight in the morning. If I worked during the day, say, from eight o'clock in the morning until eight o'clock in the evening, then I rest for twenty-four hours, then I will have another two days off. So I work one day in a forty-eight hour period.

Like in any family, my wife helps me get ready for work. She makes breakfast for me. I get up at seven o'clock if I'm working in the morning and have breakfast, depending on my mood. Sometimes I just have coffee. Sometimes I breakfast heartily. As a rule, there isn't usually much time in the morning, so more often than not my wife, you know, and I eat an omelet with sausage or whatever's fastest. If my wife happens to get up a little earlier, she may also make potatoes with butter, you know, a well-balanced diet.

I have three children, boys. The oldest is studying in, say, the third grade in a ten-year school. He's nine years old. The middle boy will be three years old in May, and the youngest is eight months. We might have more children. Well, I wouldn't say no, and my wife, she would like to also. My wife doesn't work outside the home, she has two children to care for.

You see, the thing is, my work week differs a little from the work week of a person who works say, at an enterprise or a factory. Since our work is on a timetable, it can happen that I work Saturday and Sunday. So then I'd have my days off in the middle of the week, Tuesday and Wednesday, for example, Thursday and Friday, however it falls. If it happens that I get Saturday and Sunday off, I try in fact to give my full attention to my family. I look after the children. I help my wife. Winters here in Yakutia are severe, so in winter you can't take a stroll on the street. In summer, you know, fall and spring, we frequently, especially in the fall, go to the woods for berries and mushrooms, or just for walks. In short, I try to spend as much of my free time as possible in the fresh air with my family. We go to nearby places. My wife too. And since my work isn't really physical and I'm mostly sitting still, it's good for me to get up and move.

I was active in sports, but more recently, the kids are little and there's less time. I was in track and field. Now I make time to play table tennis, Ping-Pong. The kids take up a lot of time, you see, I know that I must take part in raising them.

It seems to me that family bonds aren't determined by where you are living, but by, you could say, the internal makeup of the people who make up the unit of that family. Can I go on? What else do I want to say? Well, a lot is said now about the problem of compatibility of people, but it seems to me that if my wife and I, say, love each other, we can deal with any problems that come up. I think that the main thing is that there must be mutual understanding in the family. That is, a husband and wife should be likeminded people. She should understand me and I should understand her.

Let's see, how long ago, 1971—so I have been married for ten years now, and we still haven't had a single quarrel. Yes, I'm lucky. I don't know. Maybe we have similar characters. In general, in every situation we try to find the best way out which suits both of us, her and me. No big problems have come up for us over the time, the ten years that we've been living together. And we've solved, so to speak, those little household problems according to common sense. Well, in particular—actually it's not really a problem, it's just kind of. . . . My wife doesn't work now, and when my youngest child will turn one we can send him to a daycare center, the first, the second and the third would all be in school or daycare centers, so my wife could go back to work. Personally, I believe that a family upbringing, I mean that this is my personal opinion, that all the same a family upbringing is better. So, I'm trying to get my wife to see things my way. Well, actually we've talked about it, of course. And also, at home all the time with the children you can get bored, but all the same, considering, so to speak, that the children are still little ... I was able to convince her that she ought to be with the child at least until he turns two, that is until he can be a little independent. That is until he knows how to dress himself, eat by himself. That is until he doesn't need to be looked after. So, it'll be much easier for him in the daycare center then, than if he went, say, when he was only a year old. So my wife agrees with me, because in fact, so to say, the children are our future, we're really living for them. The point is, I respect childhood. This is what I believe, that when a child is, say, two years old, then he's more or less independent, he's already able to dress himself. It's much easier for him in the center than for a child who's, say, only one year. Yes, in my family, my mother was at home and she paid a lot of attention to us. Well, I personally consider that a family upbringing is much better for children. Being raised in the family.

I have time for reading. I try to find time for it. I read practically everything. I mean particular literary genres, like some people prefer entertaining mysteries and others like science fiction. I don't have anything like that, I like to read everything, books by Soviet authors and foreign authors, both the classics and contemporary. But in particular one of my favorite, so to speak, authors, not so much from the literary genre but for, so to speak, his style of writing, is Jack London. That's been true since childhood. When I have time I reread those works of his which I read earlier with pleasure. On the whole I'd say I read every and any literary work with pleasure. Any genre of literature, because you find just the thing you need in every book. I do have one sort of weakness, I guess, I love science fiction. I don't set it apart especially, but . . . As for music, I basically prefer light music. I also like the movies. There are movies I love. Let's see, how can I say this best? Films also come in different genres. So there are adventure films, there are westerns, there are science fiction films, plain-life films. I like all types of films, but especially, so to speak, I like best maybe films on realistic subjects, lifelike films make a strong impression on me. And I also love films—maybe it's also a leftover from childhood—about what is friendship. And since, so to say, you are a guest from the U.S.A., I was very vitally impressed by—I don't know how it goes in English, this film, but in Russian it is *Connected with One Chain* [*The Defiant Ones*]. Sidney Poitier was in it, and I don't remember the second actor. It's a good film, an outstanding film. I see lots of American films, very many. Well, I have seen one, but it's not a scientific film, it's a science fiction film, *Capricorn One*. About a flight to Mars that doesn't take place. American cosmonauts.

Religious beliefs? None. None. Well, I already told you my father was a serviceman. In any country a serviceman serves where—*

Discrimination against native peoples? Certainly not. The notion hasn't even existed for a long time and if someone touches on the subject of discrimination, it wouldn't even enter your head that what was being discussed could have anything to do with the Soviet Union. Usually we, the way I understand, if somebody says "discrimination" we immediately have the impression that it must be the U.S.A. and Negroes. That's discrimination. We don't have anything like that. Well, we all work here, Russians, Ukrainians, Tatars, a whole string of nationalities.

How can I tell you? The basic difference is under the

*Valery was cut off by the interpreter.

socialist system, like ours, for example, we have no classes in our society, a classless society. That is, we have no poor, no rich, and the means of production belong to the people. I mean, you know, we have no private property. That's the difference. Actually our state is considered one of workers and peasants. Well, even in Leonid Ilyich's [Brezhnev's] latest speech at the 26th Congress, the Party says that the primary goal is to improve the well-being, to raise the standard of living of Soviet man—that is, of all of us.

I was born under the Soviet system. I know about the capitalist system only from books, newspapers, films. For myself personally I can't imagine myself, say, in a capitalist country.

Everything, let's say, that is going on here, everything we have, I take as my due. So, for example, I lived in the west, and I decided to return to my homeland, to my place of birth, so you know, I knew that when I'd get here that I would be able to work and I'd have an apartment. Well, that is, I was moving seven thousand kilometers, but I didn't have any thoughts or concerns that I'd arrive and not be needed by anyone.* For example, I know that wherever I may go in the Soviet Union I'll be able to get a job in my field, my children will be able to go to a daycare center. My labor in fact will always be repaid according to my qualifications. So . . .

Oh, here it is once again, I want to say the same as regarding "discrimination," it's the same for the word "freedom." I don't understand how a person could not be considered free here. I consider myself absolutely free. How do I mean it? You know, nobody can be *absolutely* free in relation to the society in which he lives. There is a term in philosophy, "absolute freedom." I don't accept it. Because, say, on the scale of the state generally, absolute

---

*This is a typical Russian-language way of saying, I would be out of a job, wouldn't find an apartment, wouldn't be useful.—Translator's note

freedom, say, is anarchy. And as far as free love, I think it's immoral. That is, you know, I believe that each person has certain . . . that society itself lays responsibilities on him. In particular, I believe that any person should do his duty in relation to society as expressed by honest, conscientious labor. Well, and also to observe the laws of that society in which he lives, to be a patriot of his homeland. And what other kind of freedom does anyone need? If you do, as they say, what is for the good of your state, of your homeland, your Motherland, you're doing everything for your own good, strictly speaking; that is, the good of your family, the good of the people around you. And so, in fact, what freedoms . . . I can go wherever I want. If I want . . . in general nothing restricts us, we have no limitations. Well, maybe it's better to ask you what you mean by the concept of freedom in American terms.

How do I feel about the nuclear threat? As any thinking person, I believe that I must try to prevent it, that we must disarm. Well, the point is, that if the Third World War actually begins, it will *really* be a *world* war. Personally, I don't believe in the theory of "limited warfare" which President Carter advanced. Reagan also supports it. Because, say, you know, any limited war could always go beyond the limits and become a world war. I think, for example, that for imperialist countries, as well as capitalist, war is one of the means of relieving pressure on the state proper.

It's a complex question. If I myself lived in the United States, we could find, we'd have to find, some way out. I personally think that the ruling class in your country is so strong, that to change, say, the existing system through a revolution will never succeed in the U.S.A. So all that's left is to use peaceful methods. The disarmament movement, to get as many people as possible to participate in it. Well, it's natural that violence is used against the disarmament movement. Suppression has been and will be. Apparently the mass media, the press, radio . . . must play a role here. It is necessary not to blow up out of proportion the Soviet threat, say, but to the contrary, to explain, to interpret, the complete horror of thermonuclear war. Because with the current level of development of military technology, thermonuclear war could lead to the complete disappearance of man on Earth, or the whole planet even could disappear. I don't remember exactly, but it seems to me that Einstein said when he was asked what kind of arms would be used in the Third World War, he answered, "I don't know what kind of arms will be used in the Third World War, but in the Fourth War they'll use arrows and stone axes." In other words, civilization will disappear in the Third World War.

I think that our peoples, the American and the Soviet, must live in peace and friendship. We had a good example of cooperation during the Second World War when before our faces we had common dangers, we found a common language and were able to unite against one enemy—fascism. On the whole I think that common sense will gain the upper hand in the United States over the leaders of the military-industrial complex. And we, the two most highly developed and biggest countries in the world, will live in peace.

So I think, as a representative of the Iroquois said when talking of bad times and war, "Our paths are overgrown with grass and bushes. And the fallen trees are blocking the trails, and the sky above us is dense with clouds." So, the peoples of our countries live with the responsibility of seeing to it that the skies of our planet are never covered with clouds.

Epilogue:
Fisherman's Bottle

A crimson sunset tinted New York Harbor red. The U.S.
Air 727 gave up altitude, preparing to land. An Englishman sitting next to me on the Washington, D.C.-New York
flight pointed down at the Statue of Liberty. He was
impeccably dressed and was at first reluctant to speak to
the disheveled person sitting next to him. I had flown
straight through from Donbas to Moscow to Washington,
and boarded this businessmen's shuttle to New York. I had
been flying for twenty-four hours and twenty minutes. I
was wearing an Uzbek *chapan* over a jumpsuit, Sultan-
Murat's *chalma* around the waist, a Ukrainian coal miner's
hard hat, and was carrying a bouquet of giant calla lilies
wrapped in *Pravda* pages and a huge wooden cuckoo
clock. Gifts from Donbas miners.

"Statue of Liberty," the Englishman said to me. "America."

"I know," I said. "I'm from here."

He regarded me with surprise. "Oh, I beg your pardon. I
thought you were just arriving."

Straining under the weight of my gifts, I stood near La Guardia Airport's taxicab stand and frowned at the prospect of joining a long line of travelers queuing up for cabs. A portly redcap noticed me. "You look too tired to wait in that line," he said. He whistled and a cab pulled out of the chute and over to the curb. I got in.

Many New York taxicabs have bullet-resistant window dividers between the driver and the passenger seat in back. Through the cloudy glass, I could not see the driver's face, nor could he see mine. "Where to?" he asked me. I gave him the Manhattan address. He pulled away from the curb and almost immediately began a conversation. In five weeks, I had spoken a combination of broken Russian and broken English, and it felt strange warming up to the native tongue again. The cabdriver asked me where I had been traveling.

"The Soviet Union." I was too tired to go into detail.

"Really?" the driver said. "You're the second passenger I've had that went to the Soviet Union. What's it like over there?"

"Different. The same. It depends on what you mean."

"Okay," he said, "tell me this. Do they have cabdrivers over there?"

"Sure. And they're just like you guys. Some are honest and some cheat their fares. They're all mavericks anyway, like cabdrivers in this country."

"Give me an example of a Russian cabdriver's ripoff."

Having been taken for a few expensive rides by New York cabbies, I understood the man's curiosity. "I lost a few rubles to one cabdriver in Moscow. I didn't know the streets. The driver took me five blocks and charged me ten rubles."

"How much is that in dollars?" I told him. "Aw, that's nothing," he laughed. "I can tell you better stories. Anyway, those guys probably get ripped off by passengers like we do. You know, bad tips. Cabdriving doesn't pay like it used to. Inflation. Do Moscow's cabbies have a union?"

We talked back and forth through the bullet-resistant window for a few miles. Moscow's cabs do not have shields between driver and passenger, though my Novosti escort had told me they were once installed to protect drivers from germs. But the cabbies had rebelled and most of them were removed.

One block from my destination, the driver asked me, "What were you doing over there? Vacation?"

"I was talking to Soviet workers. About their jobs, about their lives . . ."

The cabdriver slammed on the brakes, halting the cab in the middle of St. Marks Place. He pushed his face up to the protective window and looked at me.

"Wait a minute," he said. "I know you! I was the guy who drove you to the station the day you left on this trip! I remember you talked about Siberia and reindeer herders."

Instantly, I recognized him.

Alphonsa Thomas, the New York cabbie, shook his head in disbelief. "Man, do you realize how many taxicabs there are in New York? Thousands! This couldn't happen in a million years!"

Not if you consult the odds.

At the curb, Alphonsa Thomas held the calla lilies and cuckoo clock while I unloaded luggage. A clerk I knew who worked in a nearby store came rushing outside. "Welcome home," he said, "the vacation's over."

"What do you mean, vacation?" I retorted. "I was working over there." He smiled at that.

"Your work has just begun, sister." I looked at him inquiringly. "You've been lucky," the clerk said. "You got to go behind the Iron Curtain. Now I want to know what it's like over there. How people think, how they live." He shook a finger at me. "And you owe it to me to tell everything you found out. Maybe that tape recorder of yours can answer a few of my questions."

In the tip, I gave Alphonsa Thomas a few kopecks. We shook hands warmly. "I bet you met some good people over there in the Soviet Union," he said.

Like in the United States.

A few weeks later, I stood on Alaska's shoreline, near the Bering Strait, and looked out across the water. Midsummer sun cast a golden path between Alaska and Siberia. Northern kinfolk used to cross along this route, in winter when the ice bridge formed. Now governments' guns threaten family reunions and friendly exchanges at the narrowest point between the United States and the Soviet Union. I had a vision of Igor Pogodaev, surrounded by a reindeer herd, meeting Johnson Stalker and his reindeer herd on an ice bridge. Ambassadors of friendship. Why not? Somehow the guns that divide kinfolk will have to be removed.

As if to emphasize the possibility for peaceful coexistence, a fleet of U.S. and Soviet fishing and cannery boats now operates a joint seafood venture here in the Bering Sea. The controversial fleet was the concept of a small American fishing company, Marine Resources, that formed a partnership with a Soviet cannery. Profit motives aside, the joint venture is bringing American and Soviet workers together in their common workplace, helping to usher in a new age of friendship and cooperation between the two nations. Sadly, the fleet's existence is subject to the whims and fancies of both nations' politicians, who can't seem to mend their differences.

A workingman once told me: "There are two things a welder can't mend—the crack of dawn and a broken heart." He did not mention the world. Maybe he still believes, like so many workers, that a skilled laborer can perform jobs others despair over. He speaks not of destruction but of repair, for that is the nature of his work. But is it reasonable to expect that laborers will mend the world?

They surely will not receive time off with pay to conduct such an activity. Their spare time is often occupied with union business; grievances, arbitrations, strikes and picket lines.

Labor's cause, no matter how noble, cannot be separated from the quest for world peace. In an era when the neutron bomb is capable of destroying people while leaving the products of their labor standing, workers—as patriots—are questioning the ethics of rulers who try to convince them that workers "on the other side" are preparing for a war. The simple truth is, they are not. On either side.

The picture of Doomsday had long faded from my mind's eye. As I stood on the Bering Strait, something new was forming on the horizon. The world's workers, humankind's most daring class, told me they believe in their own power and are planning for a tomorrow they believe will arrive. They are willing to work for it, and some will no doubt lead the way.

Both American and Soviet workers want more, materially and spiritually, from their bosses and their governments. Most of all, they want security. The democratic ideal that sustains both American and Soviet workers assures that they will bring the necessary changes, and not just to their own nations. The determination and optimism of these men and women can ensure security for their families and fellow workers. In spite of radioactive obstacles, they have already begun building the bridge of friendship over hostile waters. A bridge that will stand for the security of all the world's workers, as solid and strong as its builders. A bridge that will withstand changes in the climate.

Recently, Ted Mattson, an American fisherman, found a bottle with a hammer and sickle molded into the bottom washed up on Alaska's shore. There was a note inside, written in Russian. A note written by a Soviet fisherman. It said: "We are Soviet crewmen. We are from the town of Nakhodka on Primoria [Bay Ocean].

"We send a friendly greeting to whoever finds this bottle. We are interested in who finds this bottle and the letter and where they found it.

"I don't know what to say about myself. We are working and living very well.

"We don't want to fight anymore. We want to make peace for the whole world—no more fighting. We ask that all young people of all continents work harder to make peace.

"We ask that all people have sunshine in their hearts. Then there will be no more fighting."

The fisherman's bottle demonstrates that when workers want to send a message, in spite of the odds and the tides flowing against them, they will find a way. And be heard.

Kathy Kahn
Bering Strait
U.S.A.-U.S.S.R.

Acknowledgments

Special thanks to: Richard Morford, director emeritus, National Council of American-Soviet Friendship; Gennady Fedosov, director, U.S.S.R.-U.S.A. Society for Friendship; Vladimir Belyakov, information officer, U.S.S.R. Embassy.

Diane Reverand, senior editor; Melissa Pierson, assistant; Fred Sawyer, copy editor, G. P. Putnam's Sons; Fay Lila Greenbaum, translator and research consultant.

Phillip Allen, project assistant; Kathy Rothschild, Betsy Gimble, and Stanley Harrison.

And to: Elaine Markson, literary agent; Dr. John Williams of the National Endowment for the Humanities; Alexander Pushkov, N. Derevyenko, Marc Krupkin and Uri Arsieniev of Novosti Books; and Dr. Robert Coles.

A few of the many persons who guided this project are: Victor Zhuravlev, Paul Nyden, Marc Hardesty, Ray West, Estevan Flores, Maria Ambriz, Paula Ruiz, Dick Gould, Nikolai Ustinov, Sam Tafoya, George and Bonita Rodriguez, Don Beeson.

Susie Fay, Elizabeth Speten, the Munros, Donna and

Dick Kelly, Milton Cross, Pam Herman, Sam and Geneva Harben, Deb Kelly, Arnold Baskin, Paul Shapiro, Robert Gates.

And Tamara in Nerungrii.

Members of the following labor unions were helpful in providing contacts and information: Oil, Chemical and Atomic Workers' International Union; Makeevka Miners' Union; Texas Farmworkers' Union; VAZ Auto Workers' Union; Independent Drivers' Association; Amalgamated Clothing and Textile Workers' Union; Nerungrii Surface Miners' Union; Operators' and Engineers' Union, New Mexico Region.

Employees and Directors of the following enterprises were also helpful in providing information: Icicle Seafoods, Alaska; NANA Reindeer Industry; Yakut State Reindeer Farm; Yurmala Forestry; Payarik State Farm; Makeevka Mines; Lyubertsy Carpet Factory; Tashkent Textile Mill; the VAZ; Denver Yellow Cab Cooperative; Children's World, Riga; Moschnii Mine Enterprises; and Sardana Souvenir Factory.

And Amtrak's railroad crews.